THE EMPRESS IN THE PEPPER CHAMBER

The Empress in the Pepper Chamber

Zhao Feiyan in History and Fiction

OLIVIA MILBURN

UNIVERSITY OF WASHINGTON PRESS
Seattle

The Empress in the Pepper Chamber was made possible in part by a grant from the Traditional Chinese Culture and Society Book Fund, established through generous gifts from Patricia Buckley Ebrey and Thomas Ebrey.

Design by Katrina Noble
Composed in Minon Pro, typeface designed by Robert Slimbach

25 24 23 22 21 5 4 3 2 1

Printed and bound in the United States of America

UNIVERSITY OF WASHINGTON PRESS
uwapress.uw.edu

LIBRARY OF CONGRESS CATALOGING-IN-PUBLICATION DATA
Names: Milburn, Olivia, author. | Ling, Xuan. Zhao Feiyan wai zhuan. | Ling, Xuan. Zhao Feiyan wai zhuan. English.
Title: The Empress in the Pepper Chamber : Zhao Feiyan in History and Fiction / Olivia Milburn.
Other titles: Zhao Feiyan in History and Fiction
Description: Seattle : University of Washington Press, 2021. | Includes bibliographical references and index.
Identifiers: LCCN 2020051347 (print) | LCCN 2020051348 (ebook) | ISBN 9780295748740 (hardcover) | ISBN 9780295748757 (paperback) | ISBN 9780295748764 (ebook)
Subjects: LCSH: Ling, Xuan. Zhao Feiyan wai zhuan. | Zhao, Feiyan, 34 B.C.–1 B.C.—In literature. | Empresses—China—Biography—History and criticism.
Classification: LCC PL2663.L45 Z4336 2021 (print) | LCC PL2663.L45 (ebook) | DDC 895.1/352—dc23
LC record available at https://lccn.loc.gov/2020051347
LC ebook record available at https://lccn.loc.gov/2020051348

The paper used in this publication is acid free and meets the minimum requirements of American National Standard for Information Sciences—Permanence of Paper for Printed Library Materials, ANSI Z39.48–1984.∞

CONTENTS

ACKNOWLEDGMENTS

The Empress in the Pepper Chamber represents the outcome of research carried out during a sabbatical year, which was originally intended to be devoted to an entirely different research project. I would like to thank Brill for permission to reprint material from my article "Palace Women in the Former Han Dynasty (202 BCE–CE 23): Gender and Administrational History in the Early Imperial Era," *Nan Nü* 18.2 (2016): 195–223, in chapter 1. Parts of chapters 3 and 4 of this book represent a revised version of "On *Zhao Feiyan waizhuan*, China's Earliest Erotic Fiction," *Asia Major* 31.1 (2018): 91–117. I thank the journal for permitting me to reprint this material. In addition, this work was supported by the Ministry of Education of the Republic of Korea and the National Research Foundation of Korea (NRF project number 100-20180067).

I am grateful for the opportunity to have worked at the following institutions while engaged on this topic: Seoul National University; the School of Oriental and African Studies and the British Library, London; the Baptist University of Hong Kong; the National Central Library, Taipei, Taiwan; Zhejiang University, Hangzhou; and Nanyang Technological University, Singapore. In addition, I need to thank the following individuals for their assistance during my research: Bernhard Fuehrer, Oliver Chan Hon-man, Ye Ye, and Koh Keng We. I would also like to take this opportunity to thank Nadine Bregler, Han Soojung, Huang Wanzhu, Jiang Qingjun, Jo Jungeun, Kim Eunha, Min Sun-young, Tan Tianyuan, Marcus White, Xu Yuan, Yan Zinan, and Zhan Beibei. Finally, this book is dedicated to the Gupta family of Drummond Street in London, whose kindness and generosity ensured that I didn't actually starve to death while writing my PhD.

CHRONOLOGY OF CHINESE DYNASTIES

SHANG CA. 1600–CA. 1046 BCE

ZHOU CA. 1046–221 BCE

- Western Zhou ca. 1046–771 BCE
- Eastern Zhou 771–221 BCE

SPRING AND AUTUMN PERIOD 771–475 BCE

WARRING STATES ERA 475–221 BCE

QIN 221–206 BCE

HAN 206 BCE–220 CE

- Western Han 206 BCE–6 CE
- Xin (Wang Mang interregnum) 6–24
- Eastern Han 25–220

THREE KINGDOMS PERIOD 220–280

- Wei 220–265
- Shu 220–265
- Wu 222–280

JIN 265–317

NORTHERN DYNASTIES 386–581

- Northern Liang 389–439
- Northern Wei 386–535
- Eastern Wei 534–550
- Western Wei 535–570
- Northern Qi 550–577
- Northern Zhou 557–581

SOUTHERN DYNASTIES 317–589
- Eastern Jin 317–420
- Song (Liu-Song) 420–479
- Southern Qi 479–502
- Liang 502–557
- Chen 557–589

SUI 589–618

TANG 618–907

FIVE DYNASTIES 907–960

LIAO 916–1125

SONG 960–1279
- Northern Song 960–1127
- Southern Song 1127–1279

JIN 1115–1234

YUAN 1260–1368

MING 1368–1644

QING 1644–1911

THE EMPRESS IN THE PEPPER CHAMBER

Introduction

IN THE HAN DYNASTY (206 BCE–220 CE), AND INDEED THROUGHOUT the imperial era in China, the administration of the central government within the palace city was subject to sexual segregation. Palace women lived and worked in the area known as the Rear Palace (Hougong), while their male peers worked in the Front Palace (Qiangong). The Rear Palace was in turn divided into a number of different areas depending on function: low-ranking women lived and worked in the Lateral Courts (Yeting), while higher-ranking individuals had their own private residences, where they were assisted by a dedicated household staff. The empress herself was housed in a special centrally located residence called the "Pepper Chamber" (Jiaofang).[1] Since this complex was her designated abode, the same term was also used as an epithet to apply to her, and in Han dynasty usage "to be resident at the Pepper Chamber" (*zai Jiaofang*) or "to become the Pepper Chamber" (*wei Jiaofang*) were synonyms for being appointed as empress.[2] There are a handful of accounts preserved in ancient Chinese literature that describe the construction of this residence, whose name, they explain, was derived from the mixing of Sichuan pepper into the plaster with which these structures were built.[3] The clearest explanation for this practice is found in *Ceremonial Regulations for Han Dynasty Officials* (Hanguan yi) by the Eastern Han dynasty historian Ying Shao (140–206 CE). It states that the spices were incorporated into the construction of the empress's official residence in the interests of encouraging the birth of many children: "The empress is called by the epithet 'Pepper Chamber' in order to take advantage of its implication of numerous fruit. *Book of Songs* [Shijing] says: 'The fruit of the pepper plant grow lushly and fill a *sheng*-measure.'[4] The building [is constructed with] pepper-infused plaster, in order to imbue [the empress's residence] with warmth and expel evil influences."[5]

Sichuan pepper, like many other pungent spices, was considered a numinous substance, allowing communication with the spirit world. At the same time, it was also a symbol of fertility, and when the Han dynasty empress was required to take up residence in the Pepper Chamber, this was done in the hope that she might be responsible for the birth of offspring for the imperial house, in particular an heir to the throne.[6] Given that Han emperors maintained harems that housed not only their main wife but also numerous other junior consorts and concubines, the role of the empress in encouraging fertility extended to encouraging the emperor to produce children with other women as well. Above and beyond that, residence in the Pepper Chamber was considered an embodiment of the wider function of the empress as the supreme maternal role model for the entire country. The many fruit of the pepper plant crushed into the plaster in the walls of the Pepper Chamber symbolized her significance in assuring the reproductive success of all families throughout the empire.

The Empress in the Pepper Chamber is a study of the life and literary legacy of one Han dynasty empress: Zhao "Feiyan," or "Flying Swallow" (formally titled Empress Xiaocheng; d. 1 BCE), the second wife of Emperor Cheng (r. 32–7 BCE). As documented in the earliest surviving biography of the empress, preserved in *History of the Han Dynasty* (Hanshu), Zhao Feiyan was considered by many to have been a spectacular failure in every aspect of her duties as a denizen of the Pepper Chamber. First, having been born into slavery and trained in the performing arts, she was thought to be utterly lacking in the high social status and exemplary moral qualities desirable in an empress. Second, she and her sister, Zhao "Zhaoyi" ("Lady of Brilliant Deportment," an official rank; d. 7 BCE), who was also a fellow resident of Emperor Cheng's harem, were criticized for not observing the kind of modest and womanly behavior praised in ritual texts, instead wasting taxpayers' money with wild extravagance. Third, in spite of virtually monopolizing the emperor's sexual favors for many years, Empress Zhao not only failed to give birth to any children herself, but she and her sister were both accused of murdering rival women and their offspring. Fourth, and finally, on the death of Emperor Cheng, when her younger sister was forced to commit suicide because of her involvement in the deaths of a succession of baby princes, Empress Zhao Feiyan saved her own life by acting quickly to install Emperor Ai (r. 7–1 BCE) in power. However, Emperor Ai also failed to produce any children, and

Empress Zhao was eventually demoted and forced to commit suicide in the purge that took place on his demise. The political problems caused by the throne passing from one childless branch of the imperial family to another played a major role in destabilizing the Han dynasty. The legend of the evil empress, villainously scheming to destroy her rivals even if this brought ruin to the regime, was established in this first biographical account.

An alternative tradition concerning Empress Zhao Feiyan can be found in other Han dynasty and Age of Disunion (220–589 CE) texts. Again she is portrayed as failing in her duties as the occupant of the Pepper Chamber, though in quite a different way from the official history of the dynasty. Rather than describing her murdering a succession of infants, this tradition emphasizes her seductive beauty and sensual appeal, the insanely expensive luxuries that she and her sister enjoyed in their lives as pampered harem favorites, and the empress's sexual promiscuity that saw her engaged in affairs with a number of low-class men. Her wasteful squandering of national resources was one way of demonstrating her failure to act as a maternal role model to the empire. Far more serious, however, was her failure to produce children with Emperor Cheng, and hence her determination to have sex with as many men as possible—from inside or outside the palace—in the hope of becoming pregnant. Empress Zhao Feiyan is depicted as utterly unprincipled and immoral in her determination to foist some illegitimate brat upon the imperial house. She flouted the most basic norms of female behavior within a patriarchal society, and the degradation that she planned to inflict upon the throne was only thwarted by the fact that she never became pregnant. Tales from this tradition can be found preserved in texts such as *Miscellaneous Records of the Western Capital* (Xijing zaji), *Yellow Plans of the Three Capital Regions* (Sanfu huangtu), and *Records Gleaned from Lost Works* (Shiyi ji). During the Tang dynasty (618–907 CE), these stories would coalesce and be combined into one particularly important and influential text: *The Scandalous Tale of Zhao Feiyan* (Zhao Feiyan waizhuan). This is not merely one of the earliest surviving erotic works to be produced in the Chinese language; it is also highly significant in establishing a new kind of prose literature—writings purporting to tell the "true story" of life in the imperial harem. It is *The Scandalous Tale* that is the major focus of this book.

After it first came into circulation in the late Tang dynasty, *The Scandalous Tale* continued to be popular throughout the remainder of the imperial era, and would be regularly rewritten, expanded, and updated to take account of changing tastes. This text should be considered seminal in creating a wider literary genre, here termed "Silk Pillow" literature. This genre covers a variety of "unorthodox"—or in other words invented—histories, including texts with a significant erotic or pornographic component. These prose works have a number of important characteristics in common. First, the text makes use of the names of genuine historical individuals, most notably those of emperors and their consorts. Additionally, the narrative centers on the female characters, whose luxurious lifestyles and sexual exploits are described in considerable detail. Further, as with other genres of palace literature, Silk Pillow writings make strong claims of authenticity. This means that however unlikely the events reported, they are given a gloss of truth by the author's claim of personal experience or privileged information. The term is itself derived from a line in a song lyric titled "Yuchi's Cup" (Yuchi bei) composed by the Northern Song literatus Liu Yong (987–1053), which describes an elite man and his lover: "Cuddled up among silk pillows with phoenix patterns and mandarin-duck embroidered coverlet" (Choumiu fengzhen yuanbei).[7] It is particularly appropriate to derive the term describing this genre of palace prose writing from one of Liu Yong's songs, since although wildly popular with contemporary audiences, the combination of a lushly emotional atmosphere, coupled with sexually explicit passages and detailed descriptions of luxurious living meant that his work was traditionally denigrated as the acme of vulgarity by the educated elite. This assessment is not unrelated to the problem that has all too often afflicted Silk Pillow writings: either they are taken far too seriously as genuine historical sources or they are not taken seriously enough, because they are too popular, too emotionally charged, too lurid and revealing about private matters—particularly issues of sexuality—and too hedonistic to be openly admired and appreciated as the remarkable works of literature that so many of these texts are.

Fictional accounts purporting to tell the true story of the private lives of the rich and powerful are not unique to China; this genre is well established and has been the subject of a great deal of academic interest in other cultures.[8] However, the terms used to describe this kind of literature are often very vague: European examples of such writings are sometimes referred to as libelous or scurrilous pamphlets, reflecting the format in which they were published and the contention that their contents were not true.[9] In other instances, the terminology is extremely culturally specific—for example,

French Silk Pillow writings are known by the names of major targets: hence *mazarinades* attack Cardinal Mazarin (1602–1661), while *poissonades* complain about the licentiousness and luxurious lifestyle of King Louis XV's official mistress, Madame de Pompadour (1721–1764), whose maiden name was Poisson.[10] It would be highly anachronistic to use such terms to discuss Chinese literature. Therefore, the more neutral term of Silk Pillow literature will be used in this book.

Silk Pillow writings are fictional representations of life in the imperial harem, and, as such, texts like *The Scandalous Tale* tell us nothing about the life of the real Empress Zhao. On the other hand, given that the imperial harem was the subject of great interest in popular culture, and that it was a focus of enormous anxieties about gender, sexuality, the corrupting influence of wealth, and so on, these texts can be very informative about changing attitudes toward the perennially controversial issue of women in positions of power. Although the development of many of the key concepts in defining the role of the empress in imperial-era China have not been the subject of much research, the institutions of queenship have been widely studied in other cultures, and the results of such studies are relevant for understanding the situation in China.[11] However, compared to many other civilizations, an astonishingly strict control was exerted throughout the imperial era in China over information leaking from the Rear Palace, both because of concerns over national security and in the interests of preserving the mystique of the reigning dynasty.[12] As a result, with accurate information extremely hard to come by, the emperor's harem was more easily transformed into a site of fantasy: a place where every hedonistic desire could be fulfilled. Projections of this kind may have no basis in reality, but they nevertheless created stereotypes about palace women that are still widely perpetuated today.

The role of empresses in the Han dynasty, as prescribed in ritual texts, was twofold: to encourage the birth of children within the imperial harem and to support the mandate of the ruling house. During the Han, empresses were usually appointed on the basis of their illustrious lineage and political connections, but their sons were not legally prioritized in the succession. Hence, the majority of Han emperors were stepsons or children adopted by the previous emperor's main wife. These women were often quite successful in building working relationships with their fictive kin, but had much more difficulty weathering political storms. As a result, a remarkable number of empresses during this period died by violence. In practice, their distinguished ancestry proved of little benefit in the event of a purge at court; furthermore, empresses could be killed for political reasons regardless of whether they had given birth to children or not. The dangers faced by the historical Empress Zhao underpin fictional accounts of her behavior, which stress her manipulative actions and overt subservience to her husband's wishes: if she or her sister were to offend the emperor, they would find themselves vulnerable to their many enemies. However, literary representations of Zhao Feiyan were not strongly tethered to historical accounts, but evolved in the wider context of Silk Pillow writings. For at least the past one thousand years, short stories and novels that claim to give the true story of life in the imperial harem have been highly popular. They have been instrumental in creating a highly sexualized image of palace women: young and beautiful, constantly engaged in jealous scheming against their rivals interspersed with bouts of frivolous shopping and vigorous sex acts. *The Scandalous Tale*, as one of the very earliest surviving works in this genre, was significant in setting many of the standard themes associated with such writings.

The plot of *The Scandalous Tale* (translated in full in chapter 2) focuses on the triangular relationship between Emperor Cheng, his second empress, Zhao Feiyan, and her younger sister, named in this text as Zhao Hede. Recounted with a strong narrative focus on the experience of women within the Han Rear Palace, *The Scandalous Tale* describes the emperor's sexual obsession first with the empress and then with Zhao Hede and their internecine rivalry, all carried out in a setting of unimaginable luxury. Although this text is well known, and a number of translations have been produced in various Western languages, all translations to date have been expurgated. This book provides the first complete translation into English of *The Scandalous Tale*, with extensive annotations and notes, as well as translations of the three further associated short texts, attributed to the putative author, Ling Xuan; the major late Western Han to Eastern Han dynasty transition period philosopher and statesman Huan Tan (ca. 43 BCE–28 CE); and the Jin dynasty scholar and statesman Xun Xu (d. 289 CE), respectively.

A comparison between *The Scandalous Tale* and the earliest surviving biography of Zhao Feiyan, found in *History of the Han Dynasty*, indicates that they are completely unrelated: indeed, if it were not for the names being the same, it would be impossible to identify the two accounts as pertaining to the same person. *The Scandalous Tale* can clearly be related to an alternative biographical tradition that focused on Empress Zhao's extravagance and immorality. Although the difference between these two trends in writings about Zhao Feiyan has long been recognized, the connections between *The Scandalous Tale* and the histories of the Han dynasty have not. According to this novella, the eponymous protagonist was born to a granddaughter of the king of Jiangdu as a result of her affair with a lowborn musician; the text returns again and again to the connection between the Zhao family and the royal house of Jiangdu. According to *History of the Han Dynasty*, the kings of Jiangdu, descended from Emperor Jing (r. 157–141 BCE), were notorious for their violent and uncontrolled behavior; furthermore, the second and last king of Jiangdu was recorded as having inflicted appalling sexual tortures upon the unfortunate women in his household. The reiteration of the fact that Zhao Feiyan was connected by blood with the sadistic king of Jiangdu, whose incestuous relationships and murderous rages were described in great detail in the official history of the dynasty, suggests that the author or authors of *The Scandalous Tale* had some knowledge of this text.

The Scandalous Tale has been the subject of controversy for at least one thousand years, with various dates of composition being suggested ranging from the Han dynasty to the Song. This range of possible dates actually does not affect its status as one of the earliest surviving erotic texts to be written in the Chinese language. However, a careful consideration of the textual history of this novella, the language employed in the writing, and the history of its reception means that it can be proved that *The Scandalous Tale* dates in its current form to the late Tang dynasty. Related textual material preserved in earlier texts suggests that the possibility that *The Scandalous Tale* contains some older sections should not be ruled out, but linguistic analysis indicates that the present text cannot have been composed prior to the Tang. Characterization of the Zhao sisters in *The Scandalous Tale* derives much of its interest from the fact that it claims to provide a privileged perspective into the lives of some of the most important and powerful women of the time; the supposed author, Ling Xuan, is said to have obtained his information from his concubine, a relative of Zhao Feiyan who also served in the Han Rear Palace. However, in the course of the narrative, while Emperor Cheng's actions and motives are consistently laid bare to the reader, the reasons the Zhao sisters behave as they do are obscure. Hence, although the story as a whole is presented from a highly unusual feminized perspective—something that is virtually unique in fiction writings at this early period—the women characters are throughout the most mysterious, their true thoughts and feelings often hidden even from those closest to them.

The role of gender stereotyping in representations of Empress Zhao Feiyan is apparent in both *History of the Han Dynasty* and *The Scandalous Tale*, where she is explicitly described as jealous (*du*), a term loaded with strongly pejorative meanings in early imperial China. Given that only women were believed to suffer from sexual jealousy, it is impossible to escape the gender-specific connotations of this term. However, jealousy in Han dynasty texts usually refers to situations in which a woman's actions in interfering with male sexual behavior were believed to be endangering the dynasty, threatening the imperial house, or disrupting the smooth running of the government. Sexual jealousy was consistently interpreted as a political problem in Han dynasty texts. By the time *The Scandalous Tale* was written, attitudes had changed significantly. Although jealousy was still viewed as a specifically feminine emotion, it was now considered to be something that all women suffered from and a natural consequence of their gender. Once jealousy was considered a normal part of a woman's emotional life, it could no longer be problematized as it had been in the early imperial era. This in turn had a major impact on medieval and later literary representations of Empress Zhao Feiyan. Another aspect of gendering can be seen from the fact that almost all early writings about Empress Zhao were produced by men. Such a highly controversial woman would have been very difficult for other women to write about, since choosing such a topic might be seen as calling into question their own moral values. Hence, although men had been writing about Empress Zhao for two millennia, it was only in the Qing dynasty that women felt confident in tackling the subject of so subversive a female figure. The negative attitudes reported in their writings should not detract from our understanding just how revolutionary it was for women to undertake a literary response to so challenging a historical personage, who was believed to have utterly failed both as an empress and as a wife.

Thanks to the way in which *The Scandalous Tale* is presented, incorporating explicit claims of authenticity, for centuries people have believed that through reading this text they have obtained a privileged glimpse into the decadent luxuries enjoyed by imperial favorites at the height of the Western Han dynasty, and the vicious scheming that they engaged in to protect their positions. The stereotypes developed in this novella have proved to be astonishingly long-lived and pervasive. It is important to examine both historical texts and fictional writings to understand how our image of the Han dynasty Rear Palace has been constructed, and how this affects our views of the many and various women who lived there, and who—for better or worse—changed the history of China.

CHAPTER ONE

The Empress in the Pepper Chamber

ALTHOUGH CHINA WAS FIRST UNIFIED UNDER THE QIN DYNASTY IN 221 BCE, almost nothing is known about the Rear Palace in the time of the First Emperor. It is likely that at least some institutions and personnel appointments in the early imperial era were identical to those in the Qin royal palace, but so little is recorded of the palace administration during this period that this assumption is based upon Han dynasty accounts of practices that they identified as Qin-style. While the first monarch of a united China is known to have produced a number of children, the identity of their mothers was not recorded, and it is not clear whether he ever appointed an empress. Furthermore, given the quick collapse of the Qin regime in 206 BCE, it is unlikely that a strong tradition defining the role of the empress and shaping the administration of an expanded Rear Palace could have been established in such a short time. The Han dynasty would therefore have inherited some systems, but with considerable room for development and adaptation. During the course of the 400-year history of the dynasty, enormous changes would take place, which would in turn affect the way in which the powerful women of the imperial house—in particular empresses and dowager empresses—performed their roles, and how their position was envisaged.

Long before the beginning of the imperial era, there was a deeply ingrained tradition of concern about women wielding political power. Philosophers associated with widely differing schools of thought were united in agreeing that women were dangerous and malicious creatures, incapable of being educated and uncontrollable in their sexual urges, and whose involvement in the government of the country would inevitably throw the regime into chaos. Such ideas are recorded, for example, in the "On the Rectification of Power" (Quanxiu) chapter of *Book of Master Guan* (Guanzi): "If women speak of official affairs, then punishments and rewards will not be trustworthy" (Fu yan renshi, ze shangfa buxin).[1] A similar point of view is articulated in the "Signs of Destruction" (Wangzheng) chapter of *Book of Master Han Fei* (Han Feizi): "If [the ruler] listens to the commands of his mother, or employs women in [the government of] the state . . . he can bring [it and himself] to ruin" (Ting zhumu zhi ling, nüzi yong guo . . . ke wang ye).[2] Throughout the Han dynasty, conservative thinkers would argue that women in the Rear Palace should be confined solely to domestic duties, and if the appointment of an empress was considered necessary, she should be the mother of the heir to the throne. In this way, it could be made clear to one and all that her position was dependent upon his, an idea encapsulated in the saying "A mother should be honored because of her son" (Mu yi zi gui).[3] This would serve to inculcate patriarchal authority by emphasizing the transfer of power through the male line. However, when it comes to the imposition of this kind of conservative ideology in the Han dynasty, one thing is quite clear: this simply did not happen.

There are three reasons for women's ongoing participation in the government: one practical, one theoretical, and one institutional. The practical reason is that emperors got sick or went mad, or they died unexpectedly without an heir to the throne or with the succeeding monarch coming to power as a small child—any one of which situations would necessitate a regency or some kind of temporary power-sharing that might involve a woman taking control.[4] In any situation where a dynastic crisis could be mitigated by allowing a woman to assume power for a short time, misogynistic ideology would be set aside rather than risk plunging the regime into chaos and warfare. Theoretically, the empress was envisaged as a maternal role model for the entire empire and was commonly thought to hold a personal mandate to support the dynasty. Given that she was accorded this position in contemporary models of rulership, it proved impossible to keep the empress out of political decision-making. Finally, the empress was the head of the Rear Palace, a significant institution that employed many hundreds (if not thousands) of people, right at the heart of the government. She was in close personal contact with the emperor, the fountainhead of all authority in the imperial system, and played a key role in deciding which other individuals would be granted access to him. No matter how virulent the rhetoric against women wielding political power, empresses had no choice but to do so.

In the cutthroat atmosphere of Han dynasty politics, senior women in the imperial house were often casualties: of the sixteen Western Han dynasty empresses, only five died before disaster struck. The biographies found in the two relevant dynastic histories—*Records of the Grand Historian* (Shiji) compiled by Sima Qian (ca. 145–86 BCE) and *History of the Han Dynasty* (Hanshu) by Ban Gu (32–92 CE) and other members of his family—are shocking. Eight empresses were deposed, six were forced to commit suicide, one was murdered, and two survived serious political turmoil at the cost of seeing all their close relatives executed.[5] The actual rates of violence were probably considerably higher than what is recorded in the official histories of the dynasty (which does not always indicate cause of death for those who had been deposed or imprisoned), and a similar pattern is observable among other senior palace women as well, suggesting that the denizens of the Rear Palace were regularly engulfed in the waves of killing that took place during political purges. This exceptionally high level of violence affecting the most powerful female figures in the empire is not seen in other dynasties—even the Eastern Han dynasty seems to have seen a significantly reduced rate of murder of empresses.[6] This suggests that the position of Western Han dynasty empresses was unusually precariously balanced—had they been more powerful, they would have been too politically significant to kill; had they been less so, they would not have been worth executing since they posed no threat to anyone.

The Role of the Empress in Theory

In Han dynasty texts, the role of the empress was consistently defined in maternal terms, though the term later developed to define her role, "Mother of the Country" (Guomu), had not yet been coined.[7] Surviving Han dynasty accounts stressed the importance of her "nurturing" (*yang*) activities; she was supposed to "act as the mother of All-under-Heaven" (*wei Tianxia mu*); and her duties were said to involve "maternally watching over All-under-Heaven" (*mulin Tianxia*), "maternally watching over the myriad states" (*mulin wanguo*), and "acting as a maternal role model for All-under-Heaven" (*mu yi Tianxia*), the last term being often abbreviated simply to "acting as a maternal role model" (*mu yi*).[8] These terms were used regardless of whether or not the empress concerned had personally given birth to children, since this maternal rhetoric was directed at social and not biological motherhood.[9] Since the laws of succession of the Han dynasty did not require the heir to the throne to be the son of the empress, many empresses did in fact avoid becoming mothers—whether by choice or necessity—relying instead for their long-term future on alternative sources of power such as their role in bringing up the heir apparent and assisting him in establishing his own authority; the exalted position of their own natal families; their rank within the uppermost echelons of the hierarchy of the imperial house; or the political capital gained by presiding over the smooth transfer of power from one emperor to the next. An empress might have good reasons for wishing to avoid the experience of pregnancy and childbirth: Lady Xian (d. 66 BCE), the mother of Empress Huo Chengjun (d. 54 BCE) and grandmother of Empress Shangguan (d. 37 BCE), calculated the danger as follows: "It is extremely risky for women to give birth, with ten dying for every one that survives."[10] In such circumstances, it was clearly desirable to have other women endangering their lives by producing offspring, providing that the empress could successfully assert her maternal and nurturing role with respect to whichever male child was eventually chosen as heir to the throne. Birth mothers could be sidelined, but if they proved recalcitrant, they might be killed.

If the empress was always represented in Han dynasty texts as a motherly figure, the emperor, by contrast, was never presented in a paternal role as the father of the country and only comparatively rarely shown as a parent, such as in the locution "The ruler of the country is the father and mother of his people."[11] Instead, the emperor was designated in Han dynasty texts by an extremely ancient title, that of "Son of Heaven" (Tianzi). In some instances, the role of the Son of Heaven is described as intrinsically parental and gender-balanced: "The Son of Heaven is the father and mother of the people, and thus he can act as the monarch of All-under-Heaven" (Tianzi zuo min fumu, yiwei Tianxia wang), but this kind of formulation seems to be confined to theoretical discussions in texts that do not consider any role for the Son of Heaven's consort.[12] The title "Son of Heaven" developed at a very early stage in Chinese history; it appears in a number of ancient bronze vessel inscriptions as well as in the transmitted textual tradition.[13] Alternative designations for the Han dynasty emperor, such as "Sovereign" (Shang), place more emphasis on his position as the individual situated at the apex of the bureaucratic and social pyramid.[14] Conceptualizations of the role of the emperor that place him alone at the summit of power ignore the role of his consort, the empress, as the "Mother of All-under-Heaven." The significance accorded in the title of "Son of Heaven" to the emperor's religious role, as the representative of the supreme deity upon earth, means that he could be considered the lowest figure of the celestial hierarchy.[15] Indeed, there is some evidence that the monarch was occasionally envisaged as the offspring of a deity and a human woman: that is, literally a "Son of Heaven."[16] However, if the marriage of the monarch and his consort is viewed as a microcosm of the entire world, then this relationship serves as the conjunction of two different realms, where the celestial and terrestrial hierarchies meet.

In an alternative view of the gendered relationship standing at the heart of government, common to a number of Confucian texts, the emperor was portrayed as the leader of all men in the empire, and the empress as the head of all women. As is standard in such representations of imperial authority, it was modeled upon a worldview in which the state was considered an extension of the family—and the family a miniature version of the state—and predicated upon a belief that the emperor and empress, manifesting virtuous behavior within their own relationship, would then in turn bring about the moral transformation of the people. This image reflected an idealized understanding of the nature of the marriage between the Zhou king (and Son of Heaven) and his consort the queen, which can be seen in ritual texts of an earlier era: "The Son of Heaven takes charge of the education of men, while the queen presides over the obedience of women; the Son of Heaven regulates the way of yang, while the queen controls the power of yin; the Son of Heaven takes charge of the government on the outside, while the queen presides over the women of the household. When education and obedience are inculcated, then inside and out are in harmony, and both state and family are well governed."[17]

There were certainly some ceremonial and religious aspects of the empress's role in which she appeared formally at the head of a parade of palace women; for example, in the annual spring ceremonies involving sacrifices to the deity Gaomei, she was present with all the female residents of the Rear Palace. In these fertility rites, women who had recently engaged in sexual relations with the emperor were the focus of the ceremony and treated with special honor.[18] When the empress performed sericulture and lustration rituals, she was accompanied by the wives of senior government officials, indicating that these were also gendered ceremonies.[19] However, it appears that most Han dynasty texts emanating from government officials did not favor a gender-segregated interpretation of the position of the empress. The clearest expression of this is the account of the death of the unfortunate Empress Song (d. 178 CE) in the Eastern Han dynasty. She was forced to commit suicide after having been accused of using witchcraft against her husband, Emperor Ling (r. 168–189 CE); then, following her untimely death, the emperor dreamed that he was accused of failing as the Son of Heaven. Terrified, Emperor Ling consulted a member of his staff, Xu Yong, about the significance of this dream and was told in no uncertain terms of the support his late wife enjoyed among the people whom she had represented so loyally: "Empress Song personally officiated with Your Majesty at the shrines to the imperial ancestors, and she maternally watched over the myriad states. She did this for many years and all within the seas was transformed [by her beneficent influence]: no one ever heard of her making a mistake or doing an evil deed.[20] But you listened to the words of flattery and jealousy, and thus the innocent were punished: she suffered the extreme penalty and disaster overtook her family. Your vassals—male and female—across the empire are all angry and upset about this."[21]

In spite of having successfully performed her duties, Empress Song was the victim of slander and ended up suffering the death penalty. The people of the empire felt deeply unhappy at this development: they had witnessed the downfall of the person who was their representative at the highest echelons of government. Furthermore, it is worth noting that it is both male and female subjects (*chenqie*) of the Han who are said to be angry, since Empress Song represented both men and women in her formal duties. This kind of usage reaffirms the impression that Han people saw the empress as the apex of earthly authority, representing all people within the realm, not just women and certainly not merely the denizens of the Rear Palace.

The use of the title "Son of Heaven" for the Han emperor implies a connection with the dynasty's "Mandate of Heaven" (Tianming); again this is a very ancient concept that significantly predates the unification of China.[22] However, if successive emperors in the Han imperial house were thought to have inherited the Mandate of Heaven from their ancestors, empresses were thought to be in possession of a personal role in affirming that mandate which justified their authority. This can clearly be seen in proceedings to depose an empress, which frequently invoked the loss of the Mandate of Heaven by these women individually: this was true of Empress Chen (d. ca. 110 BCE), the first wife of Emperor Wu (r. 141–87 BCE), and Empress Huo Chengjun, the second wife of Emperor Xuan (r. 73–49 BCE). In each case, an identical formula was used in the document declaring their deposition: "[She] cannot uphold the Mandate of Heaven."[23] Again, right at the end of the Eastern Han dynasty, when the warlord Cao Cao (155–220 CE) deposed Empress Fu Shou (d. 214 CE) to allow one of his own daughters to be promoted in her stead, she too was said to be unfit to uphold the Mandate of Heaven.[24]

The position of empress was to be held only by a truly exceptional woman, for the emperor's family Mandate of Heaven was reinforced by the empress's own great personal distinctions and virtues.[25] Here, it is relevant to consider another of the honorifics that could be accorded to an empress: the title of "lesser ruler" (Xiaojun). This ancient title was defined in *Guliang's Tradition [of the Spring and Autumn Annals]* (Guliang zhuan) as follows: "A lesser ruler is not a ruler. So why is the term 'ruler' used? She is the main consort of the lord and that is why she can be called a 'lesser ruler.'"[26] When Han dynasty empresses were designated as "lesser ruler," it indicates that, while perhaps not as politically important as the Son of Heaven, they were nevertheless monarchs (*jun*) and not subjects (*chen*). As a result of the emphasis placed upon the empress as a support to the dynasty, their biographies—and indeed those of other senior women in the Rear Palace including dowager empresses and other senior consorts—frequently stress their special qualifications for upholding the mandate. For Zhao Feiyan, this would be one of the key justifications for the attacks launched on her throughout her time in the Rear Palace: as a former slave and dancing girl, she was too lowly and inferior to be able to assist in supporting Emperor Cheng's mandate.

The Role of the Empress in Practice

The two most important aspects of the empress's role in theory—acting as a maternal role model and supporting her husband's mandate—had a major impact on the way that empresses acted in practice. Given that there could only be one empress at a time, the onus was upon finding the single most useful person to appoint as the emperor's primary consort.[27] It was undoubtedly the case that a wife with a strong connection to a powerful lineage could play a crucial role in raising her spouse to the throne, allowing him to defeat other rivals. The marriage practices of the Han imperial house strongly favored social endogamy, with emperors usually selecting spouses from a small group of aristocratic houses—exactly the same group of families from whom marriage partners for princesses were also commonly selected. Thanks to close political connections reinforced by repeated intermarriage, their interests could be presumed to be closely tied to those of the imperial house. The choice of empresses from a small number of very prestigious lineages with different surnames allowed the Liu family to maintain patterns of surname exogamy related to preunification practice.[28] By marrying the daughters of paternal sisters, or the descendants of maternal brothers or cousins, the emperor consolidated the power held by his closest blood relatives, whose interests thus became ever more intimately linked with his own.

Given that the emperor, as Son of Heaven, was a semidivine being, he would have been regarded by most people as an unimaginably alien "other." For such a person to marry an "ordinary" woman would have been profoundly troubling; by seeking a consort from an affinal lineage, the emperor reinforced the mystique and separateness of the imperial house.[29] The Han dynasty emperors who chose to marry wives of low birth—Emperor Wu, Emperor Xuan, and Emperor Cheng—did so as a test of their authority: this is made particularly clear in the case of Emperor Xuan, given that he threatened to abdicate if his personal choice of a spouse was not accepted by government officials.[30] At the same time as asserting the right to select their own consort, these emperors were also affirming their ability to raise into the aristocracy any family they might choose. This was successful in the case of Emperor Wu's and Emperor Xuan's consorts. Emperor Wu's second empress, Wei Zifu (d. 91 BCE), had a life that began and ended in miserable circumstances: she started out as a slave-entertainer and was eventually demoted and forced to commit suicide during the witchcraft scandals that decimated the court in the years 91–90 BCE.[31] However, the extended Wei family did become fully incorporated into the ruling elite, not least because Wei Zifu served as empress for thirty-eight years, and the last five Western Han emperors were directly descended from her. Meanwhile, Empress Xu Pingjun (89–71 BCE), the first wife of Emperor Xuan, was also criticized for her humble origins when she was first appointed: her father had been convicted of a crime for which he was punished by castration—this ensured that, later on, protests were made against his being raised to a marquisate when his daughter was appointed empress.[32] Again, the Xu family would subsequently become integrated into the highest echelons of Han dynasty society, and when her niece was selected as Emperor Cheng's first wife, there is no suggestion that the family was still considered too lowborn to provide imperial consorts. Empress Zhao was also criticized for her very humble origins on her initial appointment. This was, however, a dangerous argument to push too far: prior to her appointment she already held senior rank in the Rear Palace, and her father had been granted a marquisate.[33] In other words, the Zhao family had already been promoted into the aristocracy, and henceforward should be considered a distinguished lineage. After all, if not even an emperor could successfully raise the family of his main wife above their base origins, did that not suggest serious limits to his authority?

The empress did not just act as the mother of the country, supporting the imperial mandate; she also represented the apex of power within the Rear Palace.[34] This institution was the site of the emperor's harem, but above and beyond that, it also controlled a number of important government offices and bureaus. Of the manufacturing divisions administered by the Rear Palace, the Weaving Room (Zhishi) is perhaps the best known.[35] This division was responsible for the production of high-quality textiles for government and palace use, made from silk thread submitted as tax payment. Furthermore, a very large number of women who were not expected to engage in sexual relationships with the emperor worked within the Rear Palace: they ranged from lowly charwomen and cleaners up to senior female officials. Even consorts who failed to produce offspring for the imperial house should probably best be considered as servants of the dynasty rather than as concubines.[36] Some women recruited to work in the palace ended up in a sexual relationship with the emperor, but the Rear Palace and the polygynous harem were overlapping and not identical institutions.

During the Han dynasty, men and women who were employed by the state would have held a rank (*jue*) in the orders of honor, and a job title depending on their role in the bureaucracy. The orders of honor were graded from the lowest level of one to the highest level of twenty, and served as a mechanism to tie the interests of the wider population to those of the regime, with promotions being offered to celebrate major events in the reign of each emperor, such as his accession or the appointment of an empress or an heir to the throne. Many aspects of an individual's life were affected by the rank he or she held, including the kind of house they could live in, the amount of land they could hold, and the taxes they paid.[37] The very highest rank in the orders of honor (effectively rank twenty-one), that of *zhuhouwang*, or "king," was reserved for members of the imperial family, and hence was commonly omitted from consideration in discussions of ranking since it was usually not possible to be promoted up to this level.[38] A woman employed by the regime outside the Rear Palace was graded by the same system as men: for example, Xu Fu, who was employed by the first Han emperor as a fortune-teller, achieved the remarkable feat of being granted the title of Marquis of Mingci in her own right—the same *liehou*, or "adjunct marquis," rank she would have held had she been a man.[39] Given that this was the highest rank anyone outside the imperial house could achieve, Xu Fu was as honored as any Han dynasty individual could possibly be. However, as the dynastic histories and Han dynasty administrative texts make clear, women in the Rear Palace made use of a different system of ranks from those that pertained in wider society, and this has often been somewhat misunderstood. The most detailed description of this hierarchy is that given in *History of the Han Dynasty*, and it is here translated in full:

> When the Han arose they continued to use Qin nomenclature and titles, so the mother of the emperor was called *huang taihou* [dowager empress], his grandmother was called *taihuang taihou* [grand dowager empress], his wife was called *huanghou* [empress], and his concubines were all called *furen* [consorts].[40] In addition there were the titles of *meiren* [beauty], *liangren* [virtuous lady], *bazi* [consort of the eighth rank], *qizi* [consort of the seventh rank], *changshi* [senior palace maid], and *shaoshi* [junior palace maid].[41] Then Emperor Wu established the official titles *jieyu* [lady of handsome fairness], *xing'e* [lady of graceful beauty], *ronghua* [lady of lovely countenance], and *chongyi* [lady of complete deportment], so that each had their own rank and position, and when Emperor Yuan [r. 48–33 BCE] added the title of *zhaoyi* [lady of bright deportment] there were fourteen ranks in all.[42] A *zhaoyi* was comparable to a *chengxiang* [chancellor], and her rank was equivalent to that of *zhuhouwang*. A *jieyu* was comparable to a *shangqing* [senior minister], and [her rank] was equivalent to that of a *liehou*.[43] A *xing'e* was comparable to an official with a salary of a full two thousand bushels of grain, and [her rank] was equivalent to that of a *guanneihou* [marquis within the passes]. A *ronghua* was comparable to an official with a salary of a true two thousand bushels of grain, and [her rank] was equivalent to that of a *dashangzao*

> [senior imperial provider]. A *meiren* was comparable to an official with a salary of two thousand bushels of grain, and [her rank] was equivalent to that of a *shaoshangzao* [junior imperial provider]. A *bazi* was comparable to an official with a salary of a thousand bushels of grain, and [her rank] was equivalent to that of a *zhonggeng* [head of the middle watch]. A *chongyi* was comparable to an official with a salary of a thousand bushels of grain, and [her rank] was equivalent to that of *zuogeng* [head of the left watch]. A *qizi* was comparable to an official with a salary of eight hundred bushels of grain, and [her rank] was equivalent to that of a *youshuzhang* [chief of the right host]. A *liangren* was comparable to an official with a salary of eight hundred bushels of grain, and [her rank] was equivalent to that of a *zuoshuzhang*. A *changshi* was comparable to an official with a salary of six hundred bushels of grain, and [her rank] was comparable to that of a *wudafu* [grand master]. A *shaoshi* was comparable to an official with a salary of four hundred bushels of grain, and [her rank] was comparable to that of a *gongsheng* [master of chariots]. A *wuguan* [all-purpose maid] was comparable to an official with a salary of three hundred bushels of grain. A *shunchang* [lady of obedient constancy] was comparable to an official with a salary of two hundred bushels of grain. A *wujuan* [lady without impurity], *gonghe* [lady of reverent gentleness], *yuling* [lady of pleasing spirit], *baolin* [lady of the precious bevy], *liangshi* [maid of virtuous employment], and *yezhe* [lady of night attendance] would all be comparable to an official with a salary of one hundred bushels of grain. A *shangjiarenzi* [senior woman of the household] and a *zhongjiarenzi* [ordinary woman of the household] were comparable to an official with a salary measured in pecks.[44]

Although this account states that there were fourteen ranks within the Rear Palace hierarchy, the text in fact names twenty-one, the same as in the regular Han dynasty orders of honor. Ban Gu seems to have understood the usual Han dynasty orders as normative, and attempts to relate the two systems, which does not work. There is some equivalency between the two, but it seems that in the Rear Palace there was a much larger number of low ranks than pertained in society as a whole (see appendix 1). Since there were fewer middle- and high-ranking positions in the Rear Palace hierarchy, women's salaries, responsibilities, and power would have undergone a marked increase with each promotion. However, appointment to the very uppermost ranks was clearly dependent on imperial favor. The account given in *History of the Han Dynasty* also suggests that the title of *zhaoyi* was created by Emperor Yuan to honor women in the Rear Palace who were the mothers of kings, creating a distinction between these women and holders of the next highest rank of *jieyu*, who enjoyed the same salary but did not necessarily have children.[45] In fact, women holding the title of *zhaoyi* seem to have been treated more as quasi empresses in situations where the emperor was unable to promote them further for personal or political reasons. This means that in Emperor Cheng's harem, the positions of Zhao Feiyan and her younger sister, Zhao Zhaoyi, were effectively unassailable, since between them they occupied both the position of empress and that of empress-in-waiting.

While the description given in *History of the Han Dynasty* is unique for the level of detail it gives about the ranking of women in the Rear Palace, it is not the only Han dynasty text to mention this system. For example, *Old Ceremonial Regulations for Han Dynasty Officials* (Hanguan jiuyi) by the early Eastern Han dynasty scholar Wei Hong (fl. 25–57 CE) gives a closely related account of the system. However, here the emphasis is on the ritual (*li*) position accorded to these women. Furthermore, although much of this discussion centers on titles known to have been used in the Western Han dynasty Rear Palace, reference is also made to the title of *guiren*, or "noble lady," which does not appear in the *History of the Han Dynasty*. This title was an Eastern Han dynasty creation, instituted by Emperor Guangwu (r. 25–57 CE) in his simplified and streamlined five-rank harem hierarchy.[46] The *Old Ceremonial Regulations for Han Dynasty Officials* account reads as follows:

> A *jieyu* . . . is treated with ritual comparable to that for a *chengxiang*. A *xing'e* . . . is treated according to the ritual appropriate for a general, or the *yushi dafu* [head of the censorate]. A *zhaoyi* . . . is [treated with ritual] comparable to that for an official with a salary of a full two thousand bushels of grain. A *guiren* . . . is treated by ritual in a manner comparable to an official with a salary of two thousand bushels of grain. *Meiren* are not limited in number. Persons of rank lower than that of *jieyu* all live in the Lateral Courts [area of the palace].[47]

As this account makes clear, all the most senior members of the palace hierarchy would have maintained their own households, and the management of a more or less extensive staff was an important part of their day-to-day duties. In excavations of the site of the Weiyang Palace, the location of the Pepper Chamber has been discovered. The associated fourteen other buildings have been tentatively identified as the residences of individuals holding the rank of *zhaoyi* and *jieyu*: that is, palace women whose seniority entitled them to their own private accommodation.[48] *Old Ceremonial Regulations for Han Dynasty Officials* goes on to explain that numbers of upper-echelon palace women were restricted, but that there were numerous junior positions: "There is only one empress. From *jieyu* to *guiren* rank, there may be up to ten at each level. *Meiren* are comparable to *daizhao* [expectant officials], and there is no limit to the number. Emperor Yuan and Emperor Cheng both had thousands."[49]

At present, one of the biggest lacunae in our understanding of the workings of the Rear Palace is a very incomplete understanding of the duties performed by women, particularly those of lower rank. While the grading of different ranks in the Rear Palace is reasonably well documented, this provides information with respect to the male hierarchy and does not inform us about the work that these women actually carried out. It is only the most senior women in the Rear Palace—the empress, dowager empress, and grand dowager empress—who have their actions recorded in the dynastic histories. From the very beginning of the dynasty, these women exercised considerable power in the day-to-day running of the empire: the large number of surviving edicts they issued dealing with a wide range of different issues demonstrates that they could assert their authority in many areas of policy.[50] Thus, although some Han dynasty sources claim that "the status of the empress was comparable to that of a king" (*huanghou zhi bi guowang*) rather than an emperor, this locution seems to underestimate her potential significance in the government, particularly in the case of dominant figures like Empress Lü (d. 180 BCE).[51] It is more likely that a contemporary audience would recognize the value accorded to the position of empress in the announcement made by Emperor He (r. 88–105 CE) when he appointed Deng Sui (d. 121 CE) as his principal consort, which stresses that her duties comprised both ritual and managerial roles that were likely to prove extremely challenging: "The honorable position of the empress is equal to my own; she must support the imperial ancestral shrines and be Mother to All-under-Heaven—this is not easy at all! Only Deng Guiren has the virtue to control the Rear [Palace and Lateral] Courts, so she could assume this office."[52]

The greatest political significance of the senior women of the Rear Palace lay in their role as regents in the event of a minor emperor coming to the throne—and here it should be noted that very few Han dynasty emperors came to the throne as adults—and overseeing periods of transition. In particular, they played a crucial role in supervising the sometimes highly delicate process by which the throne was transferred from one emperor to the next. In the event of the death or deposition of the emperor, authority was supposed to pass to the heir apparent. If no heir apparent had been appointed, a member of the imperial house from one of the kingly lineages should be installed as the new emperor. These individuals, to use historian Andrew Eisenberg's term, form the "politically relevant imperial descent group."[53] The decision as to which member of which lineage should be invested as the new emperor would be formally made by the most senior women in the imperial house: sometimes after consultation with senior officials in the Front Palace and sometimes in private. Women also presided over the process by which a supposedly incompetent emperor was stripped of power.[54] Therefore, although much of the rhetoric found in contemporary prescriptive texts is unremittingly hostile to any expression of a public role for women, in fact empresses, dowager empresses, and grand dowager empresses were accorded a significant role not only in the internal administration of the Rear Palace, but also within the government of the empire.

Empresses in Imperial-Era Fiction

Throughout Chinese history, ordinary people have always greatly enjoyed the image of the Rear Palace as a site of decadent luxury, inhabited by incredibly beautiful women, wearing the most glamorous and expensive clothing, and riven by sexual jealousy toward each other. The insatiable demand for accounts of this kind would result in genres of literature exclusively focused on the life of women in the Rear Palace, of which palace poetry (*gong ci*) has probably received the most attention.[55] Conventionally, this type of verse described the plaint of lovely ladies living in circumstances of exceptional magnificence and privilege who nevertheless suffer from the emotional poverty of their existence, in some cases exacerbated by active cruelty or neglect. Though other people tried to write palace poetry, they could be criticized for doing so, since it was often held that only a personal experience of life within the confines of the imperial harem would qualify an individual to produce works in this genre.[56] Anybody other than a palace woman attempting to do so would have to imagine living in such circumstances, and given that the power of palace poetry over the reader's imagination comes from the excitement of reading about the beautiful inhabitants of the emperor's harem coupled with the unexpected vignettes of "what it is really like" living within the palace walls, an obviously invented account of this kind of life would be completely unsatisfactory.

Although there has been considerable academic interest in palace poetry, the same is not true for prose genres that describe the experiences of women living inside the Rear Palace. Such works include unorthodox histories (with titles indicating that they are "alternative histories" or "scandalous chronicles" such as the terms *biezhuan*, *waizhuan*, or *yeshi*), from which it is but a short step to erotic writings about palace women, and then to pornographic ones.[57] These texts, which are characterized by detailed descriptions of magnificent surroundings and an interest in sexual and emotional relationships—hence their collective designation here as "Silk Pillow" literature—have a number of important characteristics in common regardless of where they fall in the spectrum of unorthodox history-to-pornographic writings. Prose works of this kind make use of the names of genuine historical individuals, usually those of emperors and their consorts. The narrative centers on the female protagonists, or attempts to articulate a feminine voice. Again, as with other genres of palace literature, Silk Pillow writings make claims of privileged access to information about the imperial harem. Either the author was resident in the Rear Palace, was given details of life there by someone who was, or was smuggled in, or the author somehow or other obtained an ancient manuscript recording these events from a first-person perspective that had been lost from the imperial archives. Finally, Silk Pillow literature has often been banned, either because the sexual elements were unacceptable to conservative rulers or because there was the perception that historical individuals were being used to criticize contemporary monarchs.[58] As a result, it has often been difficult to gain access to these texts. In spite of the legal restrictions that have been applied to them in various periods, such writings have served to create a lasting stereotype about powerful women in the Rear Palace, which has often overshadowed the facts recorded in more reputable sources.

The significance of the depiction of Empress Zhao in *The Scandalous Tale of Zhao Feiyan* lies in the fact that this is one of the earliest surviving fictional accounts of life inside the imperial harem, and so would establish many features subsequently considered definitive in literature of this kind. *The Scandalous Tale*, which fits squarely into the Silk Pillow genre, would merely be the first of many writings to describe the sex lives of Emperor Cheng, Empress Zhao Feiyan, and her sister as this text was revised, expanded, and updated for new audiences. Other Silk Pillow writings about Han dynasty empresses include the anonymous *A Beauty of the Han Palace* (Hangong chunse), a collection of short tales produced during the late Qing whose main protagonist, the beautiful and charming Empress Zhang (d. 163 BCE), was forced into a companionate but ultimately unconsummated incestuous marriage with her uncle, Emperor Hui (r. 195–188 BCE).[59] This text stresses the relentless sexual harassment and abuse the unfortunate empress suffered after her husband's premature demise, part of an extended feminist critique of the treatment meted out to women throughout Chinese history. Another work that concentrates more on the luxurious details of life in the Rear Palace and less on explicit details of the sex lives of its inhabitants is *Miscellaneous Matters from the Han Dynasty: Secret Text No. Eight* (Han zashi mixin), a Ming dynasty novella that purports to describe the process by which Empress Liang Nüying (d. 159 CE), the wife of Emperor Huan of the Eastern Han dynasty (r. 146–168 CE), was appointed.[60] This literary pastiche is closely modeled upon the account of the marriage between Emperor Mu of the Jin dynasty (r. 344–361) and his wife, He Fani (339–404), preserved in *History of the Liu-Song Dynasty* (Songshu).[61] However, the account of the future empress being stripped of her clothing and inspected inch by inch (a scene apparently invented by the author of this text) ensured that *Miscellaneous Matters from the Han Dynasty: Secret Text No. Eight* would achieve considerable popularity when it entered circulation in the late Ming dynasty.

There are evident concentrations of Silk Pillow writings around certain individual monarchs and the women in their harems, though the process by which this accretion occurred is often not clear. For example, there is an important series of texts concerned with the private life of Emperor Yang of the Sui dynasty (r. 604–618). Among early works in this genre there is *Record of Gleanings from Lost Texts of the Daye Reign Era, 605–618* (Daye shiyi ji), traditionally attributed to the historian and scholar-official Yan Shigu (581–645), which describes the difficult relationship between the debauched emperor and his jealous wife, Xiao Fei, a character modeled on Empress Xiao (d. 648).[62] Another early work is *Record of the Labyrinth* (Milou ji), which features Emperor Yang engaged in various extreme sexual practices with a succession of unnamed partners described as "palace maids" (*gongnü*).[63] This erotic novel forms an important early discussion in Chinese literature of various different fetishes, since it describes Emperor Yang fulfilling bondage and imprisonment fantasies, as well as performing voyeuristic sex acts while entirely surrounded with mirrors. What makes *Record of the Labyrinth* disturbing is that while these activities represent the fulfilment of intensely exciting fantasies for Emperor Yang, the women concerned are genuinely imprisoned, and in the bondage sequences they are tied up so they cannot move.[64] The reader is left in no doubt as to the high costs of such demeaning and objectifying treatment for the women concerned, since *Record of the Labyrinth* follows the descriptions of Emperor Yang's pleasures with an account of the death of Consort Hou, who commits suicide in despair at the emptiness of her life.[65] Later works such as *Romantic History of Emperor Yang of the Sui Dynasty* (Sui Yangdi yanshi) by the pseudonymous Qidong yeren (preface dated 1631) develop the character of Consort Hou, and thus the doomed relationship between the unhappy pair eventually ended up being incorporated in historical novels about the period, such as *Romance of the Sui and Tang Dynasties* (Sui-Tang yanyi).[66]

Unsurprisingly, the only female emperor in Chinese history, Wu Zetian (r. 690–705), would become the key female protagonist in a number of Silk Pillow texts. The most important of these is *The Tale of the Lord of Perfect Satisfaction* (Ruyijun zhuan), a late Ming dynasty erotic novel that intersperses discussions of political legitimacy with explicit sexual acts between the aged Wu Zetian and her much younger lover.[67] The consorts of Emperor Xuanzong of the Tang dynasty (r. 721–756) would also figure prominently in Silk Pillow writings. Texts of this kind include *The Scandalous Tale of Yang Taizhen* (Yang Taizhen waizhuan), attributed to Yue Shi, and in the Ming dynasty *The Seductive History of the Jade Consort* [*Yang Guifei*] (Yu Fei meishi), written by the pseudonymous Yanyansheng—though the latter text appears to have been completely lost.[68] (The same author also wrote a much-admired Silk Pillow novella titled *The Remarkable History of the Zhaoyang Palace* [Zhaoyang qushi], about Empress Zhao Feiyan and her sister.) Focusing on another of Xuanzong's supposed lovers, *The Tale of the Plum-Blossom Consort* (Mei Fei zhuan), a novella tentatively dated to the Song dynasty, has provoked much debate as to whether the protagonist should be considered a genuine historical individual or not.[69] Similar concerns are raised in the historicity of tales about Li Shishi, a Song dynasty courtesan from Bianliang, who is supposed to have engaged in a sexual relationship with Emperor Huizong (r. 1110–1126). In *The Scandalous Tale of Li Shishi* (Li Shishi waizhuan), an anonymous work in one *juan* (fascicle) supposed to date from the Song dynasty, Empress Zheng (1079–1139) remonstrates with her husband about his affair and proclaims: "Courtesans are inferior and base, and hence they should not approach the sacred imperial body" (Jiliu xiajian, buyi shangjie shenggong); her opposition means that the emperor cannot openly continue the relationship.[70] Instead, he sends his courtesan-lover a stream of expensive gifts and has a secret tunnel dug leading from the palace to the brothel in which she is resident. Alternatively, *Forgotten Events of the Xuanhe Reign Era of the Song Dynasty, 1119–1125* (Da-Song Xuanhe yishi), a very moralistic text, uses the relationship between the emperor and the courtesan to stress the decadence and corruption of Emperor Huizong's court; after the execution of her husband for complaining about his wife's relationship with the emperor, Li Shishi is taken into the imperial harem and given the title of Ming Fei.[71] Subsequently, the relationship between Li Shishi and the emperor was immortalized in *The Water Margin* (Shuihu zhuan), thus finding a place in one of the greatest works of Chinese fiction.[72]

While Consort Hou and Li Shishi would make their way from Silk Pillow literature into historical fiction, other such works would also have an important effect on the writing of history. Empress Chen Jinfeng (d. 935) of the Min dynasty is the main protagonist of *The Scandalous Tale of Jinfeng* (Jinfeng waizhuan) by Xu Tong (1561–1599). This text describes a variety of voyeuristic practices: Emperor Huizong of the Min dynasty (r. 933–935) finds it arousing to be watched by others as he has sex with the empress, and Empress Chen Jinfeng herself engages in promiscuous sexual relationships with other men.[73] This fictional text would provide a sensational tale of imperial decadence to be incorporated into a supposedly reputable historical work: *Spring and Autumn Annals of the Ten Kingdoms* (Shiguo chunqiu) by Wu Renchen (ca. 1628–ca. 1689).[74] Silk Pillow writings set during the Yuan dynasty include *Mr. Yuan's Record of the Lateral Courts* (Yuanshi yeting ji), attributed to the scholar and bibliophile Tao Zongyi (1329–1410), a text that has no obvious plot or narrative structure at all, but that strings together vignettes of the luxurious appointments of the palace with what appear to be completely fictional accounts of the lives of various favorite consorts and concubines of Külüg Khan (r. 1307–1311) and Toghon Temür (r. 1333–1368), also known as Emperor Wuzong and Emperor Huizong of the Yuan dynasty, respectively.[75] Here, the disadvantages of writing a Silk Pillow text before the compilation of the dynastic history released archival material into the public domain can clearly be seen—the author seems to have been entirely ignorant of what actually went on inside the palace.

Early Qing dynasty works focus particularly on the supposed sexual immorality of Empress Borjigit Bumbutai (1613–1688); such anti-Manchu writings seem to have circulated widely at the time but were confiscated and destroyed by the authorities whenever they were found, and hence very few survive to modern times.[76] Eventually, there would even be examples of writings about Chinese palace women by authors from foreign countries, particularly centered on the figures of the Dowager Empress Cixi (1835–1908) and Dowager Empress Longyu (1868–1913). These include Georges Soulié de Morant's *T'seu Hsi: Impératrice des Boxers* and Victor Segalen's *René Leys*.[77] Meanwhile Sir Edmund Backhouse (1873–1944) would record his fantasy of a passionate sexual relationship with Dowager Empress Cixi in his *Décadence Mandchoue*.[78] It seems that the fascination with pampered and yet sexually voracious women sequestered behind the walls of the imperial palace had a wide cross-cultural appeal. Silk Pillow literature continues to be produced in China right up to the present day; the only major change that this genre has seen in modern times is that it is now commonly presented as fictional. However, when modern Silk Pillow texts are filmed or televised, it is still common to see strong assertions of historical verisimilitude in the attendant publicity materials, with an emphasis on the expert historians consulted, the authenticity of the costumes and jewelry, and filming at locations associated with the personages that are being dramatized.

One of the most striking features of Silk Pillow writings is the emphasis on psychological realism. Since so many of these texts consider issues of love, passion, sexual obsession, and even fetishism, the authors of such works proceed to give very detailed and realistic accounts of the feelings of the persons concerned. Where history writings concentrated from a very early stage in their development upon extracting moral judgments from the events that they recorded, Silk Pillow literature tends to eschew simple constructions of praise and blame. Although historical figures are described, and some of these individuals feature within traditional histories as "good" characters or "bad" ones, such interpretations do not necessarily cross over into literary representations. Portraying individuals trapped in unhappy political marriages, overcome with love or lust for an inappropriate sexual partner, or obsessed within some kind of fetishistic practice, these fictional narratives show them to be unable to extricate themselves from the situations in which they find themselves. The handling of complex and delicate states of mind found within Silk Pillow literature is not replicated in other genres of Chinese fiction writing until significantly later. This fact forms one crucial rationale for separating out these writings as an independent genre. When grouped with historical texts, as has all too often been the case, the fictional elements are highly problematic. If lumped in with other kinds of fiction, then the inclusion of erotic and sexually explicit material makes more conservative readers uncomfortable. Finally, if considered as erotic literature, then the presence of extensive discussions of the historical background and the detailed analysis of sexual and relationship problems and the emotional burdens that these impose are out of place—they militate against reading these writings as titillating. It is by placing these works of literature together that allows them to appear as an important genre in their own right.

There has been very little study to date of the textual history and dating of the vast majority of Silk Pillow writings, and hence the development of this genre is at present not well understood. Many of these texts are burdened with spurious attributions, and variant dates have been proposed for a single text that are centuries or even a millennium or more apart. However, it seems as though many key early works, including *The Scandalous Tale* itself, are products of the ninth century, and hence can be closely connected in time with the first appearance of other types of palace literature. Further research is much needed to clarify the way in which our understanding of imperial-era history has been distorted by popular writings of this kind.

Conclusion

In the Han dynasty, empresses played an important role both in the administration of the Rear Palace and in the government of the empire. At some level, these two roles were interchangeable, because the Rear Palace was in itself a branch of the government, and a source of prestige for the regime. By some accounts, during the Han dynasty there were thousands of women employed there at any one time—these included the daughters of the most noble families in the empire, as well as the finest women writers and poets, the loveliest singers and dancers, and so on. Though very few people would ever be privileged to see them in person, the fact that they were known to be living and working within the Rear Palace brought honor to the emperor and the dynasty as a whole.[79] On rare occasions, these women were given the opportunity to appear in public, in particular for religious festivals. For these events, involving magnificent parades through the streets of the capital, palace women formed a dazzling display in their rich silk robes and beautiful jewels. By their presence on these occasions, they were a living embodiment of the power and prestige of the dynasty. The Rear Palace formed a reservoir of female talent and excellence that was in its own way as important for adding luster to the regime as the wise ministers and brave generals serving in the Front Palace.

When women entered the Rear Palace as young girls, they were cut off from their families and from society as a whole, and many would spend the rest of their lives behind its walls. In the process, they were transformed within the popular imagination into incredibly beautiful young women, living emotionally impoverished or sexually tormented lives in surroundings of unimaginable magnificence. This is a stereotype in which neither the wretched palace skivvy nor the busy woman official has a place. However, it is crucial to accept that many people prefer this fantasy version of imperial life, and this preference has had such an impact on the writing of history that for many empresses and palace women, it is very difficult indeed to separate fact from fiction. So all-pervasive have the stereotypes first promulgated in *The Scandalous Tale* become that they affect our understanding of every dynasty in Chinese history, not just the Han, and every empress, not just Zhao Feiyan.

CHAPTER TWO

The Scandalous Tale of Zhao Feiyan

THE SCANDALOUS TALE OF ZHAO FEIYAN IS A LANDMARK IN TRAditional Chinese fiction, being an extremely early surviving example of Silk Pillow writing—a genre defined by its focus on the experience of life within the Rear Palace, particularly that of women.[1] This text has proved enormously influential; many expressions still in common use in Chinese ultimately derive from *The Scandalous Tale*, and it also had a major impact on the subsequent development of fiction writing, first and foremost in China, and then in East Asia as a whole. A number of scholars of traditional Chinese fiction writing have discussed the importance of this text as a precursor of later Ming dynasty erotic novels, in particular the classic *The Plum in the Golden Vase* (Jinpingmei); furthermore, an interesting study by literary scholar On Shionoya (1878–1962) considers the significance of *The Scandalous Tale* for early Japanese fiction as well, stressing its influence on texts such as *The Tale of Genji* (Genji monogatari).[2] In addition, *The Scandalous Tale* circulated widely in Korea, with many surviving woodblock editions of the text being found on the peninsula, and in recent years scholars have begun to elucidate the influence of this text on early Korean fiction.[3] It is likely that further research will serve to uncover yet more instances of the way in which this novella exerted a profound influence on the development of early fiction writing traditions in East Asia.

This short narrative concerns three main characters, all based upon genuine historical individuals: Emperor Cheng of the Han dynasty; his second empress, Zhao Feiyan, a former dancing girl; and her younger sister and fellow denizen of Emperor Cheng's harem, Zhao Hede (known in historical texts only by her title: Zhao Zhaoyi). The story begins with an account of the origins of the two girls, the offspring of an illicit relationship between a granddaughter of the king of Jiangdu and a musician in her husband's household. After their father's death, the pair travel to Chang'an, the Han dynasty capital, where eventually they enter the service of the Princess of Yang'a. From there, Zhao Feiyan is recruited into the harem of Emperor Cheng. Immediately she is much favored by His Majesty and is thus appointed as his empress. However, her failure to produce children (here attributed to the toxic potions she takes to preserve her youthful beauty) means that she is forced to accept the entry of her younger sister into the emperor's harem to reinforce her own position. At the same time, she engages in a wide variety of promiscuous sexual relationships in the hope that she may yet become pregnant. Emperor Cheng becomes more and more infatuated with Zhao Hede, to the point where his relationship with the empress is threatened: indeed, at one juncture in the narrative she seems to be on the verge of suicide over the failure of her marriage. The novella concludes with the decline of the emperor's health, his ever-increasing reliance on Zhao Hede for sexual satisfaction, and finally his death through accidental poisoning with a toxic aphrodisiac that she has administered. The portrayal of imperial extravagance and lust, the manipulation of the emperor by his two favorites, and the tragic end of their obsessive triangular relationship would prove enormously influential on later writings about sexuality and gender. Given its popularity, it is not surprising that *The Scandalous Tale* was repeatedly rewritten and updated through the late imperial era, to bring this story to new audiences.

The Scandalous Tale has long been admired for its beautiful use of language and the psychological complexity of its characters. Within the narrative, the main male character, Emperor Cheng, is caught in a triangular relationship—no mention is made here of the many other women known to have formed part of his harem: his first wife, Empress Xu (d. 8 BCE), and his other junior consorts mentioned in the dynastic histories, including the famous scholar and poet Ban Jieyu (d. 6 BCE), and two great-aunts of Empress Ma of the Eastern Han dynasty (40–79 CE), both of whom also held the title of *jieyu*.[4] Other major female figures in the life of Emperor Cheng, such as his mother, Dowager Empress Wang Zhengjun (71 BCE–13 CE), the most powerful woman of the day, and his late father's two favorite consorts, Fu Zhaoyi (d. 3 BCE) and Feng Zhaoyi (d. 6 BCE), are also omitted from this tale. By focusing upon the intense and exploitative relationship between the emperor and the Zhao sisters, the reader realizes the extent to which he is manipulated and lied to by this precious pair. At the same time, they are entirely dependent on his enduring sexual interest in them: should he ever lose this, they will be at the mercy of their enemies. If the reader is clear about the deceptions practiced upon Emperor Cheng, and the motives behind them, the same transparency does not pertain to the relationship between the various female characters themselves. In every situation described in *The Scandalous Tale*—dramatic or mundane—the true feelings of the women concerned are not explained. It is this that sets up a strong tension in the narrative. The reader is informed at the very beginning of the text that the two Zhao sisters are trained actresses and performers; hence they are intrinsically untrustworthy, since their entire education is aimed at instructing them in how to dissimulate their true feelings and manipulate the emotions of their audience.[5] And yet, the text does not explicitly eliminate the possibility that there are occasions when Zhao Feiyan and her sister do express their real feelings. Thus when Empress Zhao seems to attempt suicide on realizing she has been entirely supplanted in the emperor's affections by her sister, this may be a cynical play for sympathy, or it may be a genuine expression of despair at the failure of her marriage. When Zhao Hede consistently refuses to participate in Emperor Cheng's voyeuristic sexual practices, this could be a deliberate action to maintain a high level of excitement for the emperor, or it might be the result of her own feelings of distaste. It is left as a matter for readers to decide for themselves.

Today, *The Scandalous Tale* is usually printed with three other short texts, purporting to be written by distinguished historical figures and full of information concerning the history of this novella. The first, variously known as *Ling Xuan's Authorial Preface* (Ling Xuan zixu 伶玄自序) or *Ling Xuan's Authorial Postface* (Ling Xuan zixu 伶玄自叙), is a fine and important work of literature in its own right.[6] This describes how in his old age, Ling Xuan, who had previously held the position of chancellor of Huainan (*Huainan xiang*), acquired a concubine named Fan Tongde. This woman, who was a close relative of Zhao Feiyan and also served in the imperial palace, then informed him of the events recorded in *The Scandalous Tale*. Ling Xuan's text is conventionally joined by two other short postfaces, attributed to a pair of exceptionally important scholars: Huan Tan and Xun Xu. These documents purport to describe the vicissitudes suffered by the manuscript of the novella during the late Han dynasty, and record an almost miraculous tale of its survival. The attribution of these short pieces to such distinguished figures in Chinese intellectual history was no doubt intended to enhance the prestige of *The Scandalous Tale*, but the historical details given in these two texts have proved completely impossible to verify. Many of the scholars who work on *The Scandalous Tale* have considered the prefaces as evidence of dating. Usually either the prefaces are all accepted as genuine, in which case it is treated as a Western Han dynasty text in spite of the evidence to the contrary, or all the prefaces are dismissed as forgeries.[7] For the purposes of this study, the prefaces will not be considered as evidence for the date of the text because they are not necessarily intrinsic to *The Scandalous Tale*. However, given the exceptional literary qualities of Ling Xuan's authorial preface, and the importance of this text for reinforcing the same direction of narrative found in *The Scandalous Tale*, it is entirely possible that both were originally written by the same person.

This translation represents the first publication of a full translation of *The Scandalous Tale* into any Western language (the complete Chinese text is given in appendix 2). Although there have been a number of partial translations already published in German and English, these do not cover the entire text. In these earlier renderings of the text, the cuts have been twofold. First, the sexually explicit material was removed, a decision provoked by more conservative attitudes. Removing this material changes readers' perception of the narrative and makes it impossible to appreciate the way that this text influenced subsequent erotic writings in China. Second, the descriptions of extravagant gift-giving between the sisters and the emperor were also omitted as boring and superfluous. Again this serves to mislead the reader as to the nature of the story. While for some audiences the descriptions of sex acts might be thought shocking, for others the accounts of female financial profligacy would have been every bit as fascinating and titillating. In this regard, *The Scandalous Tale* can be considered a very early precursor of the endlessly popular sex-and-shopping genre.[8] The authors of Silk Pillow texts expected their readers to be interested not only in the more or less unusual sexual practices described, but also in the luxurious settings in which these activities took place. Although at this remove of time it may be difficult for modern readers to fully appreciate this aspect of the story, *The Scandalous Tale* is intended to be doubly shocking, and to leave out these sections alters the story beyond recognition.

The significance of *The Scandalous Tale* lies in its importance as an exceptionally early example of erotic fiction, and of literature about life in the imperial harem. Nevertheless, it has been the subject of astonishingly little academic research. Part of this is no doubt due to ongoing concerns about the problem of dating and authenticity: as long as it continues to be dismissed as a "forged text" there will be little study of it. At the same time, it does not fit comfortably into any standard categorization of literary development, and there are but few other Tang (or earlier) fictional writings that deal with such candor about matters of sexuality: this is a strange tale by an unknown master of a triangular relationship marked by obsessive desires, internecine rivalry, and lies set against a backdrop of unimaginable power and wealth.

TRANSLATION OF *The Scandalous Tale of Zhao Feiyan*

The father of Empress Zhao Feiyan was Feng Wanjin.[9] Her grandfather was [Feng] Dali. He worked on tuning musical instruments, and served the king of Jiangdu as orchestral master.[10] [Feng] Wanjin was not willing to continue in the traditional occupation of his family; he studied the performance of music and singing—forgetting about traditional forms and melodies, composing complex tunes and sad songs instead. This he called "music of supreme refinement." Those who heard him [perform] were deeply moved. The granddaughter of the king of Jiangdu was the Princess of Gusu.[11] She was married to Zhao Man, the commandant of Jiangdu.[12] Man favored Wanjin: if they did not dine from the same dishes, he would not eat his fill.[13] Wanjin was thus able to have an affair with the princess.[14] The princess became pregnant. [Zhao] Man was a man of violent and jealous temper; furthermore, he had contracted a sexually transmitted disease as a young man and so did not have relations with women. The princess was terrified. Announcing that she was seriously ill, she went to live in the royal palace. She gave birth there to twin girls, whom she handed over to [Feng] Wanjin. The older was named Yizhu; the younger twin was called Hede.[15] Both of them took the surname Zhao, even though they had no claim upon it.[16]

From a very young age, Yizhu was a clever and alert child. Among the possessions of the household was a copy of *Pengzu's [Technique for] Taking the Pulses* [Pengzu fangmai],[17] and so she became well versed in the skill of moving the *qi*.[18] As she grew up, her slender figure grew ever more lissom and elegant. People called her "Flying Swallow" [Feiyan]. Hede [had skin] so glossy and smooth that when she left her bath, she was not even wet. She was extremely eloquent and her soft, slow [voice] was a delight to hear. The two girls were both exceptionally lovely. However, when Wanjin died, the Feng family lost everything.[19] Feiyan and her younger sister wandered around until they eventually made their way to Chang'an. At this time, people called her Lady Zhao, and some people said that she was an illegitimate daughter of [Zhao] Man. She [lived] next door to the Princess of Yang'a's household provisioner, Zhao Lin.[20] [Zhao Feiyan] decided to entrust herself to Lin's care, and on a number of occasions she made fine embroideries with elaborate patterns to present to Lin. [Zhao] Lin was embarrassed but accepted them.[21] She lived in Lin's house and declared herself to be [Zhao] Lin's daughter. Lin had a daughter who had been employed within the imperial palace. When she became seriously ill, she was sent home to die. Feiyan may perhaps have assumed the identity of the dead woman.

Feiyan and her younger sister served in the household of the Princess of Yang'a, performing menial duties as required. [Feiyan] taught herself to sing and dance by imitating [the performances] she watched in secret, concentrating carefully and capturing the characteristics [of each artiste]. She would listen right through to the end of the day without eating a thing. The salary she received for her work was minimal, and the work was hard, but whatever money she had was all spent on face creams and hair oils, lotions and powders, and she did not begrudge the money, however much the cost. All the other servants considered her an idiot. At this time Feiyan was engaged in an illicit sexual relationship with a huntsman in the nearby Feathered Forest.[22] Given that Feiyan was extremely poor, she shared a coverlet with

Hede. One night, when it was snowing, she waited for the huntsman outside her home. Feiyan was exposed to the elements, but she controlled her breathing and allowed her *qi* to circulate freely, so her body remained comfortably warm and she did not even shiver.[23] The huntsman thought that this was remarkable indeed, and considered her to be a goddess [come down to earth]. Thanks to the good offices of the princess, [Zhao] Feiyan entered the palace, whereupon she was summoned by the emperor to his bed. Her aunt, Fan Yi, was the directress of tapestries at the Chengguang [Tower], and hence knew about the affair between Feiyan and the huntsman—she was terrified about this [becoming known].[24]

When she was favored [by His Majesty], Feiyan closed her eyes and hugged herself tight, the tears trickling down her cheeks. She shook with fear as she refused to allow His Majesty near her. The emperor caressed Feiyan for three nights, and at the end was still unable to have sex with her. However, he did not blame her in the least [for her behavior]. Those in the palace who had previously often been favored by His Majesty asked the emperor about the situation.

The emperor said: "She is more than voluptuous, and [her body] is so soft it feels as if she is boneless. She holds back out of respect, appearing sometimes far and sometimes near, as is appropriate for a gentle and well-behaved young woman. In her modesty, she can be compared to Lady Cao!"[25]

When [His Majesty] finally achieved sexual congress [with her], her blood flowed abundantly.

[Afterward, Fan] Yi spoke privately to Feiyan: "Did the huntsman never have sex with you?"

"I engaged in internal meditation for three days," Feiyan replied, "and then my flesh was restored.[26] His Majesty's penis is thick and long, so he hurt me very much indeed with it."

From this point onward, Feiyan received special favor in the Rear Palace, and was entitled Empress Zhao.

The emperor was staying within one of the chambers of the Mandarin Ducks Hall.[27] He was checking through the registers of the imperial house and [Fan] Yi was there to present these documents to His Majesty. Yi then reported that [Zhao] Feiyan had a younger sister named

Hede, who was also beautiful, pure, and trustworthy, though she could not compare with Feiyan herself. The emperor ordered his retainer, Lü Yanfu, to take a richly ornamented palanquin to collect Hede.

Hede refused, saying: "If my noble sister does not summon me, I would not dare to go. I am willing to be beheaded and thus requite His Majesty [for the honor he has shown me]."

[Lü] Yanfu returned and reported this. [Fan] Yi took one of the empress's name cards in a five-colored brocade-patterned [case] to use as proof to summon Hede on the emperor's behalf. Hede had just washed her hair, and she now anointed it with Jiuqu gharuwood perfume before tying it in a knot of the kind called a "New Chignon." She drew on fine eyebrows, in the manner called "Distant Hills."[28] She painted a little rouge [on her lips], in the style called "Dawdling Approach" makeup. Her clothing was purposefully simple: an embroidered skirt with a short-sleeved [jacket] and plum-patterned socks. His Majesty was gracing the Cloud Luminous Hall with his presence when he ordered Fan Yi to present Hede.[29]

"My noble sister is a violent and cruel woman," Hede replied. "It would not take much for her to forget that we are family. I would rather die than be humiliated."

Without so much as a second glance she turned on her heel [and walked out]. Her words were at once restrained and incisive. Those present whispered their admiring comments [to each other]. As a result, the emperor had to allow Hede to go home.

In the time of Emperor Xuan, there was an erudite [attached to] the Spreading Perfume [Hall] named Zhuo Fangcheng.[30] This white-haired instructor [of the women] in the palace was known by the respectful title of Lady Zhuo. She was standing behind the emperor and muttered: "This woman is a Water disaster. The destruction of Fire is now certain."[31]

His Majesty [now] made use of Fan Yi's plan, and sent the empress to live at a new residence: Extending Shoots House.[32] He bestowed upon her hangings [with a design of] purple flower sprigs amid swirling clouds,[33] an armrest of multicolored jade, and a mountain-shaped incense burner in nine levels, made of gold.[34] [Fan] Yi now warned the empress, saying: "His Majesty has been childless for a long time.

How can you be here in the palace without making your plans for the future? Why not present [a woman] to His Majesty at an opportune moment, in the hope that she may bear him a son?"

The empress admired [Fan] Yi's plan, and that very night she sent Hede to the emperor. The emperor was very pleased. By touching every part of her body, [he discovered that] she was in every way delightful. He called [her body] his "Realm of Soft Warmth." He said to [Fan] Yi: "I plan to grow old in this realm; I simply cannot imitate Emperor Wu in his search for the Realm of White Clouds."[35]

"Long life to Your Majesty!" [Fan] Yi shouted. Then she congratulated him, saying: "You have indeed obtained a goddess [for your harem]."

The emperor bestowed upon Yi twenty-four bolts of exceptionally high-quality silk brocade with a shagreen pattern.

Hede was favored to a quite remarkable degree, receiving the title of Zhao Jieyu. As she held the rank of *jieyu* she was in constant attendance upon the empress, and always greeted her with the same level of ceremony as a child [would show to a parent]. [One day] when the empress was sitting by the *jieyu*, she spat by mistake upon her sleeve.

[Zhao] Jieyu said: "The way your spit has stained my blue sleeve really looks like lichen on a rock. Should I have ordered the Imperial Manufactories to make such a thing, they would not necessarily have been able [to produce] something like the lichen design on this dress. I will call this 'Rock Lichen Broad-Sleeves.'"[36]

The empress, living at Extending Shoots House, engaged in promiscuous sexual relationships with attendant gentlemen and palace slaves who already had many children. The *jieyu* did everything she could to protect her. She repeatedly told the emperor: "My older sister has an aggressive character; if someone were to trump up charges against her, the Zhao family would all be killed." Every time [she said this] her tears would flow as she was overwhelmed with a sense of impending tragedy. For this reason, if anyone reported the empress's debauched behavior, His Majesty would immediately kill them. The attendant gentlemen and the palace slaves concerned wore the fanciest clothing and the richest scents. They would do exactly as they wished while staying at Extending Shoots House and no one dared to say anything about it. However, in the end the empress never had any children.

The empress bathed in "Five Skandhas" perfumed waters, in which seven spices had been mixed, and sat upon a seat made of *tongxiang* and gharuwood.[37] She burned "Summoning the Gods" 100-spice incense cakes.[38] The *jieyu* bathed in waters perfumed with the ginger lily, to which she added "Dewdrop Millefiori" powder.[39] The emperor frequently spoke in private to Fan Yi, saying: "Although the empress is noted for her remarkable fragrance, it cannot compare with the natural perfume of the *jieyu*'s body."[40]

There was a former concubine of King Yi of Jiangdu, Li Yanghua, whose aunt was the wife of Feng Dali. When Yanghua got old, she went to live with the Feng family. The empress and her younger sister both treated Yanghua as if she was their own mother. [Li] Yanghua was very skilled at the arts of personal adornment, and she regularly instructed the empress to repeatedly immerse herself in gharuwood perfumes, not to mention musk internal muscle relaxant pills.[41] The *jieyu* also [took] these internal muscle relaxant pills. If these are used continuously, it makes a woman's periods increasingly weak. On one occasion the empress mentioned this to Shangguan Wu, the directress of medicinal preparations at the Chengguang [Tower]. She beat her chest [in horror] and said: "If that is so, how can you possibly have any children?" She instructed the empress to decoct the finest flowers and cleanse [her system] with this. However, this ultimately had no effect.[42]

The barbarians of Zhenla presented a 10,000-year-old clamshell and a night-shining pearl.[43] Both of these items shone like the moon, and anyone illuminated by them—no matter whether they were beautiful or hideous—became supremely lovely. His Majesty the Emperor gave the shell to the empress and the pearl to the *jieyu*. The empress had the shell set as decoration in her five-layer gold gauze hangings. After some while, the emperor said to the *jieyu*: "When I see the empress by daylight, she is not as lovely as when I see her at night. Every morning I feel confused, as if I were missing something."

When the *jieyu* heard this, she immediately renamed her pearl the "Pillow-Side Night-Shining Pearl" and gave it to the empress as a gift. She never said anything to the empress about what the emperor had told her.

When [Zhao Feiyan] first received her appointment to the exalted title [of empress], the *jieyu* wrote a letter to the empress, saying: "Heaven and Earth have united in triumph for my noble older sister to be so much blessed. In glory you ascend to your rightful place, bringing honor on our ancestors. I cannot contain my delight and so I respectfully present these twenty-six items to you in congratulation:[44]

One carriage cushion patterned in gold.
One bowl in the shape of a lotus flower, made of gharuwood.
One five-colored concentric ornamental knot.
One bolt of extra fine quality silk brocade with a design of mandarin ducks.
One glass screen.
The "Pillow-Side Night-Shining Pearl."
One rug of clove-scented black wildcat fur.[45]
[One rug] of *tongxiang*-scented tiger-skin.[46]
One sandalwood statue.[47]
Two [carved] fish small enough to fit in the palm of the hand, made from ambergris.[48]
One single-poled lotus-painted palanquin.
A heptafoil mirror in the shape of a water caltrop.[49]
Four refined gold finger rings.
One unlined red silk 'Vanishing' gauze dress.
Three sets of name cards [covered with] perfumed and patterned fine silk.
One heptagonal jar of shining top-quality lard-based hair pomade.
Three perfume braziers made from precious metals, for use in bed.[50]
Two pairs of patterned rhinoceros-horn chopsticks, to detect the presence of poison.
One box for face cream made from green jade."

She ordered her servant, Guo Yuqiong, to present these items. The empress responded with some hangings of five-colored cloud-patterned silk brocade and a gharuwood jug. The *jieyu* wept as she complained to the emperor: "If I had not been given these things by my sister, I would have died without knowing of their existence."

The emperor apologized to her, and informed [the region of] Yizhou that they should keep back three years' revenue in order to make a set of hangings of seven layers of silk brocade, ornamented with gharuwood, for the *jieyu*.[51]

The *jieyu* received the emperor at the Taiyi Pool.[52] He had ordered a thousand-man boat to be constructed, which was called the "Boat of Union." In the middle of the pool, he had built the "Immortals' Realm Belvedere," forty feet high.[53] The emperor admired the view from the top of the belvedere—His Majesty was dressed in a watered silk robe, so finely sewn that the seams were invisible, while the empress was dressed in an iridescent purple skirt that had come as tribute from Nanyue, [topped with a jacket] of green agate–colored light flower-patterned silk.[54] The empress sang and danced to the tune "The Whirlwind Travels Far Away."[55] The emperor beat time on a jade jar with a patterned rhinoceros-horn hairpin. He ordered the empress's beloved gentleman in attendance, Feng Wufang, to play the flute to accompany the empress as she sang. In the middle of this, as they were enjoying the music, a storm began to brew. The empress faced into the wind and sang even louder, while Wufang drew deep breaths [with which to play] his elegant and refined [melody].

The empress's skirt [blew up to reveal] her legs. "Look at me! Look at me!" she cried. Then the empress spread out her sleeves [like wings] and said: "I am an immortal! I am an immortal! But you have abandoned your old love in favor of a new! Have you indeed forgotten your love?" [She seemed about to throw herself from the top of the belvedere, and in the process she tore her skirts.][56]

"Wufang, catch the empress for me!" the emperor shouted. Wufang stopped playing and [was in time to] grab the empress's shoe.[57] After a while the wind died down.

The empress wept and said: "You have been kind to me, Your Majesty, and prevented me from becoming an immortal." She heaved a long sigh, redolent with sadness, as the tears trickled down her cheeks.

The emperor then felt even more ashamed [of how he had behaved] and loved the empress with greater fervor. He bestowed vast sums on Wufang and allowed him to enter the empress's residence [whenever he wished]. Some of those ladies in the palace that he had favored in the past now pleated their skirts to make knots; they called this style "Restraining the Immortal Skirts."[58]

The *jieyu* was increasingly honored and favored, so she was granted the title of *zhaoyi*. She requested permission to live close to Extending Shoots House. The emperor ordered the Junior Consort House to be constructed for her.[59] [At the same time] he had built the Dewdrop Hall, the Wind-Blown Hall, the Transmitting Glory Hall, and the Peace-Seeking Hall: all of these were front halls. As rear halls he also had the following buildings constructed: the Warm Chamber [Hall], the Cool-Pitcher Chamber [Hall], and the Perfumed Waters Chamber [Hall].[60] The entranceway connecting to the inner chambers was ornamented with gold and white jade, with jade discs [decorating the walls] inside and out. This was called the "Gate for Communicating with Immortals."[61]

The empress had been elevated to such a position of nobility and favor that she increasingly felt free to throw off all restraint. She sent people out to find esoteric masters far and wide, to seek a means to remain young and ward off senescence. At that time the Beibo barbarians in the southwest sent tribute.[62] Their envoy would eat a single meal and then he would not lie down or rest for a day and a night together. The official in charge of subordinate states reported this circumstance to the throne. Furthermore, strange lights were repeatedly observed [in his vicinity]. The empress heard about this and asked him what technique he used.

"My arts are as one with Heaven and Earth," the barbarian replied, "and equal to life and death. I can come and go through existence and nonexistence and pass through myriad transformations without ever changing."

The empress ordered Fan Yi's nephew, Buzhou, to give [the barbarian] one thousand pieces of gold. The barbarian said: "Anyone who wishes to study my esoteric techniques cannot engage in debauchery or lie." The empress therefore did not go back [to pursue her studies].

On a subsequent occasion Fan Yi was waiting upon the empress as she performed her ablutions. Their conversation was very cheerful. The empress reported to Fan Yi what the barbarian had said.

Yi clapped her hands and said: "That reminds me of when we were back at Jiangdu, when Auntie Li Yanghua was raising fighting ducks in a pond and she was troubled by otters eating the ducks. At that point Granny Rui from Xiazhu Village got hold of a wildcat that could catch otters and presented it. However, Granny [Rui] said to Aunt [Li]: 'This wildcat won't eat anything else, it only wants ducks.' Aunt [Li] was furious and strangled the wildcat. This barbarian's magic arts seem to be something of the same kind."

The empress shrieked with laughter and said: "Why should I have to sully myself by strangling that foul barbarian?"

There was a palace slave with whom the empress engaged in illicit sexual relations named Yan Chifeng: a strong and healthy young man who was able to climb over any wall. He was also pursuing an affair with the *zhaoyi*. Just when he was leaving the Junior Consort House, the empress happened to come to visit. At that time, it was the fifth day of the tenth lunar month. Everyone in the palace was therefore busy, because they were about to go to the Ling'an Temple. On this day ocarinas were played and drums were banged as they moved in a procession through the streets shoulder to shoulder and sang "The Arrival of the Red Phoenix" [Chifeng lai qu].[63]

The empress asked the *zhaoyi*: "For whom does the Red Phoenix [Chifeng] come?"

"Of course the Red Phoenix [Chifeng] comes for you," the *zhaoyi* replied. "How could it be for anyone else?"

The empress was furious and upended her cup all over the *zhaoyi*'s skirt. "Even rats bite people sometimes!" she exclaimed.

"[This rat] has got past your fine clothes to see what you are really like; that is all," the *zhaoyi* retorted. "Why should it bite someone as well?"

The *zhaoyi* was normally very humble when she was in attendance on the empress and did not expect to be interrogated so viciously.

Having considered the matter carefully, she decided not to say anything more. Fan Yi pulled the hairpin out [of her chignon] and kowtowed until she drew blood. Then she made the *zhaoyi* bow to the empress. As she made her bow, the *zhaoyi* wept and said: "Have you forgotten how we shared a blanket through the long nights, suffering so much from the cold that we could not get to sleep, and then you would make me hug your back? Today we have both achieved honors far beyond anyone else, and we have outsiders to contend with. How can we sisters fight among ourselves?"

The empress also wept and held the *zhaoyi*'s hand. She took out a purple jade nine-phoenix-chick hairpin and used it to pin up her chignon. That was the end of the matter.

The emperor heard something of what had transpired, but he was afraid of the empress and did not dare to question her. He asked the *zhaoyi* about it, and she replied: "The empress is jealous of me, that's all. Since the Han dynasty governs under the power of Fire, she refers to Your Majesty as a Red Dragon or [Red] Phoenix." His Majesty believed this and was very pleased.

One day the emperor went out hunting early in the morning. Meeting with snowy weather, he became seriously ill. His potency weakened and he could no longer maintain an erection. However, each time he clasped the *zhaoyi*'s foot, he could not control his desires and would immediately become violently aroused. The *zhaoyi* usually [responded] by turning away to lie on her side, so the emperor could no longer get hold of her foot.

Fan Yi said to the *zhaoyi*: "His Majesty has ingested all sorts of amazing elixirs obtained from esoteric masters in the hope of achieving an erection and none of them have worked. However, the moment he takes hold of your foot, he is ready for action. This is a great blessing that Heaven has bestowed upon you, *guifei*.[64] But why do you turn away and lie on your side, avoiding penetration by His Majesty?"

"It is fortunate that by turning away and lying on my side he cannot penetrate me," the *zhaoyi* said. "This is why I have been able to keep His Majesty interested in me. If I had treated the emperor as my older sister did, he would have become bored and left me. In that case how could I hope to excite him again?"

Meanwhile, the empress in her arrogance and profligacy became slightly unwell, whereupon she immediately refused to feed herself, insisting that the emperor wield the spoon and chopsticks [for her]. When the medicine had a bitter taste, if it were not the emperor who gave it to her, she should keep it in her mouth and then spit it out, refusing to swallow.

The *zhaoyi* entered the Perfumed Waters Chamber one night and the glory of her skin outshone the lamps. His Majesty watched her secretly through a crack in the curtains. The servants reported to the *zhaoyi*, and she grabbed a towel and gave orders that the lamps be doused. On subsequent occasions, the emperor agreed to give the servants gold so that they would not tell her [he was watching], but her personal maid was not part of this agreement. She came out of the curtains only to bump into the emperor. She immediately went back in to report [his presence] to the *zhaoyi*, who then got out of the way as quickly as she could. From this time onward, the emperor put lots of gold in his sleeve when he went to spy on the *zhaoyi* amid the curtained Perfumed Waters Chamber. If he encountered one of the servants or her personal maid, he immediately dragged them off [to a corner] and gave them [gold]. The servants became greedy for this imperial largesse, and they came in and out without stopping. The emperor could spend more than a hundred pieces of gold in a single night.

The emperor's illness caused him to gradually become weaker. The imperial physicians tried everything they could think of but could not help him. At one point they obtained some *shenxu* paste, which they gave to the *zhaoyi*.[65] She immediately presented it to His Majesty. After he took a pill [made from this paste], he was able to have sex once. One night, the *zhaoyi* was drunk, so she gave His Majesty seven pills. That night the emperor took the *zhaoyi* in his arms as he took his place amid the ninefold curtains. He laughed hysterically without cease. When it got light, the emperor arose and began to dress. Semen flowed unstoppably [from his body], and a short time later, His Majesty went into a coma. [The *zhaoyi*] pulled on some clothing and [went over] to inspect the emperor. His remaining semen then bubbled up, spattering the bedclothes. A short time later the emperor died.[66] The palace women reported this to the dowager empress. The dowager empress ordered that the *zhaoyi* be placed under restraint.

"I treated His Majesty [with the same care and devotion] as if he were a baby, and the favor I received was a source of wonder to all the world," the *zhaoyi* wailed. "How can I obey the director of the Lateral Courts and talk about our most intimate affairs?"[67] Then she beat her breast and screamed: "Your Majesty! Where have you gone?" After that, she spat blood and died.

Introduction to the Three Postfaces

The Scandalous Tale is conventionally published with three postfaces. These short texts are intended to create an air of verisimilitude to the text as a whole; this is a feature of the Silk Pillow genre, in that prefaces or postfaces are commonly included to explain how the author had access to information about the private lives of female members of the imperial house who lived hidden away within the harem, and to give the text a history that will encourage readers to believe that it is not a work of fiction. Such protestations of factual accuracy are far from unique to Silk Pillow writings; for example, Tang dynasty *chuanqi* (tales of strange events) would still attempt to give a factual gloss to the events described, even when the text concerns the appearance of ghosts, supernatural phenomena, and miraculous feats, by suggesting that the account was written down from an eyewitness report or naming a historical individual supposedly involved.[68] In the case of *The Scandalous Tale*, the first postface is attributed to a personage named Ling Xuan, who is not recorded in any surviving Han dynasty text. He is specifically said to have held the post of chancellor of Huainan, the author apparently not being aware that the kingdom of Huainan was only extant from 202 BCE to 122 BCE. It is impossible that Ling Xuan, who is described elsewhere in the postface as a contemporary of Yang Xiong (52 BCE–18 CE), could have held this post. It was this point that made the Song dynasty scholar and expert on *chuanqi* tales Hong Mai (1123–1202) declare the text a later forgery.[69] Although this text claims an authenticity that on closer inspection turns out to be spurious, the importance of Ling Xuan's postface lies in the fact that it is closely tied in to the text of *The Scandalous Tale*, assuring the reader that the latter represents a genuine eyewitness account of these events because Ling Xuan's concubine is said to have served in the palace harem in the time of Emperor Cheng and been a confident of Empress Zhao herself. The lack of corroborative information in the dynastic histories and other contemporary texts is dealt with by attributing this to jealousy—other scholars and historians deliberately omitted Ling Xuan from their accounts, and refused to credit his privileged information.

The second postface, attributed to Huan Tan, an important philosopher and statesman who served in the governments of the very late Western Han dynasty, the Xin dynasty, and the early Eastern Han dynasty, continues the theme of authenticity.[70] First, this postface provides a provenance for the text that takes it up to the beginning of the Eastern Han dynasty. Additionally, it purports to document the rediscovery of *The Scandalous Tale* during the Red Eyebrows rebellion, when it was found in a lacquer chest bound with metal bands. The terms in which this is described explicitly link it with "The Metal-Bound Casket" (Jinteng) chapter from *Book of Documents* (Shangshu).[71] This particular piece was attributed to the authorship of the Duke of Zhou, and the story of how he placed it in a chest is also recorded in a number of ancient texts.[72] "The Metal-Bound Casket" stresses that the Duke of Zhou was the victim of unsubstantiated rumors concerning his supposedly treasonous conduct, only to be vindicated by the discovery of the text that he had earlier hidden away. It is appropriate for *The Scandalous Tale* to claim a connection with these events, for the text purports to be the "true story" of Empress Zhao's relationship with Emperor Cheng.

The third and final postface is attributed to the authorship of Xun Xu, and takes the provenance of *The Scandalous Tale* up to the Jin dynasty.[73] Associating the text with Xun Xu, one of the most distinguished scholars of the day, further adds to the impression of authenticity—if so eminent a scholar accepted *The Scandalous Tale* as a genuine Han dynasty document, how could the reader fail to do likewise? This attribution is particularly significant given the role accorded to Xun Xu here in the transmission of the text, since he is said to have transcribed it from a damaged bamboo book. This description of his role serves to implicitly connect *The Scandalous Tale* with the discovery of a major cache of ancient texts in Ji Commandery in around 279 CE, where Xun Xu was chosen to head the group of scholars collating them.[74] The postface seems to be suggesting that *The Scandalous Tale* is every bit as significant in the history of Chinese literature as *Bamboo Annals* (Zhushu jinian), *The Tale of Mu, the Son of Heaven* (Mu Tianzi zhuan), and other important ancient texts found at Ji Commandery. Cumulatively, all three postfaces stress the same points: *The Scandalous Tale* is a genuine Han dynasty text, whose authenticity was accepted by the finest scholars of their day. The reader is supposed to be reassured that no matter how unlikely, this is indeed an account of life in the imperial harem written by someone with firsthand experience, who personally witnessed the relationship between Emperor Cheng, Empress Zhao Feiyan, and her sister, Zhao Hede.

LING XUAN'S AUTHORIAL POSTFACE

Ling Xuan had the style name Ziyu,[75] and came from Lushui.[76] He was an excellent scholar, knowledgeable in music and good at composition, but in spite of this he remained a modest and simple man, without any arrogance at all. Yang Xiong was the only person to be aware of [his fine qualities].[77] However, [Yang] Xiong was ambitious and proud, thus he was determined to bring him down. Ziyu refused to continue their acquaintanceship, whereupon [Yang] Xiong became very vindictive and determined to destroy him. Ziyu, from a minor official position in the Ministry of Works, was promoted to the rank of court gentleman, before becoming a regional inspector in the provincial administration, and then chancellor of Huainan. He was throughout a man of great refinement.

In the time of Emperor Ai, Ziyu resigned his position on the grounds of old age, at which point he bought a concubine named Fan Tongde. This Tongde was the daughter of [Fan] Buzhou, the nephew of [Fan] Yi. She was very talented and beautiful, was learned in history texts, and deeply admired *Records of the Grand Historian* by Sima Qian.[78] She was able to recount many stories about Zhao Feiyan and her younger sister. Ziyu was living in a retired way, and when he commanded her to talk to him, he found himself endlessly fascinated. Ziyu said to Tongde: "These people turned everything they touched into dust and ashes! They exhausted their vital energies, giving rein to every desire and lust, just as if they were bewitched. Surely they knew they would end in [graves surrounded by] abandoned fields and rank grass?" Tongde spread her sleeves and then turned her head to look at the shadows in the lamplight.[79] Holding her chignon in her hand, bitter tears coursed down her face.[80] She could not hide her distress, and Ziyu felt the same.

Tongde said respectfully: "When a man becomes debauched by a woman's beauty, it is because he is possessed of great intelligence. Intelligence leads to understanding, understanding to emotional change; if emotional change occurs with nothing to prevent it, then [it will be like water] running through a canal or down a waterway: it goes where it will. Though you may talk about ritual propriety and proper ceremony, success and failure, you cannot prevent this emotional change. It is only through the emotional impact of reaching the zenith and nadir [of a worldly career], or through death itself, that you may keep [such a person] within bounds. Today I spoke of Empress Zhao and her younger sister: they achieved the summit [of worldly success]; you were distressed by the tragedy of [their graves surrounded by] abandoned fields and rank grass: this is the greatest sadness. When I used my body to throw shadows it was to remind you that you cannot remain forever at the zenith, nor can you speed yourself on the journey to the depths. A predestined meeting may suddenly be cut short by death. Even though the *jieyu* knew this, did she not suffer great loss?[81] Fortunately they have you, my lord, to record their biographies. Let me hold the inkstone and erasing knife, as I recite what will be recorded."

Thus [Ling Xuan, also known as Ziyu] compiled *The Alternative History of Empress Zhao*.[82] When Ziyu was acting as commandant of Hedong, Ban Zhu was a member of his staff, and [made use of his position] to become extremely friendly with the prefect, from whom he received considerable bribes. Ziyu summoned [Ban] Zhu and enumerated his crimes, upbraiding and humiliating him. [Ban] Zhu's older cousin's son, [Ban] Biao, was writing a continuation of Sima [Qian's] *Records of the Grand Historian*; he omitted Ziyu and did not allow him to be recorded.[83]

HUAN TAN'S STATEMENT

In the time of Wang Mang,[84] there was a certain Bian Li from Maoling,[85] who was an expert in the Xiahou tradition of *Book of Documents*.[86] In the second year of the Gengshi reign era (24 CE), the Red

Eyebrows passed through Maoling, and Bian Li abandoned his maps and books to flee into the mountains to hide.[87] Liu Gong entered his hut,[88] and found a lacquer chest bound with metal bands. He opened it up and thus obtained Xuan's book. In the second year of the Jianwu reign era (26 CE), Jia Ziyi showed this book to me,[89] and said: "Xuan was Bian Li's instructor in the *qin*."[90]

XUN XU'S STATEMENT

As for *The Biography of Empress Zhao* by Ling Xuan, the bamboo strips [on which it was written] were crumbling and destroyed, and the meaning of the text had become garbled, so that it could not be completely understood.[91] [Various scholars] and I carefully collated and verified the text, removing all that was incomprehensible, putting together the remainder into [a text of] one *pian* (chapter). There is no account given here of what happened to Empress Zhao and Fan Yi in the end; so I suspect that there is a section missing from [Ling] Xuan's [original].

CHAPTER THREE

Zhao Feiyan's Biography in Historical Sources

THE RELATIONSHIP BETWEEN HISTORY AND FICTION IN *THE SCANdalous Tale of Zhao Feiyan* is a complex one. The earliest known biography of Zhao Feiyan is that included in *History of the Han Dynasty*—a text compiled by various members of the Ban family, who had good reason to dislike the woman since they would have blamed her for disrupting the relationship between Ban Jieyu and Emperor Cheng, which ended in accusations of witchcraft and Ban Jieyu's fall from grace. This text is of great importance as by far the earliest surviving biographical account of Zhao Feiyan; however, it is unfortunate that this consistently hostile portrayal cannot be balanced by reference to other sources of comparable antiquity. If alternative accounts ever existed, they have been lost. In addition to *History of the Han Dynasty*, there are a number of other early Chinese texts that incorporate biographical material concerning Zhao Feiyan and her younger sister. These texts include *Miscellaneous Records of the Western Capital* (Xijing zaji), *Yellow Plans of the Three Capital Regions* (Sanfu huangtu), and *Records Gleaned from Lost Works* (Shiyi ji). Dating to the late Han dynasty or Age of Disunion (220–589), but possibly including some material of a much earlier date, these three texts all contain scattered anecdotes concerning the life of Zhao Feiyan that are related to stories that appear in *The Scandalous Tale*.[1] However, the relationship between these texts is not simple: the author or authors of *The Scandalous Tale* did not simply copy tales already included in these earlier works. Instead, in each case, the material preserved in *The Scandalous Tale* (though related to what is found in these medieval writings) is nevertheless sufficiently rewritten or reworked to the point where the precise nature of the relationship is not obvious. It is also striking that where these texts—most notably *Miscellaneous Records of the Western Capital*—include passages identical to those found in *History of the Han Dynasty*, this material has not been transferred into *The Scandalous Tale*. This difference in their respective contents suggests that these Age of Disunion writings were not used as a direct source for the novella.

In addition to parallels between Han dynasty and Age of Disunion texts and *The Scandalous Tale*, the connection between the account given of the life of the kings of Jiangdu in *Records of the Grand Historian* and *History of the Han Dynasty* and that found in this novella is also of relevance. Although the latter text frequently stresses the connection between the Zhao family and the royal house of Jiangdu, previous scholarship has not considered this issue at all. According to both *Records of the Grand Historian* and *History of the Han Dynasty*, the two kings of Jiangdu were notoriously unpleasant individuals, and in the case of the last king of Jiangdu, he was a sadistic murderer, who devised a series of horrifying sexual tortures for members of his household who had displeased him in any way. His debauchery was also appalling: this included committing incest with a number of his father's consorts and his own sisters. Although *The Scandalous Tale* is not directly linked to the biography of Zhao Feiyan given in *History of the Han Dynasty*, and consistently gives an entirely unrelated portrayal of events in her life, when the author or authors of *The Scandalous Tale* stress her long-standing personal connection with the kings of Jiangdu (which encompasses not only herself but various other female members of her family), it is possible that readers were intended to make a link with the gruesome events recounted in the dynastic histories. By establishing an explicit blood relationship between Zhao Feiyan and members of this notorious family, the text provides some kind of explanation for her promiscuity: What else is to be expected of a great-granddaughter of this royal house, herself the illegitimate and secret offspring of an affair between a princess and a favorite musician? The relationship between history and fiction in *The Scandalous Tale* is not a straightforward one, which can only be comprehended by a detailed study of the various related texts, to demonstrate the way in which each adds to the multifaceted portrayal of its remarkable protagonist.

The Portrayal of Zhao Feiyan in *History of the Han Dynasty*

The earliest surviving account of the career of Zhao Feiyan is the short biography that appears in *History of the Han Dynasty*, written by Ban Gu and other members of his family.[2] It is not to be expected that the portrayal of Zhao Feiyan in a text authored by any member of the Ban family would be favorable, given the numerous clashes between her and Ban Jieyu, Ban Gu's great-aunt, which ended when the latter withdrew from the Rear Palace and joined the household in attendance on Dowager Empress Wang Zhengjun. Ban Jieyu originally entered the Rear Palace with the rank of *shaoshi*; having obtained Emperor Cheng's favor, she was promoted to the position of *jieyu* and bore His Majesty two sons. At this point, the star of the Ban family must have seemed to be greatly in the ascendant, since it was well known that many of those who held the rank of *jieyu* were subsequently promoted to the position of empress. However, in this case it was not to be. Ban Jieyu's children both died young, and when Emperor Cheng's first empress—his cousin, Empress Xu—was demoted in 18 BCE, it was Zhao Feiyan who was appointed in her stead. In Ban Gu's account of these events, the deposition of Empress Xu and his great-aunt's fall from grace were brought about by the machinations of Zhao Feiyan, who slandered them both with vicious accusations of witchcraft.[3] The lurid crimes attributed to her and her sister are likely to be a reflection of the deep disappointment of the Ban family at the frustration of their ambitions.

The first section of Empress Zhao's biography, given in the "Biographies of Consort Houses" (Waiqi zhuan) chapter of *History of the Han Dynasty*, stresses both her poor family background and her education in the performing arts. The emphasis on these two aspects should be seen in the context of Emperor Cheng's other wives and consorts who are accorded their own biographies. Emperor Cheng's first empress was personally chosen by Emperor Yuan as the principal wife of the heir apparent. Empress Xu was the daughter of Xu Jia, who held the titles of commander in chief, general of the chariots and cavalry, and Marquis of Ping'en (*da sima cheji jiangjun Ping'en hou*), and was thus Emperor Cheng's maternal second cousin once removed—Xu Jia was the brother of the first Empress Xu, murdered in 71 BCE to clear the way for a daughter of the all-powerful Huo family to become empress. Empress Xu was therefore a first cousin of Emperor Yuan; however, her close relationship to his murdered mother overrode any consideration that she belonged to a senior generation when it came to arranging a marriage with the heir to the throne.[4] Ban Jieyu also came from an aristocratic family, claiming descent from a distinguished branch of the royal family of the preunification kingdom of Chu that had produced many senior government officials.[5] Both ladies were said to have possessed exceptional personal qualities: Empress Xu is described as a woman of great intelligence and well versed in history, while Ban Jieyu is accorded expertise in classical texts, not to mention an excellent knowledge of traditional ritual practice.[6] Engaging in performing arts, on the other hand, was traditionally considered a very low-class activity; actresses, singers, and dancers were regarded very much in the same light as prostitutes, if not worse, since they were trained to appear to be something that they were not. To persons of high status, Zhao Feiyan was damned by the form of her education: no matter how intelligent, she would be considered someone expert in duplicity and sullied by a connection with the stage.[7] When coming to the biography of Zhao Feiyan in *History of the Han Dynasty*, the reader is certainly meant to draw the conclusion that she was neither socially nor educationally suitable to be the principal wife of the emperor of the Han dynasty:

> Empress Zhao, the consort of Emperor Cheng, was originally a palace slave in Chang'an.[8] When she was born, her father and mother did not nurture her, but when she was still alive after three days, they decided to bring her up. When she was grown, she was attached to the household of the Princess of Yang'a, where she learned to sing and dance: she was given the soubriquet Feiyan, or "Flying Swallow." Emperor Cheng once happened to leave [the palace] on an incognito journey, during which he passed by [the residence] of the Princess of Yang'a, whereupon she gave a musical performance. His Majesty saw Feiyan and was pleased with her. He summoned her to enter the palace, where she was much favored. Her younger sister was also summoned to enter [the palace], and they were both given the title of *jieyu*.[9] The honor with which they were treated startled the Rear Palace.[10]

In her unusual vitality even as a baby, Zhao Feiyan indicated that she was born to no common destiny. The reader is prepared for her meteoric rise by the description of her abandonment: it was believed that a newborn who survived such treatment was predestined for some very special fate, either for good or for evil.[11] The choice originally made by her poor and exploited parents—and their slave background could make them nothing else—was probably the result of harsh necessity: they could not afford to bring up their child. Having been convinced to do so, it is said to have been pure chance that brought the girl to the attention of the emperor. As with other entertainers turned empresses, Zhao Feiyan met the emperor outside the confines of the Rear Palace—study of the careers of such women suggest that regulations preventing emperors from coming into contact with such lowborn individuals were less strictly applied in royal households.[12] However, once infatuated with her and her sister, Emperor Cheng would brook no opposition to his plans to raise them to the very top of the Rear Palace hierarchy. Thanks to the machinations of his maternal relatives, the marriage between Emperor Cheng and Empress Xu had collapsed some years earlier; by the time that His Majesty discovered that the allegations made against her were false, their relationship had been ruined beyond repair.[13] As a result, though Emperor Cheng was unwilling to overtly go against his mother's wishes, he had no intention of allowing the Wang family to dictate his future marital choices: "When Empress Xu was deposed, His Majesty wished to appoint Zhao Jieyu in her stead. Dowager Empress [Wang Zhengjun] despised her on the basis of her extremely humble background, and made trouble over this. The dowager empress's older sister's son, Chunyu Chang (dates unknown), held the rank of palace attendant, and he took messages back and forth [between Dowager Empress Wang and her son]. When he obtained a [favorable] edict from the dowager empress, His Majesty enfeoffed Zhao Jieyu's father [Zhao] Lin as Marquis of Chengyang. After a month or so, he then established the *jieyu* as empress."[14]

As with Zhao Feiyan herself, Chunyu Chang is accorded a very unflattering portrayal in *History of the Han Dynasty*, though he was one of Emperor Cheng's most trusted advisers.[15] In spite of the fact that he was related to the Wang family on his mother's side, Chunyu Chang seems to have been devoted to the interests of Emperor Cheng and the Xu family, not least because he was engaged in a long-running affair with Xu Mi, Empress Xu's sister. In 8 BCE, it was the discovery by the Wang family of Chunyu Chang's commerce with the deposed Empress Xu and his determination to effect a reconciliation between the imperial couple that led to the ex-empress being forced to commit suicide. The former empress Xu had indicated a willingness to accept junior consort status, but any attempt on her part to return to favor would have been perceived by the Wang family as a profound threat.

Zhao Feiyan's biography consistently emphasizes the prejudice she faced within the imperial family. Dowager Empress Wang Zhengjun had originally entered the palace as a *jiarenzi*, or "woman of the household." Having been selected to join the harem of the future Emperor Yuan in around 52 BCE, she bore him his first son. However, her relatively junior rank on entry into the Rear Palace should not be seen as implying low status, since she was a member of an aristocratic family that claimed descent from the pre-Qin ruling house of Qi.[16] Furthermore, the dowager empress was far from being the only member of the imperial house who was concerned that Zhao Feiyan came from too humble a background to be appropriate for elevation to the honor that she now held. Elsewhere, *History of the Han Dynasty* quotes the text of a memorial sent to the throne by Liu Fu, a minor member of the imperial family descended from the kings of Hejian: "Now you have given rein to your desires, showing your partiality to a woman of base extraction, wanting to make her the Mother of All-under-Heaven—you have shown your contempt of Heaven and your lack of shame toward your fellow man: no delusion is greater than this. There is a village saying: 'Rotten wood cannot be used to make pillars; a serf cannot become a master.'"[17]

Liu Fu's horror at the prospect of a dancing girl being placed in a position of such authority is echoed in other memorials condemning the appointment of Zhao Feiyan as empress. *History of the Han Dynasty* also records the reactions of the foremost intellectual of the day, Liu Xiang, to the news that a former slave and entertainer was about to become the most important woman in the empire; this is said to have been a crucial factor in his decision to compile *Biographies of Exemplary Women* (Lienü zhuan) to provide proper moral instruction to the emperor:

> [Liu] Xiang saw that customs had become lax, extravagant, and debauched, and that women of the ilk of Zhao [Feiyan] and Wei [i.e., Li Ping] had risen from poor and humble backgrounds to trample on proper rituals and regulations.[18] Xiang believed that the instruction of a monarch should begin with internal [training] and then proceed to external matters, and that one should begin with things that touched him personally. Thus he selected [exemplary tales concerning] the wise queens and virtuous wives recorded in *Book of Songs* and *Book of Documents*, [illustrating] principles that would bring glory to the country and make a family illustrious, and placing them in order, he compiled

> *Biographies of Exemplary Women*, in eight *pian* in total, with a view to warning the emperor.[19]

Feminist scholars in recent years have thoroughly researched a number of historical figures from various different cultures whose careers and posthumous reputations show a striking similarity with the treatment accorded to Empress Zhao. In particular, these women share the characteristic that they were actresses, entertainers, or courtesans before they were raised to power by marrying a monarch as his official consort. Although such women were often treated with considerable respect in immediately contemporary sources, after their deaths they were commonly accused of engaging in the most extreme sexual practices, participating in orgies, and behaving with rampant promiscuity.[20] The career of Empress Theodora of Byzantium (ca. 500–548 CE) involved a quite different cultural and historical setting from that of Zhao Feiyan, but both women rose from extremely humble entertainment backgrounds to positions of considerable power—Han dynasty authors seem to have lacked the imagination of Procopius (ca. 500–560 CE) in *Secret History* (Apókryphe Istoría [Ἀπόκρυφη Ἱστορία]), where he accuses Empress Theodora of participating in astonishing lewd floor shows in her early years as a performer, as well as engaging enthusiastically in prostitution and debauchery, not to mention developing a lifelong interest in sorcery and black magic.[21] Although such extreme topics do not appear in the earliest texts to talk about her, very similar concepts would be explored in literature about Empress Zhao Feiyan from the Tang dynasty onward.

Although Zhao Feiyan is much more famous as a femme fatale than her younger sister, *History of the Han Dynasty* suggests that during the reign of Emperor Cheng, it was Zhao Zhaoyi who was in some ways the more important figure. Certainly, all early accounts of Zhao Feiyan's biography suggest that she was quickly eclipsed in imperial favor by her sister and that her position as empress did not reflect a particularly close or loving relationship with Emperor Cheng. The charges of enormously extravagant expenditure—often considered a particular feature of the reign of Emperor Cheng—are also laid specifically to Zhao Zhaoyi's account. *History of the Han Dynasty* includes a long and detailed account of her residence, which does indeed seem to have been very luxuriously appointed, though it may be that the statement "These were things that had never been seen in the Rear Palace before" is something of an exaggeration, if other accounts of the magnificence of the Han imperial palaces are to be believed:

> Once [Zhao Feiyan] had been established as empress, her favor decreased somewhat, but her younger sister remained the sole focus of His Majesty's attentions, as a result of which she was appointed as a *zhaoyi*. She lived in the Zhaoyang Residence, where the central courtyard was [painted] vermillion, and the main hall was coated in many a layer of lacquer, while the doorways were all faced with copper that was then covered with a layer of pure gold gilding.[22] The steps were made of white jade, while the close-studded wall timbers were decorated with gold rings, set with jade discs from Lantian, and ornamented with pearls and kingfisher feathers.[23] These were things that had never been seen in the Rear Palace before. The two sisters monopolized power for more than a decade, but in the end neither of them ever gave birth to a child.[24]

Complaints made about the two Zhao sisters in Emperor Cheng's own lifetime seem to have centered on the low social status of their family and the drain that their spending on luxurious living imposed on the financial stability of the imperial household. Their extremely low social status at birth was certainly a fact; however, Emperor Cheng seems to have been extremely conservative in the awards and grants made to both members of the imperial house and consort families in his reign.[25] This may have been the result of concerns about the overweening powers of the Wang family that increasingly threatened the stability of the central government, or it may equally have been a reflection of the careful fiscal policies of the monarch, who seems to have been just as cautious whether the expenses were charged to the state or to his own private funds. As for the charges of personal extravagance made against Empress Zhao Feiyan and her sister, similar accusations were also made against Empress Xu before her divorce: indeed, this seems to have been a popular mechanism for discrediting powerful women. As with queens in other cultures, the senior women of the imperial house were required to wear special ceremonial regalia on certain occasions and to live in residences built to particular specifications that could be extremely expensive. In addition, setting new fashions and building relationships with key allies through the giving of valuable gifts were part and parcel of their duties.[26] Yet all too often, as was the case with the Zhao sisters, they were criticized for actually carrying out these roles. However, much more serious allegations of criminal activities were not made against them until after the emperor's sudden demise:

> The following year in the spring [7 BCE], Emperor Cheng died. His Majesty had been in good health throughout his life, and there was no sign of any disease. . . . In the evening and overnight he was perfectly well, but at dawn when he was putting on his trousers and socks with a view to getting up, he dropped these garments and could not speak. By the time the water clock had gone down another ten *ke*, His Majesty had died.[27] The people placed the blame for this on Zhao Zhaoyi. The dowager empress ordered the commander in chief [Wang] Mang, the chancellor, and the minister of works as follows: "His Majesty has died suddenly and the people are clamorous in their suspicions [at this turn of events]. Director of the Lateral Courts Fu and others were present in the Rear Palace, serving [His Majesty] at dinner or simply in his presence: they can assist the censor, the chancellor, and the chamberlain for law enforcement in investigating the emperor's actions and the circumstances of his sudden attack of sickness." [At this point] Zhao Zhaoyi killed herself.[28]

As events transpired, Zhao Feiyan was lucky to survive the death of Emperor Cheng and the downfall of her younger sister. She was saved by being appointed dowager empress by Emperor Ai. However, when six years later, in 1 BCE, Emperor Ai himself died childless as well, she was immediately demoted. The edict to this effect was issued by Grand Dowager Empress Wang Zhengjun, at the instigation of her nephew Wang Mang, and the wording is given in the dynastic history as follows: "Formerly, when the dowager empress and the *zhaoyi* both served His Majesty the Emperor, these sisters monopolized imperial favor and were the only ones to serve him in his bedchamber. [Empress Zhao] has plotted to seize power; she has killed [His Majesty's] children and thereby threatened [the imperial] family; and she has turned her back on [the will of] Heaven and offended the ancestors—she is entirely lacking in the virtues of a Mother of All-under-Heaven. Let her be demoted from the position of dowager empress to that of Empress Xiaocheng, and moved to live in the North Palace."[29]

While it seems something of a non sequitur that Empress Zhao could be both monopolizing Emperor Cheng's sexual favors and at the same time killing babies born to other women in the harem, these allegations served to legitimize the process by which she was deprived of rank. A few months later,

Empress Zhao was further demoted to the status of a commoner, at which point she immediately committed suicide. As part of the same political purge, the widow of Emperor Ai was also reduced to the rank of a commoner on the same day, but she would wait until she arrived at the site of her husband's tomb before killing herself. The order that forced the former empress Zhao's death, which is described in *History of the Han Dynasty* as "an execution" (*zhu*), reads:

> The empress is well aware that her crimes are terrible indeed, [for not only is she responsible for] court protocols becoming lax, she has failed to behave as a [good] woman should; she has not been able to perform the rituals of mutually nurturing [the palace], but has conducted herself with the viciousness of a wolf or tiger.[30] This has enraged the [imperial] house and infuriated all within the [Four] Seas. However, she still occupies the position of a lesser ruler, which is indeed not what august Heaven desires. Since even the smallest mistake can have terrible consequences for great plans, so those who cannot be touched by benevolence must be removed in the interests of justice. Today, let us demote the empress to the status of a commoner, to be sent to [Emperor Cheng's] tomb.[31]

The biography of Zhao Feiyan in *History of the Han Dynasty* also incorporates an extensive quotation from the report commissioned by Grand Dowager Empress Wang Zhengjun on the death of her son; though rather than addressing the issue of imperial health and the precise circumstances of Emperor Cheng's demise, it is instead concerned exclusively with the crimes of Zhao Zhaoyi. In particular, the report concentrates on the fate of two women in the Rear Palace, Xu Meiren and Cao Gong—the latter identified as a woman official employed to instruct Empress Zhao in *Book of Songs*. Both were said to have borne sons for Emperor Cheng, and it was claimed that the children were killed by order of Zhao Zhaoyi. The woman official Cao Gong is also said to have been forced to drink poison.[32] Perhaps the most scandalous revelation contained within this report is that the emperor participated in the murders of his own children. It would seem likely that in much the same way that anyone who died after dining with the Borgias was automatically assumed to have been poisoned (no matter how old or infirm or what epidemic diseases were rife at the time), any woman in Emperor Cheng's harem who died during the Zhao sisters time in power was said to have been killed by them. Furthermore, it is worth noting that the events described are presented in the context of quotations from the original report, rather than written into the main text itself.[33] It is entirely possible that Ban Gu did not quite believe the account produced by the Wang family, consisting as it does of unsubstantiated allegations, backed up by supposedly verbatim reports of "secret" conversations held a half dozen or more years earlier.

The account of the life of Zhao Feiyan in *History of the Han Dynasty* is by far the earliest. It is likely that the basic outline of events is correct, though the personal prejudices of the Ban family seem to have resulted in her being presented in a consistently hostile light. To a more neutral observer, it might seem that the faults of the Zhao sisters lay more in their failure to kill the right people and sheer bad luck than in any special malevolence. After all, had Zhao Feiyan and her sister murdered enough members of the Wang family, their lives would have been a great deal easier, and it is unlikely that in such a situation the two women would have been forced to commit suicide. Furthermore, if Emperor Ai had concluded a long and successful reign by siring many sons, Zhao Feiyan would have been hailed as the savior of the dynasty, overseeing the peaceful transfer of power from one branch of the imperial line to another. However, when the *History of the Han Dynasty* account is compared with *The Scandalous Tale*, it is clear that the two are almost entirely unrelated. Indeed, if it were not for the fact that the names of the main characters are the same, it would be extremely difficult to recognize the two texts as pertaining to the same individuals. Where *History of the Han Dynasty* describes the wickedness of the Zhao sisters in terms of poisoning and garroting their enemies, slanderous accusations of witchcraft against rivals, and the murders of defenseless infants that culminated in their execution, *The Scandalous Tale* focuses instead on their extravagance and sexual promiscuity, and concludes with the accidental poisoning of Emperor Cheng and the death from shock of Zhao Zhaoyi. Their crimes are thus of a completely different order of magnitude.

The Portrayal of Zhao Feiyan in *Miscellaneous Records of the Western Capital*

The textual history of *Miscellaneous Records of the Western Capital* is extremely problematic, and this is unfortunate given the close relationship between some sections of this text and *The Scandalous Tale*. A better defined date of composition for the former text might throw much light upon the circumstances in which the latter was written. In its present format, *Miscellaneous Records of the Western Capital* consists of 132 individual notes or anecdotes concerning life in the capital city—in particular the imperial palaces—during the Western Han dynasty. The text is accompanied by an afterword purporting to be written by the Jin dynasty polymath Ge Hong (283–363), which attributes original authorship of this book to Liu Xin (d. 23 CE), the son of the great Western Han dynasty scholar and imperial librarian Liu Xiang. *Miscellaneous Records of the Western Capital* is said to have been compiled as a two-*juan* work by Ge Hong, from an edited version in ten *juan* of Liu Xin's much longer text, to fill lacunae in *History of the Han Dynasty*.[34] Unfortunately for the claims that this represents a précis of a genuine Western Han dynasty text, composed by an extremely distinguished scholar, there are no references to *Miscellaneous Records of the Western Capital* prior to the sixth century. In addition, the text was originally anonymous; the afterword attributed to Ge Hong is first mentioned in the Tang dynasty.[35] Although some scholars have favored an attribution to the Liang dynasty scholar Wu Jun (469–520), and others have assigned the text to a much more obscure figure named Xiao Ben (d. 549), there is at present no consensus on either the dating of the text or its ultimate authorship.[36] Although there appear to be no known references to the *Miscellaneous Records of the Western Capital* text itself that predate the 530s–540s, this does not mean that the text does not contain older material. Furthermore, no matter how late the date of compilation is placed, it must still be earlier than the transmitted text of *The Scandalous Tale*.[37] In fact, the complex relationship between *History of the Han Dynasty*, *Miscellaneous Records of the Western Capital*, and *The Scandalous Tale* is interesting because it suggests that the later novella may draw on much earlier material than is readily apparent in the transmitted text.

The first reference to the Zhao sisters in *Miscellaneous Records of the Western Capital* is contained in the first *juan* of the text, and consists of an extensive description of the residence of Zhao Feiyan's younger sister, after she assumed the title of *zhaoyi*. This account of the Zhaoyang Residence, here called the Zhaoyang Hall (Zhaoyang Dian), begins in exactly the same terms as the shorter *History of the Han Dynasty* description; however, *Miscellaneous Records of the Western Capital* lists the luxurious appointments of this palace in much greater detail. It is not clear whether the remainder of this account is an imaginative later recreation of the splendors of the *zhaoyi*'s residence, or whether it represents a longer quotation from the same text as that from which the *History of the Han Dynasty* description is also derived. In the quotation below, the section of the text identical to *History of the Han Dynasty* is given in italics:

> *Zhao Feiyan's younger sister lived in the Zhaoyang Hall, where the central courtyard was [painted] with vermillion and the main hall itself was [ornamented with] red lacquer. The doorways were all faced with copper that was then covered with a layer of pure gold gilding. The steps were made of white jade, while the close-studded wall timbers were decorated with gold rings, set with jade discs from Lantian, and ornamented with pearls and kingfisher feathers.* Above there were arranged nine bronze dragons, each of which was holding a bronze "Nine Star" bell in its mouth, and [decorated with] multicolored banners.[38] They were tied around the middle with bands of purple silk patterned in green, [ornamented with] gold and silver pendants. Every time there was a windy day, these banners and pennants would flutter and flash, lighting up the whole hall, while the chimes of the bells and pendants would startle all who heard them. In the middle there was arranged a painted wooden screen, with a pattern like the fine threads of a spider's web, together with a jade armrest and jade couch, a white ivory stool, and bearskin rug.[39] The fur on this mat was more than two feet long: [if Zhao Zhaoyi] fell asleep and pulled the rug over herself, she was completely hidden from view; if she sat on it, [the fur] covered her knees. The rug was impregnated with various aromatics, so that having once sat on the fur, the scent would cling to her for more than one hundred days. There were also four jade mat weights, which were all translucent and completely flawless. A number of the window leaves were made of green glass: they were also all translucent.[40] Not even the smallest hair could remain concealed on them. The rafters were all carved with dragons and serpents, coiling around [each other], every scale and claw beautifully defined. Everyone who saw [this palace] was completely stunned. The artisans Ding Huan and Li Ju [who made this] were unmatched in their skill.[41] Once the work was completed, he explained it to his sister's son, Fan Yannian,[42] but very few other people even knew about it and no one was able to continue the tradition.[43]

There is nothing in this description that obviously precludes a Han dynasty date for this anecdote, and the opening section undoubtedly derives from this period. However, although *The Scandalous Tale* drew on some of the same material as *Miscellaneous Records of the Western Capital*, this particular description of the Zhaoyang Hall is not one of them. There is no specific description in the former text of the abode of either the empress or her younger sister. This is indicative of the clear separation between *History of the Han Dynasty* and *The Scandalous Tale*, which applies to all the material related to the Zhao sisters in *Miscellaneous Records of the Western Capital.* Also found in the first *juan* of this text is another anecdote concerning Zhao Feiyan and the presentation of a long list of gifts to the empress by her sister. This mirrors one of the central episodes of *The Scandalous Tale*, which records in detail an exchange of gifts between the two women. In both texts a very detailed list of items is given, presumably to emphasize the extravagant spending and wasteful luxury in which the sisters were now engaged, having been raised out of their natural milieu as entertainer-prostitutes thanks to the besotted foolishness of Emperor Cheng. The account in *Miscellaneous Records of the Western Capital* reads:

> When Zhao Feiyan became empress, her younger sister was living in the Zhaoyang Hall. She sent a letter to Feiyan which read as follows:
>
> > "Today is an auspicious day, so may my noble elder sister magnanimously accept this document on which I have carefully listed thirty-five items for presentation, by which I express my loyal fervor:
> >
> > A hat [decorated with a design of] gold flowers and purple clocks;
> > A face veil [again decorated with] gold flowers and purple clocks;[44]
> > A floral silk brocade jacket;[45]
> > A floral silk brocade skirt;
> > A multicolored silk belt;
> > A jacket [with a design of] mandarin ducks;
> > A quilt [with a pattern of] mandarin ducks;
> > A coverlet [with a design of] mandarin ducks;
> > An embroidered vest with gold-stamped designs;
> > *Saptaratna* sandals;[46]
> > A jade bracelet with multicolored stripes;
> > A *saptaratna* hairpin in a joined-hearts design;
> > A gold *en tremblant* hairpin;[47]
> > Hepu round earspools;[48]

An amber pillow;
A pillow with a design [inlaid in] tortoiseshell;
An ornamental coral *jue*-ring;
An agate archer's thumb ring;
A mica fan;[49]
A peacock feather fan;
A kingfisher feather fan;
A *jiuhua* fan;[50]
A *wuming* fan;[51]
A mica screen;
A glass screen;
A golden mountain-shaped incense burner in
five sections;[52]
A *huifeng* fan;[53]
A mat made from coconut-palm fiber;
A double-blossomed plum tree;
A 'hidden-branch' pear tree;
Qingmu aromatic;[54]
Gharuwood aromatic;
A conch-shell cup;
Deer musk from Jiuzhen;[55]
A seven-branched lamp."[56]

This eclectic list of items is somewhat difficult to interpret, largely because so little is known of the fashions in luxury goods that were considered suitable for gift giving at the very highest echelons of society in the early imperial era. It is quite possible that with more information, we would be able to date this list with considerable accuracy, but at present one can merely say that there is nothing here to contradict a date in the late Han to early Jin dynasty.[57] The main problem with accepting a Western Han dynasty date for this list lies in the reference to *saptaratna* jewelry, which suggests the text cannot have been compiled until after the arrival of Buddhism. There is also a concern with the two aromatics mentioned: *qingmu* and gharuwood. The date that these aromatics were first imported into China remains highly controversial.[58] However, in addition to its interest as an account offering luxury products suitable as a congratulatory gift to the woman who has everything and dating to approximately the third century CE, it is also useful to compare the list of

Zhao Hede's presents in *Miscellaneous Records of the Western Capital* with that given in *The Scandalous Tale*. The context of the two lists is identical: in both texts they record gifts from Zhao Hede to the empress, and it is intended to demonstrate the extravagant taste in expensive goods that the pair developed after they were introduced into the Rear Palace. However, although the two accounts are undoubtedly related, there is not a single item on the list that is the same. Furthermore, the list from *The Scandalous Tale* records many objects that did not exist prior to the Sui-Tang period.

The importance of this list of luxurious gifts, and the account of the elegant and expensive appointments of the Zhaoyang Hall previously described, lies in the enjoyment and interest felt by many readers in vicariously experiencing the pampered life of harem favorites. That this was a very significant part of the appeal of these texts can be seen from the number of detailed descriptions of the clothing and décor they enjoyed, not to mention the highly elaborate gift-giving practice described in many literary works about the imperial harem. The audience for writings about Zhao Feiyan was expecting to be shocked and fascinated by such information, and hence extravagant shopping is mentioned not only in prose works such as *Miscellaneous Records of the Western Capital*, but also in poetry; for example, "A Poetic Essay on [Zhao] Feiyan" (Feiyan pian) by the Tang poet Wang Han (fl. early eighth century) speaks of her

> Putting on makeup before a precious mirror on a coral stand,
> Her frescoed walls adorned with a silver flute and a mica fan.[59]

Other poems about the lives of women within the Han imperial harem drew on similar themes and vocabulary; thus, "Plaint of a Palace Lady from Handan" (Handan gongren yuan) by Cui Hao (704–754) speaks of

> Great walls daubed with Sichuan pepper and elaborate frescoes,
> From the Jiuhua [Hall] walkways link the innermost rooms.
> Rock crystal hanging curtains and mica fans,
> Glass windows and tortoiseshell beds.[60]

The account of Zhao Feiyan's luxurious lifestyle given in *Miscellaneous Records of the Western Capital* was to prove highly influential on later writings describing the riches enjoyed by the female denizens of the Han Rear Palace.

There are some instances where *Miscellaneous Records of the Western Capital* includes a unique reference to Zhao Feiyan and her sister, with no counterpart in either *History of the Han Dynasty* or *The Scandalous Tale*. One such anecdote, a description of the appearance of the two women, is also found in the first *juan* of the text. There appears to be no obvious reason why some material in *Miscellaneous Records of the Western Capital* should have been matched in *The Scandalous Tale*, while other sections—such as this one—are completely omitted: "Empress Zhao was of slender build with a narrow waist, and her every movement walking forward or backward was extremely lovely; her younger sister, the *zhaoyi*, could not compare with her in this. However, the *zhaoyi* was fine boned and with a delicate skin, and she was excellent at cracking jokes.[61] The two women were as exquisite as fine jades, the most [beautiful women] of their time. They both monopolized the emperor's favor in the Rear Palace."[62]

Miscellaneous Records of the Western Capital is not entirely consistent in its portrayal of Empress Zhao. In *juan* 5, it includes a very short anecdote describing a famous musical instrument, which serves to introduce a quite different portrait of the empress as an expert performer on the *qin*. The instrument that she played is recorded not merely as an exceptionally beautiful and finely made object; it is also said to have been ornamented with images of exemplary women. To spend time contemplating such depictions was considered a deeply meritorious act in the Han dynasty and is mentioned in praise in many ancient texts.[63] However, of all the wives and consorts of Emperor Cheng, this kind of moral training was specifically associated with Ban Jieyu.[64] For Empress Zhao to participate in it as well provides a quite different perspective on her personal behavior while living in the palace. Clearly what is at issue here is not whether Empress Zhao genuinely spent time viewing images of moral exemplars, but that at least one source for *Miscellaneous Records of the Western Capital* (and this must have belonged to a very different textual tradition to *History of the Han Dynasty*!) thought that she might have done so. This anecdote thus belongs to a more positive biographical tradition than the majority of surviving material: "Empress Zhao had a precious *qin*, named 'the Phoenix.' It was decorated with dragons and cock phoenixes, [together with] hornless dragons and hen phoenixes, [not to mention] images of wise exemplary women from antiquity, all done in relievo [inlaid carvings] in gold and jade. She was an expert in performing the melody 'The Whirlwind Travels Far Away.'"[65]

In the second *juan* of *Miscellaneous Records of the Western Capital*, there is another story that has been transformed in transmission between this text and *The Scandalous Tale*. In this case, the anecdote concerns a man named Qing Anshi, who is identified as one of Empress Zhao's many lovers. Although the two texts retain considerable differences in detail, it is likely that Qing Anshi, the attendant gentleman who is so good at performing music and so much beloved by Zhao Feiyan, is actually the same character as Feng Wufang, the favored attendant gentleman who provides her musical accompaniment in *The Scandalous Tale*. Both texts are as one in their description of Empress Zhao's sexual promiscuity when she hoped that another man might father a child on her when Emperor Cheng failed. The only significant difference is in the identity of these anonymous sexual partners; *Miscellaneous Records of the Western Capital* states that men were smuggled into the palace from outside, while *The Scandalous Tale* identifies them as men who worked within the palace, either as elite officeholders or as servants in the imperial household:

> When Qing Anshi was fifteen years old, he was appointed as an attendant gentleman by Emperor Cheng. He was good at playing the *qin*, and could perform the songs "Two Phoenixes" and "Leaving behind the Hen Phoenix."[66] Empress Zhao was deeply impressed by this and reported it to His Majesty, whereupon he was allowed to come and go [inside the palace], having sex [with the empress] and receiving unparalleled love and favor. He always wore boots made of the lightest silk, and waved a cooling fan, with a cloak of purple satin. He was actually living with the empress. She wanted to have children, but in the end she never produced any offspring. Since Empress Zhao had no children, she set aside a room on the excuse that she wanted to pray and make supplications, where with the exception of her own servants and maids, no one was allowed to enter, not even the emperor. She had idle young men brought in [to the palace] in covered carriages, dressed in women's clothing. They would come to the Rear Palace for weeks at a time, and engage in lewd sexual acts [with the empress]: she never seemed to need a rest [from her debauchery]. If one of the men became exhausted, she would immediately demand that he be replaced. However, in the end she never had any children.[67]

Empress Zhao's childlessness was reported from the time of *History of the Han Dynasty* onward; this must be taken as a historical fact. There can also be no doubt that the political problems caused by the lack of an heir to the throne dominated court politics throughout the later years of the reign of Emperor Cheng, and that relationships between rival factions were poisonous. However, allegations of Empress Zhao's promiscuous sexual behavior are not found in any indubitably Han dynasty textual sources. This has led some scholars to argue that the accounts of Empress Zhao's licentiousness in *Miscellaneous Records of the Western Capital* could potentially have been influenced by later scandals in imperial houses during the Age of Disunion, in particular the activities of Jia Nanfeng (257–300), the first empress of Emperor Hui of Jin (r. 290–301, 301–307).[68] Empress Jia, married off by her family at the age of fourteen to a man whose mental problems were well known, became notorious both for her jealousy that resulted in the murder of a number of her husband's consorts and for her own adultery: she was said to have assassinated her discarded lovers lest they reveal her affairs.[69] While it is true that Empress Zhao's promiscuity forms an important narrative element in *The Scandalous Tale*, and this is clearly related to the account given in *Miscellaneous Records of the Western Capital*, there is no reason to believe that there is any factual basis to the story at all. It is very striking that where *History of the Han Dynasty* stresses the many evil acts perpetrated by the Zhao sisters, there is no suggestion that Zhao Feiyan's sexual morality left anything to be desired. Furthermore, had Ban Gu wished to mention such a subject, it would have been quite possible for him to do so—*History of the Han Dynasty* is not silent on the subject of incest, bestiality, and sexual violence committed by members of the Han imperial house. *Miscellaneous Records of the Western Capital*, on the other hand, does not mention the murders and other crimes attributed to the agency of the Zhao family at all, concentrating instead on Zhao Feiyan's orgies. This means that the two texts are drawing on quite different traditions when developing her biography.

It is necessary here to consider what the connection between these two texts can tell us about the process of composition of *The Scandalous Tale*. First, if the author of *The Scandalous Tale* was a Sui-Tang-era person intent on forging a "Han" text, it is hard to see why he would not simply use the various *Miscellaneous Records of the Western Capital* anecdotes unchanged. The changes introduced in *The Scandalous Tale* often include anachronistic details, which serve to betray the later origins of the text. Furthermore, if the author of *The Scandalous Tale* was using *Miscellaneous Records of the Western Capital* as a source, it is not at all clear why he would have eschewed all the information in this text associated with *History of the Han Dynasty*. At the same time, there are some anecdotes concerning Zhao Feiyan and her sister that are unique to *Miscellaneous Records of the Western Capital*, with no counterpart in either *History of the Han Dynasty* or *The Scandalous Tale*; it is again not clear why someone writing a history of Emperor Cheng's harem would not simply include all relevant material from *Miscellaneous Records of the Western Capital*, not least because the problems with this text were far from well known in the Sui-Tang period. The fact that the story of the presentation of gifts and other anecdotes eventually included in *The Scandalous Tale* appear in a different and sometimes demonstrably earlier form in *Miscellaneous Records of the Western Capital* suggests that elements that were eventually incorporated into this text were already in circulation long before the novella crystallized into its present form in the late Tang dynasty.

The Portrayal of Zhao Feiyan in *Yellow Plans of the Three Capital Regions*

The textual history of *Yellow Plans of the Three Capital Regions* is as complex as that of *Miscellaneous Records of the Western Capital*, and there is no scholarly consensus at present as to the date of compilation of this text. However, in spite of the debates concerning the dating, this anonymous text remains an extremely important source of information about the Han dynasty capital city, containing as it does many detailed accounts of the architecture that are not found in other surviving transmitted material. Furthermore, in a number of instances, the information provided by *Yellow Plans of the Three Capital Regions* has been confirmed by modern archaeology. The bibliophile Chao Gongwu (1105–1180), writing in the Southern Song dynasty, identified this text as identical with that titled *Yellow Plans* (Huangtu) in one *juan*, recorded in the catalogue of the imperial library preserved in the official history of the Sui dynasty.[70] There are, however, considerable problems with identifying the Sui *Yellow Plans* with the transmitted text of *Yellow Plans of the Three Capital Regions*, which consists of six *juan*.[71] In addition, as was noted by the Song dynasty scholar Cheng Dachang (1123–1195), there is considerable evidence that *Yellow Plans of the Three Capital Regions* in its present form dates to the Tang dynasty, though he admitted the presence of much older material within the text.[72] This dating is borne out by study of some of the specific geographical terms found within the text, which contain place-names that are not recorded until the Tang dynasty.[73] This indicates at the very least that the transmitted text must have been significantly rewritten at this point. Miao Changyan (*jinshi* 1142) was the first scholar to suggest that the core *Yellow Plans of the Three Capital Regions* should be considered a genuine Han dynasty text; his lead was followed by a number of other Song dynasty bibliophiles, including Chen Zhensun (1179–1262) in his *Annotated Catalogue of Books from the Straight Studio* (Zhizhai shulu jieti).[74] This theory is now generally adopted, but with some reservations. There is undoubtedly a certain amount of extraneous material contained within *Yellow Plans of the Three Capital Regions*, and hence the date of composition and the process by which the present text was compiled are still quite unclear.

There is only one short story specifically concerned with the biography of Zhao Feiyan contained within *Yellow Plans of the Three Capital Regions*. However, this anecdote describes her and Emperor Cheng amusing themselves at the Taiyi Pool, and is hence related—though not directly—to *The Scandalous Tale*. The same anecdote is also found, with very minor textual differences, in *Records Gleaned from Lost Works*, indicating that the two are derived from the same source, and hence the two texts will be considered together here. In the translation below, the characters found in *Records Gleaned from Lost Works* and not in *Yellow Plans of the Three Capital Regions* are given in italics:

> Emperor Cheng would often amuse himself on holidays in the autumn at the Taiyi Pool with Zhao Feiyan: there was a vessel made from *shatang* wood, *so expensive it was quite unbelievable*. It had mica ornaments on the bird-shaped figurehead on the prow—this was called the Cloud Boat. They also carved great paulownia-wood [blocks] in the shape of dragons and serpents, ornamented to make them look real; these were placed on either side of the Cloud Boat as outriggers. The rudder and oars were made from purple cassia wood. Having watched the clouds as they sculled across the waters, they would amuse themselves by plucking caltrops in the canal. His Majesty was worried that the rocking [of the boat] might alarm Feiyan, so he ordered the Sharpshooters in attendance to keep the Cloud Boat steady on the waves with a golden anchor.[75] Every time a light wind blew, Feiyan would immediately want to follow the wind and go out into the waters; His Majesty used a jade-green belt to tie up Feiyan's skirts, and then they went back. *Later on Feiyan gradually found herself becoming alienated [from His Majesty]*. She would often

> ask in alarm: "How can I expect you to tie up my skirts again, when I am of such humble birth?" To this day there is the Escaping the Winds Tower at the Taiyi Pool, which is where Feiyan tied up her skirts.[76]

This anecdote, as with so many others concerning the relationship between Emperor Cheng and Zhao Feiyan, stresses the incredible extravagance of the circumstances in which they lived, and his besotted love for her. So great was Emperor Cheng's devotion that he was prepared to perform even the most menial tasks for his beloved wife. The two surviving versions of this story are almost identical, though the context in which Zhao Feiyan makes her comment about the emperor's solicitude in tying up her skirts is different. In *Yellow Plans of the Three Capital Regions*, it is presented as though Zhao Feiyan expostulated on her humble birth every time the emperor assisted her. In *Records Gleaned from Lost Works*, by contrast, it is presented as a cause for anxiety after losing His Majesty's favor. As with *Miscellaneous Records of the Western Capital*, *Yellow Plans of the Three Capital Regions* and *Records Gleaned from Lost Works* provide a parallel with *The Scandalous Tale* that is close enough to be identifiable, and yet is equally somewhat removed from the form in which it appears in the later novella. The appearance of two similar versions of the same story in early medieval texts, and a significantly different version in *The Scandalous Tale*, again suggests that the latter text was drawing upon much older material. An early medieval tradition concerning Empress Zhao was thus rewritten and adapted for a new audience.

The Portrayal of Zhao Feiyan in *Records Gleaned from Lost Works*

Records Gleaned from Lost Works is a collection of stories compiled during the Northern Dynasties by Wang Jia. The focus of this collection was to gather together otherwise neglected stories of strange and unusual happenings from high antiquity to the Jin dynasty into one useful compendium; the result is often described as one of the most important early collections of *zhiguai*, or "miraculous tales."[77] The earliest bibliographical information concerning this text dates to the Liang dynasty, in a preface composed by an individual named Xiao Qi (dates unknown), which describes the text as having originally consisted of nineteen *juan* and 220 individual tales; however, by this time the book had suffered considerable textual loss. As a result, when he re-edited this collection, only ten *juan* remained.[78] The attribution to Wang Jia is today generally accepted, though in the late imperial era there were some scholars who called it into question—most notably the late Ming dynasty literary theorist and bibliophile Hu Yinglin (1551–1602), who suggested that *Records Gleaned from Lost Works* was in fact written by Xiao Qi and merely attributed to Wang Jia.[79] Recent scholarship, however, takes issue with the account given in Xiao Qi's preface, suggesting that he misunderstood the nature of the text and thus considered it to be fragmentary. *Records Gleaned from Lost Works* is a text that operates on two levels. It consists of many tales that are concerned with the ruler's acquisition of marvels, which come to him either as the result of tribute from distant regions or through active searches with the assistance of an adept. This is coupled with an underlying narrative concerning the succession of the Five Phases from one historical era to another—the sections pertaining to Emperor Cheng are found under the element Fire.[80] Although this underlying structure is not particularly relevant to understanding the stories found in this text that concern Zhao Feiyan, these particular tales do fit in with one major theme of *Records Gleaned from Lost Works*: the demands made by rulers for strange and marvelous objects to ornament their palaces were excessive. The determination to acquire such rarities, even when it appears benign, is in fact grossly expensive and disruptive and hence indicative of the rottenness at the heart of the system.

In among the many stories of strange phenomena found in *Records Gleaned from Lost Works*, there are two short anecdotes concerning the relationship between Emperor Cheng and Zhao Feiyan, both of which focus on events that occurred in the lavish buildings located within the royal palace complex in the immediate vicinity of the Taiyi Pool. The first of these has already been described, but in the second vignette (which has no counterpart in *The Scandalous Tale*), the focus is on the emperor's pleasures and the strange and unusual buildings and objects that he has constructed for his own delight:

> Next to the Taiyi Pool, [Emperor Cheng] erected the "Roaming Free Palace," with lacquer pillars supporting hangings of black satin.[81] All the paraphernalia and clothing, not to mention the carriage in which he rode there, were all plain black, and he delighted in going there at night, scorning the light of lamps and candles. All the beautiful women officials in the palace were

dressed in black clothes, and Ban Jieyu and her juniors each wore a dark-red silk belt. Even the strings of their hats and the *nécessaires* they wore were made of brocade or embroidered. In addition to that, they were veiled in magnolia-patterned silk gauze. Only once they arrived at the Roaming Free Palace would they take up lamps. Once the emperor had finished enjoying himself, they would still the drums yet carry on dancing, but not a speck of dust was raised by their steps.[82]

One of the very striking aspects of this account is the record of Ban Jieyu's participation. In most accounts of her relationship with Emperor Cheng, she is shown admonishing him and insisting on behaving in ways consistent with the exemplary women of antiquity even if this offends him. Yet in this account, just like the other women in his harem, Ban Jieyu is shown facilitating his bizarre interests, and joining His Majesty on his journeys through the darkness to a black palace, where they would feast and frolic. This is not at all the kind of activity with which Emperor Cheng's refined and highly educated consort is normally associated. This account continues with a further odd description of the imperial pleasures:

They constructed a "Flying Hall," one *zhang* square, much like today's palanquin, and specially selected knights from the Feathered Forest imperial guard would shoulder it and run. The emperor from his vantage point on top of the palanquin felt as though he was speeding along; hearing them [run] from in their midst was like the sound of wind and thunder: since it went so fast he called this the "Cloud Thunder Palace." The favored [inhabitants of the] palace [where he stopped] would all lay out carpets to cover the ground, since [His Majesty] disliked the racket caused by chariots making ruts and horses stamping their hooves. Even though [His Majesty] was far too fond of his plainclothes journeys and his lavish banquets, his people did not hate him, nor were they put to any trouble by this. Every time he rode back and forth on his imperial carriage, the expensive clothes and fancy foods [provided for] his beloved consorts would be abandoned by the side of the road [afterward]; the old and poor among the people of the capital would all sing out: "Long live the emperor!" This occurred in the Hongjia [20–17 BCE] and the Yongshi [16–13 BCE] reign eras, when the country was wealthy and the people were rich, and there had been no wars for a long time.[83]

This strange description of Emperor Cheng's pleasures, traveling by night in dark clothes to enjoy himself banqueting with his womenfolk in a specially built black palace, has no parallel in other texts that concern his life and reign. However, in the context of the overarching theme of this text, which concerns the worthiness of the monarch, his extravagance is balanced by his generous gifts to the poor and needy, his determination not to drag the country into expensive wars, and his willingness to listen to advice. Indulging the emperor's somewhat peculiar (but basically harmless) fantasies is thus presented as an affordable luxury for the dynasty in an era of peace, as opposed to an intolerable burden placed upon an already impoverished and suffering populace.

The account of the life of Zhao Feiyan in *Records Gleaned from Lost Works*, as with other late Han dynasty and early medieval texts, makes no mention of the many murders she and her sister are supposed to have committed within the confines of the imperial palace. Likewise, there is scant reference to her origins, or to the outrage that many members of the ruling elite clearly felt at the elevation of someone born a slave to the position of empress. Instead, these texts belong to quite a different tradition that talks about luxurious living and ostentatious spending: the emphasis is on the enjoyment of a wide variety of sensory pleasures. There are stories that attest to Zhao Feiyan's musical talents. There are stories that list the exotic perfumes with which she scented herself and the fine silks she wore, not to mention descriptions of the magnificent palaces she lived in, the lovely and rare objects that she owned, and her personal beauty. Such anecdotes attest to a truth that pertains to the historical Zhao Feiyan as well: women from entertainer backgrounds who were brought into the imperial harem were there for the pleasure that they brought to the ruler. However, stories concerning Emperor Cheng and his wife from *Records Gleaned from Lost Works* are interesting because they suggest that the expensive refinements of living for the imperial household were not necessarily viewed as intrinsically problematic. At a time when the country was wealthy and the ruler well-meaning and benevolently inclined, the regime could afford to pay for such extravagances.

The Jiangdu Connection

The Scandalous Tale makes repeated reference to the king of Jiangdu, the empress's putative great-grandfather, and his household. It might be assumed that the emphasis placed upon her royal ancestry was a sign of concern about the idea of an empress drawn from the lower classes, which could be resolved by making her a "princess," though one of illegitimate birth. However, it is unlikely that this is the sole motive for harping on the theme of a long-standing and deep-rooted connection between the Zhao family and the royal house of Jiangdu. Instead, it is important to understand the significance of the king of Jiangdu as an outstanding example of decadence and sexual debauchery in the Han imperial house. There appears to be no text prior to *The Scandalous Tale* to connect the empress and her sister with the royal family—however, in this novella the connection is made repeatedly. Not only is the empress said to be a descendant of the king of Jiangdu; she and her sister are also said to count among their intimates a number of people who once formed part of the royal household, including a junior consort of the first king. In order to understand the importance of this theme within the context of *The Scandalous Tale*, it is necessary to consider the careers of the two Western Han dynasty kings of Jiangdu. The first king, Liu Fei (168–128 BCE), was the second of the three sons Lady Cheng bore for Emperor Jing. From 155 BCE Liu Fei held the appointment of king of Runan, but following his participation in the successful campaign against Liu Bi, king of Wu (r. 194–154 BCE), his fief was moved to Jiangdu. Disappointed in all his subsequent military ambitions, Liu Fei spent the rest of his life beautifying his palaces and recruiting bravos (*haojie*) into his service. When he died in 128 BCE, he was granted the very ambiguous posthumous title of Yi, or "Willing to Reform," by his half brother, Emperor Wu.[84] Liu Fei was succeeded as king of Jiangdu by his son, Liu Jian (r. 127–121 BCE), the second and last holder of this title in the Western Han dynasty.

The account of Liu Fei's life given in the official histories of the Han dynasty provides little help in interpreting the unusual features of his mausoleum, which was excavated from 2009 from 2011. This site, covering 250,000 square meters, contains the tomb of the king himself, his two main consorts, and dozens of attendant burials.[85] For reasons about which history is silent, the first king of Jiangdu was buried not at his capital but at a site abutting the mausoleum complex pertaining to the Marquises of Tangyi—the family to which his sister-in-law, Empress Chen (the first wife of Emperor Wu), belonged. The significance of this relationship to the first king of Jiangdu is not clear, but such an unusual tomb placement would probably have required special permission from the emperor. One very striking feature of this royal tomb, which will no doubt lend further credence to the lurid allegations made about the kings of Jiangdu in the dynastic histories, is the discovery of what appears to be a sex toy: a kind of bronze dildo.[86] Although not absolutely unique in Han dynasty tomb excavations, the discovery of this exceptionally high-quality object does seem to indicate a strong interest in sexual matters on the part of this monarch.

The account of Liu Fei's life in *Records of the Grand Historian* is relatively discreet, suggesting merely a difficult character, but probably nothing out of the ordinary for a member of the imperial house. This account simply says that "he was extremely arrogant and extravagant."[87] However, when it comes to the second king of Jiangdu, Liu Jian, the two official histories of the dynasty offer significantly different biographies. *Records of the Grand Historian* states that Liu Jian engaged in incestuous sexual relationships with all of his sisters and debauched his father's favorite concubine before King Yi was even buried—although unpleasant and disrespectful toward his father's memory, such behavior was not unusual among members of the Han dynasty royal houses, particularly the descendants of Emperor Jing.[88] These activities are mentioned in passing, leading up to the second king of Jiangdu's involvement in the supposedly treasonous conspiracy headed by Liu An, king of Huainan (r. 173–122 BCE), and his associations with shamans and other religio-magical specialists, which eventually forced Emperor Wu to order the investigation of his nephew's misdeeds that culminated in his suicide.[89] Concern here is focused upon the king's political activities: incest was merely a minor matter that the authorities were happy to ignore. By contrast, although *History of the Han Dynasty* does mention some of Liu Jian's political scheming, much greater attention is paid to his sexual misconduct, beginning with his debauchery of his father's womenfolk and his incest with his sister.[90] Furthermore, it is stressed that this was a matter of official concern.[91] Interestingly, where *Records of the Grand Historian* records only one of King Yi of Jiangdu's consorts but all of his daughters falling victim to Liu Jian's sexual abuse, *History of the Han Dynasty* reverses this, indicating that many of King Yi of Jiangdu's consorts but only one of his daughters was debauched by Liu Jian. It would seem that Ban Gu felt the horror of a son encroaching upon his father's sexual prerogatives was more shocking than incest with siblings, hence the change in emphasis between the two texts:

> When [Liu] Jian was the crown prince, a man named Liang Fen from Handan brought his daughter because he wished to present her to King Yi. However,

> Jian heard how beautiful she was and summoned her secretly [to his palace], where he kept her and refused to allow her to leave. Fen told everyone: "A son is fighting with his father over a woman!" Jian sent someone to kill [Liang] Fen. Fen's family reported this to the throne, and a special commissioner was sent to investigate, but it so happened that a general amnesty was announced and so [the crown prince] was never punished for this. After King Yi died but before he was buried, Jian was resident in the mourning hut, and summoned Lady Zhuo, a beauty who had previously been much favored by King Yi, and some ten others, and engaged in debauched sexual acts with them.[92] Jian's younger sister Zhengchen was the wife of the son of the Marquis of Gai, but when she came home to attend King Yi's funeral, Jian again engaged in debauched sexual acts with her.[93]

Having introduced the reader to Liu Jian's disgusting sexual behavior, made worse by the context in which much of it was carried out—not merely during the mourning period for his recently deceased father but actually at the site of his grave—*History of the Han Dynasty* goes on to describe a number of murders carried out personally by the second king of Jiangdu. The emphasis in this account is upon the deaths of innocent and defenseless people, particularly women. The sadistic activities of the second king of Jiangdu seem to have consistently been directed against members of his own household, which made it impossible for anyone to intervene to control him:

> [Liu] Jian was traveling around the Zhangtai Palace when he ordered four women to get into a small boat. Jian then kicked out with his feet until he overturned their boat and the four women all fell into the water: two of them died. Later on when he was traveling around Leibo, the weather was very windy, whereupon Jian ordered two of his [attendant] gentlemen to get into a small boat and head out on the waves. The boat overturned and the two gentlemen were thrown into the water. They were able to grab hold of the boat and were seen now rising and now sinking [below the waves]. Jian stood at a position of vantage to watch this and roared with laughter, as he gave orders that both the men should die.[94]

Having described the sadistic treatment meted out to the unfortunate servants—male and female—by the second king of Jiangdu, *History of the Han Dynasty* goes on to record Liu Jian's horrific regime of punishments for those who offended him. Again, this account reports that this vicious cruelty was directed only at members of his own household, who would have been completely within his power. In spite of being the subject of investigation from the time that he was the crown prince, it was not until the king of Jiangdu was thought to be engaged in treasonous activities that his uncle, the emperor, finally decided to act against him. No matter how shocking the allegations, sexual misconduct, incest, and the torture of members of his household were not sufficient reason to bring a grandson of the Han emperor to justice:

> When a palace slave, woman official, or *bazi* had committed some fault, he would immediately order them to strip and stand beating a drum, or sometimes to climb up a tree, and in the worst cases it might be thirty days before they were allowed to put their clothes back on. Alternatively he would shave their heads and put them in collars to pound grain with a mallet; if they did not do exactly what he demanded, he would immediately have them beaten.[95] Sometimes he would release wolves and have them bite [the women] to death, while Jian himself watched and roared with laughter. Sometimes he would shut them up without food and have them starve to death. In this way he killed thirty-five innocent people. Jian hoped that by making people have sex with animals, he might be able to get them to have offspring, so he would force his palace women to remove their clothes and go down on all fours, to have sex with rams and dogs.[96]

In *The Scandalous Tale*, it is not made explicit exactly how the author imagined the empress and her younger sister to be related to the Jiangdu ruling house. The empress and her sister are situated within a lineage of women, interacting with their mother, aunts, and female cousins, whose relationship to them is defined in a way that their relationship to male relatives, by and large, is not. (The exception is the Zhao sisters' father, but even here, there is ambiguity: they bear the surname of their mother's husband, not of their supposed biological father.) The two women's mother, the Princess of Gusu, is simply said to have been a granddaughter of a king of Jiangdu, which might be either Liu Fei or Liu Jian. The only relationship that is defined is that of Li Yanghua—the concubine of King Yi, whose aunt was the wife of Feng Dali (Zhao Feiyan's grandmother): this makes the two women cousins. Either way, the constant reiteration in the text that Zhao Feiyan and all the other women in her immediate circle were previously intimately connected with the royal house at Jiangdu must be related in some way to the historical record. The shocking behavior of the Princess of Gusu in engaging in an adulterous sexual relationship with a musician in her husband's household, the orgies of Zhao Feiyan and her promiscuity before and after her entry into the imperial harem, and the extravagance and debauchery of Zhao Hede are things quite to be expected of persons related to so notorious a family. However, as problematic as these activities might be, they pale by comparison with the horror of what was really done to others by Liu Jian within the confines of his palace at Guangling.

Conclusion

The various different sources for the biography of Empress Zhao discussed in this chapter predate the compilation of *The Scandalous Tale*. The most famous biographical account is that found in *History of the Han Dynasty*, which portrays her as a woman capable of the most extreme acts of violence, who with the connivance of her sister was able to monopolize the emperor's favor, destroyed the lives of her rivals by accusations of witchcraft, and concluded her career of villainy by standing by while her younger sister and Emperor Cheng murdered a series of imperial offspring and their mothers with a view to consolidating the control of the Zhao family over the Rear Palace. This belongs to a quite different textual tradition to that which informed *The Scandalous Tale*. However, though this text did not draw directly upon the *History of the Han Dynasty* portrayal of Empress Zhao for inspiration, there is some evidence that the author or authors of *The Scandalous Tale* were aware of the history of this period. In particular, this can be seen in the link this text makes between the Zhao family and the ruling house of Jiangdu. *History of the Han Dynasty* is our only surviving source for the appalling crimes and sexual tortures committed by the last king of Jiangdu: although the two texts seem to be entirely unrelated, *The Scandalous Tale* stresses her blood relationship (if illegitimate) with the ruling house, and the various other connections between her family and theirs. The novella must, at some level, be connected with historical accounts of the terrible deeds perpetrated by the last king of Jiangdu.

If there is no direct connection between the official biography of Empress Zhao preserved in *History of the Han Dynasty* and *The Scandalous Tale*, there is some link between the latter text and a number of other late Han to early

Age of Disunion texts. It is clear that there were two distinct traditions pertaining to Empress Zhao current during this period: one stressed the wickedness of the Zhao family in bewitching the emperor and then murdering his children; the other was concerned with their extravagant lifestyle and sexual promiscuity. *The Scandalous Tale* is derived from this second tradition, and a relationship can be traced between sections of this text and *Miscellaneous Records of the Western Capital*, *Yellow Plans of the Three Capital Regions*, and *Records Gleaned from Lost Works*. However, the relationship is not a simple or straightforward one: the incidents in *The Scandalous Tale* have been rewritten and adapted for a later audience, and updated to take account of changing tastes. As a result, although the relationship between *The Scandalous Tale* and these earlier texts is not clear, sufficient similarities remain that they can be identified as belonging to one and the same textual tradition. This allows us to understand this Tang dynasty novella as one stage of a work in progress, in which earlier material was reworked to create an intense tale of duplicity and sexual intrigue set in the Han Rear Palace. The result has long been recognized not merely as a fine work of literature in its own right, but also as a significant precursor of many other Chinese erotic writings.

CHAPTER FOUR

Interpreting *The Scandalous Tale*

THE SCANDALOUS TALE OF ZHAO FEIYAN IS A MAJOR TEXT IN TANG dynasty Chinese literature: as a study of sexual obsession and duplicity, power and control, nothing of this level of psychological complexity would be written in the Chinese language until centuries later.[1] Although it is possible to dismiss the text as a forgery (assuming that the "author's preface" was written with an intent to deceive the reader that it was actually written in the Han dynasty), its literary value is undoubted: this is attested to in the numerous other works of literature inspired by *The Scandalous Tale*—either rewriting the novella itself or quoting it within new works of poetry and prose, or drawing inspiration from its conceit of telling the reader the "true story" of life in the imperial harem, not to mention in the entry of many words and phrases derived from this text into daily usage.[2] However, due to the lack of interest in Silk Pillow writings in academia, the existence of other comparable works in the same genre has been generally ignored, and the perception that *The Scandalous Tale* is in some way unique and unconnected to other imperial-era literary traditions seems to have confused many scholars and dissuaded them from studying this text.

The literary qualities of *The Scandalous Tale* have been used by some scholars to argue that it is too sophisticated to date from any period prior to the reunification of China under the Sui dynasty, while the erroneous belief that no other writings of this kind exist in Sui-Tang prose literature has led others to suggest that it must significantly predate this era. However, there are many reasons to believe that a Tang dynasty date for the text is correct.

First, analysis of the language used in *The Scandalous Tale* shows numerous vocabulary items that did not exist prior to the Sui-Tang period, as well as what may be an instance of observance of a Tang dynasty name taboo. In addition to that, the sudden appearance of a large number of references to the text and quotations from it in literature from the second half of the ninth century suggest that it probably entered circulation in this period. Nevertheless, *The Scandalous Tale* is a text that appears to have a very long and involved process of production, and it would be unwise to exclude the possibility that it contains some material of a significantly earlier date.

The narrative structure of *The Scandalous Tale* is highly complex. The author of the text plays with transparency and obscurity in motives, to create a highly nuanced account of the power relationships in the harem of Emperor Cheng. In this narrative, the reader is positioned between the transparency of the emperor's position and the obscurity of the palace women's motivations. The reader is at each stage informed of exactly how the emperor is manipulated by his favorites. At the same time, the reasons why the women behave as they do—their true feelings and emotions—are hidden, even though they are the major protagonists. This female character–centered narrative structure (though rare in medieval writings as a whole) is a common feature of Silk Pillow literature, since it is important for generating a sense of authenticity—*The Scandalous Tale* purports to record the experience of women living and working within the imperial harem.

The History of the Text

To date, there has only been one detailed study of the textual history of *The Scandalous Tale*: Lin Yuhong's "Research on the Composition of *The Scandalous Tale of Zhao Feiyan* and a Comparison of the Transmission of Printed Editions" (*Zhao Feiyan waizhuan* chengshu ji banben chuancheng bijiao yanjiu).[3] Unfortunately, this study omits a number of important recensions of the text, and ignores some of the major textual problems. The earliest known printed edition of *The Scandalous Tale* is thought to have been that included in the *congshu*, or collectanea, produced by Tao Zongyi, titled *Stories from the Suburbs* (Shuofu), dating to the early Ming dynasty.[4] However, although this may be chronologically the earliest known recension of the text, no copies of this printing survive. The earliest extant edition is *The Scandalous Tale* in one *juan*, edited by Gu Yuanqing (1487–1565): a recension of great importance since it has been so frequently reproduced.[5] This version has been used as the base edition for a number of collated recensions of *The Scandalous Tale*, and has also often been incorporated into numerous *cong-shu* and collections of early Chinese fiction.[6] It should be noted that not all Ming editions of the text use the same title: some favored *The Scandalous Tale of Empress Zhao* (Zhaohou waizhuan), though the contents are identical. *The Collectanea of Literature from the Han and Wei Dynasties*, compiled by Cheng Rong (fl. 1590s), contains yet another Ming dynasty edition of the text, dated to 1592: this recension was subsequently the basis of the edition found in another important collectanea titled *Secret Books from Longwei*, published in 1794.[7]

There are also a number of reprints of *The Scandalous Tale* of unknown textual origin found in modern collections of early Chinese fiction.[8] These different recensions of the text are all extremely similar; the only version that has some important textual variants is the Qing dynasty manuscript—titled *The Scandalous Tale of Feiyan* (Feiyan waizhuan)—formerly in the possession of the Wu family and held in their library, the Hall of Ancient Pleasures (Guhuantang).[9] The vast majority of textual variants found in other recensions are in the nature of alternative spellings for the same term, such as the title *jieyu*, which can be given as 婕妤 or 倢伃—this difference does not affect the meaning in any way. The Wu family manuscript has some variants that can be dismissed as errors; for example, where other recensions state, "The emperor was staying within one of the chambers of the Mandarin Ducks Hall" (Di ju Yuanyangdian bianfang), the Wu family manuscript says, "The emperor was staying within one of the chambers of the Weiyang Hall" (Di ju Weiyangdian bianfang).[10] This cannot be correct, since Weiyang was the name of a palace, not a hall; furthermore, the existence of the Mandarin Ducks Hall within the Weiyang Palace complex is attested to in a wide variety of Han dynasty texts.[11] However, where all other recensions say that when the future empress produced embroideries as gifts for her adoptive father, Zhao Lin, "Lin was embarrassed but accepted them" (Lin kui shou zhi), the Wu family manuscript says, "Lin was delighted and loved her very much" (Lin yue ai zhi).[12] Although this is likely to be the result of a graphic variant, here it is not clear at all which version is to be preferred; hence in the translation given in chapter 2 both possibilities are indicated. In the main, however, the Wu family manuscript is extremely similar to other recensions of *The Scandalous Tale*.

Comparison makes it quite clear that all the different versions of *The Scandalous Tale* in circulation in the late imperial era were ultimately derived from one single source. The nature of this source is at present beyond our reach, since no pre–Ming dynasty printed editions of the text survive and there are no early manuscript copies. However, the homogeneity is extremely pronounced, even in recensions that purport not to be related. As a demonstration of the strong links between every known edition of *The Scandalous Tale*, they all contain exactly the same mistake. In the list of presents given by Zhao Hede to her older sister, every recension of the text cites nineteen items consisting of twenty-five objects, rather than the twenty-six (items or objects, it is not clear which) that the text itself says it should contain, and they give the same description of one item: "one sandalwood statue [ornamented with] *tongxiang*-scented tiger-skin" (*tongxiang hupi tanxiang yi zuo*). This bizarre object is likely to be the creation of the amalgamation of two items in the list into one, so it appears there has been textual loss at this point. It is impossible that all the texts would contain this identical error if they were not derived from the same source. Although there are no early detailed discussions of the contents of the text, which means that it is not clear if this error was already present in the late Tang dynasty, thanks to the multitude of quotations from *The Scandalous Tale* preserved in the collection titled *Categorized Stories* (Leishuo) by Zeng Zao (d. 1155/1164), dated to 1136, it is evident that it had already appeared by the Northern to Southern Song transition period.[13] It is therefore entirely likely that it dates to an extremely early version of the text in its present transmitted form, and indicates that the wording of *The Scandalous Tale* has been stable for the last one thousand years or so.

As it stands today, *The Scandalous Tale* cannot have been written prior to the Tang dynasty since it contains a number of references to political entities and objects that simply did not exist before this date.[14] Full details of the vocabulary items that are significant for dating the text to after the collapse of the Han dynasty are to be found in the annotations to the translation; hence only references that provide clear evidence of a Tang dynasty date will be considered here. Of particular importance for dating is the account of the barbarians of Zhenla presenting a 10,000-year-old clamshell and a night-shining pearl. The earliest reference to the state of Zhenla, or Champa, in Chinese literature is found in *History of the Sui Dynasty* (Suishu).[15] This polity sent a succession of embassies, beginning with that of 616, to the Sui court; prior to this, the government in China was unaware of the major shift in power in the region that resulted from the rise of this important South-East Asian state in the region of what is now southern Vietnam and Cambodia.[16] Another indicator of a Tang dynasty date for the text is found in what appears to be an instance of a taboo on the personal name of Emperor Gaozong of Tang (r. 649–683). Where in *History of the Han Dynasty*, Empress Dowager Wang Zhengjun ordered the arrest of those concerned in the death of Emperor Cheng with the words "Director of the Lateral Courts Fu . . . can assist the censor, the chancellor, and the chamberlain for law enforcement in investigating [*zhiwen*] the emperor's actions and the circumstances of his sudden attack of sickness," in *The Scandalous Tale* this is given as "The dowager empress ordered that the *zhaoyi* be placed under restraint [*li*]."[17] This latter text thus avoids the use of the character *zhi*, which was Emperor Gaozong's personal name.[18] Furthermore, some of the objects mentioned in the text also provide clear evidence of a Tang dynasty date. For example, there is a reference in the list of presents given by Zhao Hede to her older sister to "a heptafoil mirror in the shape of a water caltrop." An object of this kind cannot have been made prior to the Tang dynasty since all early Chinese mirrors were either round or square. Such instances serve as a *terminus post quem* for the compilation of the text in its present form.

There is a small but important group of references to *The Scandalous Tale* preserved in late Tang dynasty poetry that clearly refer specifically to this text and not to any of the earlier writings about Empress Zhao. These serve to indicate a *terminus ante quem* for the compilation of the text.[19] To begin with what appears to be the earliest of these directly inspired works: the name of one of Empress Zhao's lovers, Yan Chifeng, appears in a poem by Li Shangyin (813–858): "When Empress Zhao is in her residence, Chifeng arrives."[20] This name was not associated with the life of the empress prior to the circulation of *The Scandalous Tale*.[21] Another Tang poet, Han Wo (842/844–ca. 923), is not merely the first poet to mention Zhao Hede by name; in his poem titled "On Bathing" (Yongyu), he also includes the lines

> Who would have imagined that the serving maids outside the curtains,
> Could have extorted so many gold "cakes" from the ruler?[22]

This is thought to be a reference to Emperor Cheng's voyeuristic sexual practices, when to avoid Zhao Hede discovering his activities and refusing to participate, he bribed her servants. Meanwhile, in the poem "Lines to Compare

[Du] Hong'er" (Bi Hong'er shi) by Luo Qiu (fl. 874), one line reads: "She lightly combs out her little chignon, of the kind called 'Dawdling Approach.'"[23] Again, this is a reference to the fancy makeup and styling worn by Zhao Hede in *The Scandalous Tale*, which is not attested to prior to this text.[24] To these can be added the numerous quotations from the text, under the title of *The Scandalous Tale of Empress Zhao*, preserved in *Miscellaneous Records of the Immortals in the Clouds* (Yunxian zaji) by Feng Zhi (fl. ninth century).[25] It is likely that the text was composed in its present form not long before it began to circulate in the late Tang dynasty, around the mid-ninth century. If such a highly admired and influential piece of writing was already in existence previously, it is not clear why nobody would have mentioned it.

Although early scholarship on *The Scandalous Tale* is conspicuous by its absence, the text had a significant impact on contemporary literature and was clearly much admired from the moment it became available to literati readers in the late Tang. The plethora of quotations from this text, and the vast body of poetry that it inspired, is proof of how influential *The Scandalous Tale* really was. By the time of the Song dynasty, many phrases from *The Scandalous Tale* had become common currency. The expression "Realm of Soft Warmth" (Wenrou Xiang), which Emperor Cheng applies to Zhao Hede's body, appears in a number of Song dynasty literary works; for example, in a collection of poems titled "Ten Verses Sent to Zhou Yuanweng in Remembrance" (Huai ji Zhou Yuanweng shishou), He Zhu (1052–1125) criticizes those who overindulge in sexual pleasures:

> Besotted by the "Realm of Soft Warmth,"
> They do not stop until they are ruined.[26]

That this phrase was already well established in contemporary usage can be seen from other texts, such as *New Records from Taozhu* (Taozhu xinlu) by Ma Chun (fl. 1160s).[27] Meanwhile, "Restraining the Immortal Skirts" (Liuxian Qun), a kind of dress that commemorated Zhao Feiyan's skirts torn when she attempted suicide, is mentioned in a number of Song dynasty literary works. In the poem "Summer" (Xia) by Yao Mian (1216–1262), the second of four poems collectively known under the title "In Praise of the Paintings of Four Beautiful Women in the Collection of the Official Zhao" (Zan Zhao Zhige suozang si meiren hua), it appears as a synonym for an entertainer of superlative beauty. In this poem about a painting, which appears to have depicted a beautiful woman leaving the bath in which she has been cooling herself on a hot summer's day, the last couplet reads:

> Her "Restraining the Immortal Skirts" dance in the breeze until
> her strength is exhausted,
> Unaware from whence the scent of the lotus blossom comes.[28]

Meanwhile, in his poem "Greens of Spring" (Lüyi), Zhang Yan (1248–1320?) talks of the passage of time:

> Looking back at the dances in the Han [palace] of yesteryear,
> I am afraid that [such delights] have gone, leaving little behind,
> Her "Restraining the Immortal Skirts" have been ripped to shreds.[29]

Such usage shows that quotations from *The Scandalous Tale* had become embedded in literary language.

Song dynasty literati also frequently made mention of the author's preface to the text. This addition to *The Scandalous Tale* is of uncertain relationship to the main text: from internal evidence the two are closely related, since supposedly the author's informant and inspiration for writing the text was his concubine, Fan Tongde, the great-niece of Zhao Feiyan's aunt and confidant, Fan Yi.[30] There are no references to this preface or any of the other accounts of the early history of the text in Tang dynasty writings; however, by the Song dynasty they had come to be considered integral to the text. Indeed, the presentation of *The Scandalous Tale* as a genuine Han dynasty text was no doubt crucial for its survival to the present day. Although doubts were expressed about the authenticity of *The Scandalous Tale* from an extremely early stage, the presence of these additional writings served to validate the portrayal given there of historical events. Thus, in early bibliographical accounts, there are instances where the miraculous survival of the text in the upheavals surrounding the collapse of the Xin dynasty and its rediscovery in a metal-bound coffer as reported in "Huan Tan's Statement" are accepted entirely uncritically.[31] On the other hand, it is also in the Song dynasty that the first skeptics raised their voices, declaring that the text could not be genuine. Chen Zhensun noted that there are no Han dynasty records that mention the putative author, Ling Xuan; were he associated with the famous historical figures that the preface claims, he really should have been recorded.[32] One of the key problems with many previous attempts to date the text is that they stand or fall on what it says in the author's preface or other statements attached to the text, rather than considering internal evidence of dating within *The Scandalous Tale* itself. This micro-approach has remained a problem into modern times, as many scholars have dated the text on the basis of a particular phrase, rather than taking account of the linguistic usage found throughout the whole novella.

The author's preface to *The Scandalous Tale* developed a life of its own in the Song dynasty, not least thanks to the many references to this short text in the writings of the great Northern Song poet Su Shi. In Ling Xuan's authorial preface, Su Shi seems to have found a useful image of a companionate relationship between a high-status official and his concubine, a woman of low rank who is nevertheless well educated and thus able to converse with her spouse on more or less equal terms. This positive representation inspired his verses addressed to his own concubine, Wang Zhaoyun (1062–1095), where he compares their relationship to that of Ling Xuan and Fan Tongde.[33] It is likely that Su Shi saw this text as a genuine Han dynasty survival, since such an interpretation would have provided additional weight for the sanction it gave him. It is also in the late Northern Song dynasty that Zhang Nie (1096–1148) produced a series of poems celebrating his reading of this text: "Miscellaneous Poems on Reading *The Scandalous Tale of Zhao Feiyan*" (Du *Zhao Feiyan waizhuan* zashi). In this group of seven *jueju* verses, Zhang Nie explores different themes in his reading—clearly he had access to a recension of the text that included both the novella and the author's preface. His reflections show his understanding of the text as an important historical document recording the true relationship between Zhao Feiyan and Emperor Cheng; however, he also considers the text to be providing valuable moral lessons concerning the dangers of sexual obsession and delusion:

> Layer upon layer, the snow has accumulated to cover the hills and
> the dales,
> Right then, Yizhu had arranged a meeting with her lover.
> Suddenly she sees that the plum blossom has opened in the moonlight,
> But her only concern is that she still has long to wait for her huntsman.

> Nine times [she bathed] in gharuwood perfume and dressed her hair anew,
> Her embroidered skirt and vest attested to the [lovely] body beneath.

This "Water" disaster arrived in a flash to wash away the burning "Fire,"
The only person aware of this was [the erudite] Lady Zhuo.

In the Wei Palace they sadly watched the willow-floss float away,
In the Han harem they sang together of the arrival of the Red Phoenix.
When debauchery and lust reach their acme, these things happen:
[Their graves surrounded by] abandoned fields and rank grass are indeed tragic sights.

Emperor Wu of the Han dynasty inspired great awe and the utmost trust,[34]
A [Xiongnu] Khan came to have audience at the Weiyang Palace.[35]
How could [Empress Zhao and her family] bring luck to the Master of Hongjia,[36]
Let Fan Yi's actions in the palace serve as a warning to other women!

Thanks to [His Majesty's] kindness the Swallow was lodged in Extending Shoots [House],
For the first time in her life she was able to spend winter nights as she pleased.
Why did she not practice her strange arts,
Instead of happily allowing the use of *shenxu* paste?[37]

Chifeng's false words caused deep wounds,
But His Majesty never spoke of his suspicions.
All were terrified at [Taiyi] Pool that she would leave to become an immortal,
However, I fear that she decided to stay because of her attendant gentleman.

When Hede came as a consort, the emperor was pleased indeed,
His "Realm of Soft Warmth" was far better than seeking the land of immortals.
Although Emperor Wu was deluded by the "[Realm of] White Clouds,"
He still remained in power to the end of his long life.[38]

The reading of *The Scandalous Tale* given in this group of poems is interesting for the constant harping on the idea that Emperor Cheng was inferior to Emperor Wu. This is a somewhat odd interpretation of the biographies of these two men. First, unlike Emperor Wu, who seemed to be determined to bankrupt the empire in endless campaigns of conquest, Emperor Cheng lived in an era of unbroken peace. Though military glory was in short supply, the country was also not burdened by the economic and social impact of prolonged warfare involving large numbers of casualties. It was an era of few natural disasters and no foreign threats; furthermore, although the Western Han dynasty would collapse within sixteen years of his death, the early signs of trouble were probably not seen as indications of imminent disaster by more than a handful of exceptionally pessimistic people with unusually good information concerning the inner workings of the court. Second, the difficulties caused by the fact that Emperor Cheng had no son who lived long enough to succeed him could not have been foreseen—it was only right at the end of his reign that arrangements over the succession had to be made because all of the emperor's children had died young. The decade or more of Empress Zhao's ascendancy seems to have brought stability to Emperor Cheng's personal life, in addition to which—at least according to *History of the Han Dynasty*—he also enjoyed perfect health right up until the day that he died. (*The Scandalous Tale*, by contrast, suggests that his health was impaired toward the end, but that with the assistance of aphrodisiacs he was able to continue a vigorous sex life.) Emperor Wu, in comparison, had a significantly more tortured private side—the early years of his reign were troubled by concerns about his sexuality since the emperor seemed to have difficulties in consummating his relationships, while in his later years he was driven to extreme measures by paranoid concerns that he might be the focus of witchcraft by members of his own immediate family.[39] This led to the deaths of thousands of people, including many of his own children and grandchildren. That so tormented and difficult a reign as that of Emperor Wu could be considered in any way superior to that of Emperor Cheng is only possible when the subjugation of foreign peoples is regarded as the sole measure of success—a perspective that might pertain in the Song dynasty, when Zhang Nie wrote his cycle of poems, but not necessarily at other periods of Chinese history.

Adaptations and Translations of *The Scandalous Tale of Zhao Feiyan*

There are a number of later Silk Pillow and pseudo-historical writings that serve to develop themes and characters found in *The Scandalous Tale of Zhao*

Feiyan—these works are indicative of enduring interest in fictional representations of Empress Zhao and her court. The first such text is the anonymous *Surviving Records of Empress Zhao* (Zhaohou yishi), which consists of a précis of *Miscellaneous Records of the Western Capital* and *Records Gleaned from Lost Works*, focusing upon seven stories specifically concerning Zhao Feiyan.[40] The five stories taken from the former text include the description of Zhao Feiyan's younger sister's residence, the account of the appearance of the two women, the gifts given to Empress Zhao by the *zhaoyi*, her relationship with Qing Anshi, and her ownership of a fine musical instrument. The two anecdotes taken from the latter both concern Emperor Cheng's pleasure-seeking at the Taiyi Pool. It is not clear at what date this compilation was produced, and it is often confused with other writings concerning Empress Zhao.[41]

Of more interest as works of literature are the two reworkings of the text produced during the Song dynasty. The first is *The Alternative Tale of Zhao Feiyan* (Zhao Feiyan biezhuan) by Qin Chun (Northern Song dynasty; dates unknown).[42] This takes as its starting point the period of growing estrangement between Empress Zhao and Emperor Cheng, which the novella blames on his discovery of her promiscuous sexual behavior. What follows is a lurid tale of Empress Zhao's desperation to rekindle their relationship at all costs; eventually her seduction of the emperor while drunk leads to her claiming a false pregnancy. Simultaneously, Zhao Hede occupies herself by murdering her rivals, and there is much melodramatic behavior on the part of all protagonists. The novella concludes with a strange supernatural episode: after the death of Emperor Cheng and Zhao Hede's suicide, Empress Zhao is said to have dreamed that he returned to warn her of her sister's punishment for her role in the death of his children. She is to be transformed into a turtle and suffer the cold of the sea: "Later on, the king of the Dayueshi [Yuezhi] went hunting along the coast at the northern border, and saw a giant turtle emerge from a cave, with a jade hairpin still stuck in its head. It looked back longingly from the top of the wave, as if it cared about the people [on the shore]. The king of Dayueshi sent an ambassador to ask Emperor Wu of the Liang dynasty [r. 502–549] about this, and Emperor Wu told him about what had happened to the *zhaoyi*."[43]

Although extremely well written, *The Alternative Tale of Zhao Feiyan* is a significantly less interesting work of literature than *The Scandalous Tale*. By beginning with Emperor Cheng's discovery of his wife's affairs, it completely changes the dynamic of their relationship, and with the introduction of melodrama the characterization found in this novella is much simplified. The black-and-white portrayal of a drunken and sottish emperor perverted by the two villainous Zhao sisters eliminates much of the psychological complexity that makes *The Scandalous Tale* so significant in the history of Chinese literature.[44] *The Alternative Tale of Zhao Feiyan* is also considerably more conventional in its obedience to the imperative that evil be punished: while *The Scandalous Tale* does end extremely abruptly with the sudden death of Zhao Hede of unexplained causes, she does not suffer any posthumous punishment, nor are Zhao Feiyan and her relatives subject to any obvious censure—an element in the narrative that has led some scholars to suggest that the text is incomplete. In *The Alternative Tale of Zhao Feiyan* (which admittedly does particularly stress the horror of the murders committed by the evil Zhao Zhaoyi), her many years of suffering in the form of a giant turtle are the rightful penalty for her immorality and wickedness in life. While Qin Chun's moral position vis-à-vis his characters is much clearer than that of the author or authors of *The Scandalous Tale*, this theme of retributory justice does not serve to augment the literary value of the text as a whole.

Also of interest in this context is a reference to another text, titled *The Private History of Emperor Cheng of the Han Dynasty* (Han Chengdi neizhuan), which is quoted in another Song dynasty Silk Pillow work: *The Scandalous Tale of Yang Taizhen*.[45] This text describes an incident in which Emperor Xuanzong of the Tang dynasty was reading this tale about his Han dynasty predecessor (which is sometimes later confused with *The Scandalous Tale of Zhao Feiyan*) and used it to tease his consort, Yang Guifei, about her plumpness. Although the relationship between *The Private History of Emperor Cheng of the Han Dynasty* and *The Scandalous Tale* is unclear since the story given here does not appear in any transmitted version of the latter text, this quotation does make reference to the traditions that informed the creation of *The Scandalous Tale*. A further connection is implied with both *Yellow Plans of the Three Capital Regions* and *Records Gleaned from Lost Works*, which also mention the Escaping the Winds Tower:

> His Majesty was reading *The Private History of Emperor Cheng of the Han Dynasty* . . . when the consort happened to arrive. She rearranged the collar of the emperor's robe and asked: "What are you reading?" The emperor smiled and said: "Don't ask. If you knew, you would find it really annoying." She looked and read this: "When Emperor Cheng of the Han dynasty obtained

> [Zhao] Feiyan, her body was so light that she could not withstand the slightest breeze. Since he was afraid that she would be blown away, the emperor had a rock crystal platter made, and he ordered palace servants to hold it as she danced and sang. He also constructed the Saptaratna Escaping the Winds Tower. When they were there, he would have perfumed [weights] placed on top of her, for fear that otherwise her four limbs would not be able to withstand [the breeze]." His Majesty asked: "How strong a puff would it take to blow you away?"[46]

A further reworking of *The Scandalous Tale* was produced during the Southern Song dynasty by the pseudonymous Huangdu Fengyue Zhuren, or "Master of the World of Sensual Pleasures at the Imperial Capital," titled *A New Tale from the Women's Quarters* (Lüchuang xinhua). This novella is based upon two specific incidents from *The Scandalous Tale*, which in turn informs the two-chapter format of the text. Thus, the first chapter is titled "Zhao Feiyan Conducts an Affair with Chifeng" (Zhao Feiyan sitong Chifeng), and the second, "Emperor Cheng of the Han Dynasty Ingests *Shenxu* Paste" (Han Chengdi fu shenxujiao).[47] Although the content is largely derived from *The Scandalous Tale*, the format in which this novella is presented represents a major step forward to later Ming and Qing dynasty fictional formats. With the introduction of seven-character chapter titles, and couplets to summarize the contents, *A New Tale from the Women's Quarters* recasts older material in a newly developed, more structured narrative style, placing this Silk Pillow novella right in the avant-garde of late Southern Song literature.[48]

A further series of novellas based upon the story of the relationship between Emperor Cheng and Zhao Feiyan were produced in the Ming dynasty. In *juan* 7 of his *Compilation of [Tales] of Beautiful Women with Unusual Characteristics* (Yanyi bian), the major late Ming man of letters and literary theorist Wang Shizhen (1526–1590) includes a number of texts that incorporate different reflections upon the relationship between the emperor and the Zhao sisters. In particular, this collection includes *Biography of Empress Zhao, Consort of Emperor Xiaocheng* (Xiaocheng Zhao huanghou zhuan), which was created by excerpting relevant material from *History of the Han Dynasty*, together with *The Scandalous Tale*, *The Alternative Biography of Zhao Feiyan and [Zhao] Hede* (Zhao Feiyan Hede biezhuan), which is *The Alternative Tale of Zhao Feiyan* under another title, and two very short texts, *Six Stories about Feiyan* (Feiyan shi liutiao) and *The Roaming Free Palace* (Xiaoyao gong).[49] The first of these texts consists of excerpts from *Miscellaneous Records of the Western Capital* concerning Zhao Feiyan, and is thus virtually identical with *Surviving Records of Empress Zhao. The Roaming Free Palace* consists of a single anecdote: a direct quotation of *Records Gleaned from Lost Works*. This collection thus comprises some of the most important literary works concerning Empress Zhao to be written during the imperial era.

In a separate development, there is a major late Ming dynasty rewriting of *The Scandalous Tale*—with some material derived from *The Alternative Tale of Zhao Feiyan*—titled *The Remarkable History of the Zhaoyang Palace*, which is attributed to the pseudonymous Yanyansheng. The earliest edition of this text in two *juan* dates to 1621, and one known copy survives in the Van Gulik collection at Leiden University in the Netherlands.[50] The significant distinction between this text and previous reworkings of *The Scandalous Tale* lies in its portrayal of the two main female protagonists as nature spirits that have taken human form: Zhao Feiyan is a swallow-spirit (*yanjing*) and Zhao Hede a fox-spirit (*hujing*). *The Remarkable History of the Zhaoyang Palace* is also notable for the significant pornographic sequences found in this text. For example, when Zhao Feiyan first enters Emperor Cheng's harem, she expresses concerns about her unworthiness and hopes that he will love her forever, only to have the emperor cut this short because he wants her to take her clothes off. Just as in *The Scandalous Tale*, the consummation of their marriage is attended by considerable physical difficulties, but *The Remarkable History of the Zhaoyang Palace* describes this in a great deal more detail:

> [His Majesty] aimed his rod at her vagina and pushed, but he was not able to force his way in. Feiyan closed her eyes, unclenched her fists, and the tears trickled down her cheeks. Pretending to shiver uncontrollably, she clutched Emperor Cheng and said: "That is so painful! How am I supposed to endure it?" Emperor Cheng moistened himself with spittle but he still could not enter her. . . . Emperor Cheng humped away at her for half an hour, showing her ever more love and affection. He bit Zhao Feiyan on the neck and said: "Darling, not being able to enter you is so exciting. What am I to do?" Feiyan replied: "Just be patient for a little longer." Emperor Cheng continued trying to penetrate but was in the end unable to enter her, so he summoned a palace woman named Cao Gong, thrashed around lustily, and thus reached orgasm.[51]

As this particular incident demonstrates, the author of *The Remarkable History of the Zhaoyang Palace* generally follows the outlines of the plot of *The Scandalous Tale*, but incorporates significantly more sexually explicit material. Furthermore, *The Remarkable History of the Zhaoyang Palace* makes some attempt to reconcile this story with the biography of Empress Zhao found in *History of the Han Dynasty*, which recounts that Cao Gong was the name of a woman official serving in the Rear Palace who gave birth to Emperor Cheng's son, only for her and her child to be murdered by the Zhao sisters. In the same tradition, the collection *One Hundred Banned Chinese Novels* (Zhongguo jinhui xiaoshuo baibu) includes a text titled *A History of the Lovely Ladies of the Zhaoyang Palace* (Zhaoyang yanshi), again attributed to Yanyansheng, in four *juan*. This is clearly a different work from *The Remarkable History of the Zhaoyang Palace*, since this short erotic novella does not describe its main protagonists as a swallow-spirit and a fox-spirit. In content, it seems to be an amalgam of *The Scandalous Tale* and *The Alternative Tale of Zhao Feiyan*, updated for Ming dynasty tastes.[52] However, the title and supposed authorship associates it with *The Remarkable History of the Zhaoyang Palace*, which seems to have been very popular at this period.

A number of translations of *The Scandalous Tale* have already been produced in various European languages. The first, by Lin Yutang, was published in 1942, under the title "The Private History of Queen Feiyen," in his compilation of translations from Chinese literature titled *The Wisdom of China and India*.[53] There are a number of problems with this translation, not least that Lin Yutang seems to have accepted a Han dynasty date of compilation for the text without question, and the text as a whole is severely expurgated. As explained in the introduction: "It gives us a very intimate glance into the licentious court life of China, which probably has not varied in the last two thousand years. The unconscious realists beat the conscious realists in realism, and I have had to delete passages that would be considered downright obscene by Western literary standards. It is a pity, because if sex were not so much hedged about, there might be less psychosis. On the other hand, I do not want the book to be banned in Boston."[54]

A second translation into German was published in 1959 by Wolfgang Bauer and Herbert Franke, in their collection *Die goldene Truhe*, under the title "Der Kaiser und die beiden Schwestern."[55] This entire collection of early Chinese literature was subsequently translated into English by Christopher Levenson, and published as *The Golden Casket*.[56] Again, the text is presented in an expurgated form and attributed to the Han dynasty. Given that considerable advances have now been made in clarifying the publication history of this text, and that attitudes as to what is and is not acceptable mainstream reading have changed, it would seem time to have a new and full translation of the text. *The Scandalous Tale* covers a wide variety of sexual tastes and difficulties: it shows Emperor Cheng engaged in fetishistic and voyeuristic practices with Zhao Hede, not to mention providing the very earliest discussion in Chinese fiction of the use of aphrodisiacs. It also mentions emotional problems, particularly in the relationship between the emperor and Empress Zhao. At the beginning of their marriage, she finds sex with His Majesty painful; later on he becomes bored and seems to consider her constant acquiescence with his sexual demands unexciting. At the same time, the empress is under a great deal of stress in her marriage caused entirely by her inability to conceive a child. It is this fact that forces her to introduce her younger sister into the imperial harem, and it also leads her to engage in a large number of sexual relationships with other partners. Her apparent promiscuity is thus explicitly linked with her gynecological problems. This emphasis allows *The Scandalous Tale* to move away from being mere titillation, and instead focus on sexuality as an extension of personality, and to use detailed descriptions of sexual behavior to develop character and strengthen narrative development.

The Characterization of the Zhao Sisters in *The Scandalous Tale of Zhao Feiyan*

It is often stated that imperial-era fictional writings prioritize the "male gaze"—these works of literature were written by men, for an audience of other men.[57] While it is likely that whoever wrote *The Scandalous Tale* was indeed a man, the introduction of female agency in the author's preface is interesting, because it points to the fact that this is not a text in which all events are reflected through the prism of the male gaze. In the author's preface, it is claimed that Ling Xuan wrote the text at the dictation of his concubine Fan Tongde: it was she who was informed of these events by an eyewitness, and that person was another woman, Fan Yi. In the conceit of the author's preface, *The Scandalous Tale* gives readers a privileged view of life in the women's quarters of the Han imperial palace: a space that no man could ever hope to enter, not only because it was forbidden ground, but also because the dynasty concerned had fallen many centuries earlier. Furthermore, this is a view mediated through the eyes of its inhabitants, the women who lived and worked in Emperor Cheng's harem.[58]

This novella is thus an example of palace literature; it describes the private life of members of the imperial family and it is written from an "inner" perspective, by those who experienced this kind of life firsthand, who by definition had to be women.[59] As studies of other forms of palace literature such as the palace plaint (*gong yuan*) have made clear, readers were very strongly interested in the "authentic" experience of women in the Rear Palace, and although many men did write such works, they did so in the context of a strong focus on the female voice, and an emphasis on representing the life experiences and emotional states of palace women. The ventriloquizing of palace women by literati men was regarded by many as inferior to writings actually produced by the denizens of the Rear Palace, which may indeed explain the emphasis on Fan Tongde's participation in the production of *The Scandalous Tale*.[60] Even when emperors wrote of life in the Rear Palace, these texts were considered superficial, since they failed to address one basic fact: the inhabitants of the Rear Palace were female, and it is in their lives and emotions that readers of palace literature are interested.

The female perspective in the narrative structure in *The Scandalous Tale* results in one of the most interesting aspects of the characterization.[61] Emperor Cheng is undoubtedly a significant character in the narrative, but from start to finish he is entirely in the dark as to the real personalities of Zhao Feiyan and Zhao Hede. He is throughout successfully deceived by their lies, and dies without ever realizing what has been going on around him. The reader, on the other hand, is repeatedly reminded that they are manipulating him—for example, when the emperor's health begins to fail, it is only by grasping Zhao Hede's foot that he can achieve an erection. However, once he has become aroused, Zhao Hede does not allow him to penetrate her. When Fan Yi questions her about this, Zhao Hede explains her reasoning in trenchant terms: "It is fortunate that by turning away and lying on my side he cannot penetrate me. This is why I have been able to keep His Majesty interested in me. If I had treated the emperor as my older sister did, he would have become bored and left me. In that case how could I hope to excite him again?"[62] Zhao Hede here shows a keen understanding of the importance of appearing to resist the emperor's wishes so as to create the maximum levels of excitement for him. Without a good appreciation of psychology, she would have made the same mistake as Zhao Feiyan, which would have done irreparable damage to her position within the Rear Palace. Furthermore, the way in which the women in Emperor Cheng's harem have their own agenda is reinforced here and elsewhere by the author's careful use of language: when speaking to each other, the women often use extremely vulgar terms, but this is not true when they speak to the emperor. Although the narrative is not explicitly constructed as the expression of a female voice, it is the unusual feminized perspective that gives the novella a great deal of its power.

In the case of Zhao Hede, the levels of duplicity involved are sometimes extremely difficult to gauge. Although often she is shown protecting her elder sister, they are at the same time rivals for the emperor's affections, and there are occasions when internecine rivalry is undoubtedly a factor in their relationship.[63] Zhao Hede never loses an opportunity to turn events to her own advantage. For example, when she presents a long list of extremely valuable items to her older sister as gifts, Empress Zhao responds with a mere two items: "some hangings of five-colored cloud-patterned silk brocade and a gharuwood jug." It is not at all clear whether the empress is being mean with such a small return, or whether her gifts are entirely appropriate, since we lack the information to be able to fully appreciate the nature of this exchange. However, once Zhao Hede receives these items, she bursts into tears and tells the emperor: "If I had not been given these things by my sister, I would have died without knowing of their existence."[64] The reader is clearly meant to understand that this is untrue—after all, the previous section concerned the enormously expensive gifts that she has just been giving to her older sister. Presumably, had she wanted to keep such objects for herself, she could have done so. However, her tears have the desired effect, and the emperor orders that a vast sum of imperial tax revenue be diverted to supply Zhao Hede with new bedroom furniture, thus allowing her to take advantage of his generosity.

During her time within the Rear Palace, Empress Zhao Feiyan experiences two particularly traumatic events: the first is when she realizes that she has lost imperial favor, and the second, when she discovers that one of her lovers is unfaithful to her since he is simultaneously engaged in a sexual relationship with her younger sister. In one scene of the narrative, Zhao Feiyan appears to attempt suicide in front of the emperor by trying to throw herself off a high building. The terms in which this is described make it unclear whether it is a serious attempt prompted by despair at being displaced by her own sister in imperial affections or a gesture intended to play on the emperor's feelings. However, if it is to be understood as a genuine attempt at suicide, the finale is tragic. In trying to kill herself, her skirts are torn, but afterward this becomes a fashion among other women in the Rear Palace. Thus, what may be an act of real agony of feeling is trivialized by the reaction of others who see Empress Zhao's unhappiness as an excuse to buy new clothes.

At another juncture in the narrative, the discovery that her lover, Yan Chifeng, is also having an affair with Zhao Hede provokes a confrontation between the two sisters, in which Zhao Feiyan expresses her displeasure by throwing a cup full of wine over Zhao Hede's dress. This comparatively mild response of the empress to an extremely humiliating and painful discovery is interesting because it highlights another area of potential duplicity. Throughout the text, Zhao Hede consistently stresses to the emperor how violent her sister's temper is, how uncontrolled she is when angry, how important it is for those who love her to remain on good terms with her and conciliate her whenever necessary. This is the one episode in *The Scandalous Tale* in which Zhao Feiyan has an opportunity to show her rage, and instead she makes a gesture of displeasure that it is easy for Zhao Hede to explain away to a curious emperor. This raises the question: When Zhao Hede emphasizes her sister's ungovernable anger if crossed, is this really true? Or does Zhao Hede exaggerate the empress's temper with a view to frightening Emperor Cheng and making her own character seem charmingly lighthearted and cheerful in comparison?

The Scandalous Tale also presents Zhao Hede in situations where her true motives and emotions can only be guessed at. Toward the end of the narrative, there is one sequence that concerns her response to His Majesty's voyeurism. If her thwarting of the emperor's sexual advances when he caresses her feet is a deliberate attempt to keep him interested in her, the same is not necessarily true when he is engaged in spying on her in her bath. Every time she discovers that the emperor is watching her, the *zhaoyi* immediately wraps herself up; however, in this instance her motives are not clarified. This raises the possibility that she finds his behavior objectionable but cannot explain her discomfort and distaste. The emperor is supremely powerful, and it is only through their success in fulfilling his fantasies that the Zhao sisters are able to survive. As shown by the denouement of the novella, once the emperor is dead, the pair are at the mercy of their enemies. Hence it is crucial that they should obey Emperor Cheng in every way possible, since their lives are at risk the moment that he loses interest in them.[65] The two sisters are thus forced to acquiesce in the emperor's demands that they act out his desires, and their own feelings in the matter have to be set aside.

The Scandalous Tale of Zhao Feiyan and the Tang Imperial House

One theory that has been suggested to explain the composition of *The Scandalous Tale* and the terms in which this describes the Han imperial house is that this text is a veiled critique of the behavior of the Tang emperors. In particular, it has been proposed that this text was inspired by the relationship between Emperor Xuanzong of Tang and Yang Guifei.[66] There is no direct evidence that the author of *The Scandalous Tale* intended such a connection: the text explicitly claims over and over again that it is a genuine Han dynasty document, which would automatically preclude a roman à clef reading, and the history of the text, with its various Age of Disunion precursors, means that it is unlikely to have developed as a satire or criticism of any of the Tang emperors and their private lives. However, this does raise an interesting point concerning Silk Pillow writings in general: What constraints affected authors producing such texts about the imperial house then in power? How did these writings negotiate the conflicting demands of maintaining the dignity of the emperor with the genre's characteristic frankness about sexual matters? An understanding of how this difficult balance was struck in the Tang dynasty allows us to appreciate *The Scandalous Tale* as a work of historical fiction: by focusing on a famous triangular sexual relationship involving the emperor of a former dynasty, the author could approach his subject in a significantly more open way.

During the course of the Tang dynasty, a variety of writings would be produced that took as their subject the relationship between Emperor Xuanzong and Yang Guifei, perhaps the most famous being "The Song of Everlasting Regret" (Changhen ge) by Bai Juyi (772–846), and the prose reworking of this lengthy poem titled *The Tale of Everlasting Regret* (Changhen zhuan) by Chen Hong (fl. 805).[67] The highly romantic portrayal of events found in these two pieces concentrates on the theme of true love, and the emperor and his consort are said to be predestined to be together (thus eliminating any need to even mention Yang Guifei's first marriage to Li Mao, king of Shou [d. 775]).[68] Reference to contemporary political events is kept to a minimum so as not to disturb the impression of a romance that transcends death; after her demise, when an adept is finally able to track down Yang Guifei's soul, he discovers that she still treasures the golden hairpin and silver box that the emperor gave her as tokens of his affection. Such an emotional, tugging-at-the-heartstrings account of the life and death of Yang Guifei would have been perfectly acceptable to the Tang imperial house given that any criticism is drowned in an all-pervasive romanticism. It would not be until the Song dynasty that writings like *Tale of the Plum-Blossom Consort* could be produced, in which Emperor Xuanzong is portrayed as a henpecked weakling and Yang Guifei as a fat and vulgar harridan, or *The Scandalous Tale of Yang Taizhen*, in which the author attempts to balance historical accuracy with the plethora of fascinating tales that had sprung up about his heroine, to produce a dual account in which a sober record is intercut with more or less overtly fictional material.[69] The main narrative found in *The Scandalous Tale of Yang Taizhen* tells the story of a very troubled marriage and a highly disturbed and self-destructive main protagonist, who periodically engages in compulsive behavior such as kleptomania. In one particularly odd incident, the consort steals a jade flute belonging to Emperor Xuanzong's older brother. When her theft is discovered she is expelled from the palace and ordered home to her own family, though she is eventually forgiven after making exaggerated gestures of penitence.[70] Such worrying patterns of behavior may have been historically accurate, but would have no place in a Tang dynasty panegyric on the romance between Emperor Xuanzong and his beloved consort.

Another interesting Tang dynasty example of the difficulties of negotiating a balance between telling the "true story" of life in the imperial harem and respecting the dignity of the ruling house can be seen in "The Scandalous Tale of the Tongchang Princess" (Tongchang gongzhu waizhuan), concerning the life and death of Princess Wenyi of the State of Wei (849–870), the daughter of Emperor Yizong of Tang (r. 859–873) and his favorite concubine, Guo Shufei, or "Pure Consort" Guo (d. after 878).[71] This story is found within a larger collection of fifty-one Tang dynasty tales, titled *The Duyang Miscellany* (Duyang zabian), produced by Su E (*jinshi* 886).[72] "The Scandalous Tale of the Tongchang Princess" represents an extraordinary tale of an emperor's obsessive love for his favorite daughter that found expression in an endless stream of incredibly expensive gifts during her life, and in equally excessive doting on any relics of her memory after her death. This tale serves as a useful reminder of the difficulties faced by authors writing about the reigning imperial house. It is clearly unproblematic to depict the emperor and Guo Shufei as affectionate parents who were profoundly saddened by their daughter's untimely demise. It is also acceptable to mention critically the gross amounts of money the emperor spent on his daughter. A Tang dynasty author could even suggest that the emperor's mourning was excessive—he treated those connected even tangentially with his dead daughter with a favor that they had done nothing to deserve. All of these subjects are explicitly discussed in "The Scandalous Tale of the Tongchang Princess" and represent unproblematic themes.

However, there are other aspects of the relationship between the princess and her parents that could not be mentioned. Numerous accounts record that after the death of the Tongchang Princess, Emperor Yizong ordered the execution of her entire medical team, whom he blamed for not preventing her demise. Hundreds of their relatives were thrown into prison, and senior government officials who protested at this, including Chancellor Liu Zhan (d. 874), were demoted or dismissed from office.[73] The execution of these unfortunate people is not the only controversial issue avoided by the "The Scandalous Tale of the Tongchang Princess." As long as the Tang dynasty survived, it was equally difficult to write openly about the corruption and incompetence in office displayed by the princess's husband, Wei Baoheng (d. 873), which was excused because he was married to the emperor's beloved daughter. Above all, it was impossible to mention the inappropriately close relationship between Guo Shufei and her son-in-law that caused intense gossip about a possible affair between the two. Although *New History of the Tang Dynasty* (Xin Tangshu) expresses skepticism about these rumors, this text nevertheless reports that the pair behaved reprehensibly in their illicit meetings.[74] However, as long as the Tang dynasty endured, any suggestion of a sexual relationship between them risked a charge of lèse-majesté.

It is entirely possible that Tang dynasty readers did indeed treat *The Scandalous Tale* as a critique of the imperial house, but evidence for this kind of reading is lacking. It is, however, quite clear that any author who wished to write openly about the manipulation of an emperor by his scheming and venal favorites, not to mention tackling the subject of sexual infidelity within the confines of the imperial harem, would be well advised to do so with a historical setting. By taking a series of historical characters and developing them as fictional characters, adapting the story where necessary, it was possible for the author of *The Scandalous Tale* (and indeed many other later Silk Pillow writers) to explore the themes in which they were really interested: sexual problems and relationship difficulties among persons confined within the walls of the imperial harem, where the emotional impoverishment they experience stands in powerful contrast to the immense luxury of their surroundings.

Conclusion

Although many different recensions of *The Scandalous Tale* survive, this represents one single unitary literary tradition, with very minor textual variants. That does not mean that the transmitted text is unproblematic—there appears to have been some textual loss, probably at a very early stage in the manuscript transmission of this text, and it is also quite possible that the abrupt ending means that the conclusion of the story is missing. Textual analysis of *The Scandalous Tale* indicates that it reached its present form during the Tang dynasty and it should therefore be understood in this cultural context. After it first entered circulation in the late ninth century, it was subject to many revisions and reworkings over the course of the next millennium, which is indicative of the ongoing popularity of this scandalous tale. Many of these adaptations of the original introduce a moral evaluation into the text that is completely lacking in the original, with framing narratives stressing the cosmic retribution Zhao Feiyan and her sister endured for the evil acts they committed within the Rear Palace. Very few later authors were prepared to leave their work as ambiguous as *The Scandalous Tale*, with its panoply of amoral female characters who flourish right to the very end.

One aspect of Silk Pillow writing, established very early on in the history of the genre and clearly present in Tang dynasty examples such as *The Scandalous Tale of Zhao Feiyan* and "The Scandalous Tale of the Tongchang Princess," is the degree to which the authors are happy to stress the negative aspects of the lives of their main characters. In *The Scandalous Tale*, the material comforts that the two sisters enjoy are balanced by their unhealthy dependence upon Emperor Cheng's favor and their competitiveness toward each other—though both women are shown able to relax and to some extent "be themselves" in the company of their female relatives and friends. Meanwhile, in "The Scandalous Tale of the Tongchang Princess" the wretchedly ill princess is made to live in ludicrously expensive discomfort when she is dying because her father wishes to use money as a measure of his affection for her. Later Silk Pillows would draw further upon this trend, showing their female protagonists experiencing a wide variety of emotional, sexual, and psychological difficulties, not to mention relationship problems with spouses, parents, or children. Since these women experience no material worries, and writings in this genre tend to ignore the existence of real political issues, ethnic tensions, government crises, and so on, the characters are left with personal and interpersonal issues to explore. The role played by Silk Pillow texts in creating strongly character-driven narratives and thus significantly enhancing the richness of Chinese prose fiction traditions should not be ignored.

CHAPTER FIVE

Gendering Empress Zhao

WHEN MEN AND WOMEN READ THE ACCOUNT OF THE LIFE OF Empress Zhao recorded in *History of the Han Dynasty*, they reacted with horror. Such was probably the authors' intention, since this biographical description harps upon her failures as an empress: residing in the Pepper Chamber, it was her duty to provide a maternal role model to the entire empire, and if she did not bear children herself, it was nevertheless incumbent upon her to facilitate other women producing offspring for the imperial house. Empress Zhao is here described as utterly devoid of any nurturing impulse; instead, she and her sister are said to have played an active role in bringing about the collapse of the dynasty, first by murdering the emperor's children and then by participating in the transfer of power to another childless branch of the family. Reading later accounts of her life, culminating in *The Scandalous Tale*, was also appalling to many imperial-era men and women. The empress and her sister are accused of being engaged in constant promiscuous sexual relationships with other men, while at the same time wasting taxpayers' money on their frivolous whims. However, the way that Empress Zhao was presented in historical and literary accounts was highly reflective of contemporary ideas about women and gender.

Gender would also affect readers' responses to the characterization of Empress Zhao in *History of the Han Dynasty* and *The Scandalous Tale* in a variety of ways; indeed, there are instances when women talked about Empress Zhao in terms that make it clear that her fate had meanings for them that it did not have for men. For example, the last words of Wang Yunxiu (d. 777) are indicative of the way in which one aristocratic woman drew a powerful lesson from the fate of Emperor Cheng's wives and consorts. On the execution of her husband, the senior Tang dynasty statesman Yuan Zai (713–777), for gross corruption in office, Wang Yunxiu demanded to be killed too.[1] She began by providing an account of the exceptional power and privilege she had always enjoyed: "As the thirteenth daughter of the Wang family, I was the daughter of the military commissioner of Taiyuan for twenty years, and the wife of Grand Councillor [Yuan Zai] for sixteen years." Then she continued to the crux of the matter: "Who can even begin to record what actually happened in the Changxin and Zhaoyang [Palaces]? Death can also be a kind of good luck!"[2] For this Tang dynasty elite woman, the moral of the story of Zhao Feiyan was clear: no fate could be worse than placing yourself at the mercy of your enemies.

In traditional Chinese thought, sexual jealousy (*du*) was a gendered emotion, regarded as a failing unique to women.[3] Although an alternative term was developed to designate sexual jealousy experienced by men (*mao*), many references to this emotion in early imperial-era Chinese texts express a strong belief that only women were capable of feeling jealous. Nevertheless, in spite of the fact that sexual jealousy was so strongly associated with women and regarded as a particular menace among a polygamous ruling elite, some wives were nevertheless praised for their generous and unjealous treatment of other consorts. Indeed, during the Han dynasty, it seems to have been widely accepted that an individual woman might be incapable of jealousy. However, during the Age of Disunion, attitudes changed. At this time, all women were thought to be jealous; it was merely a matter of degree. Given the shift in understanding that had taken place within this time period, it is important to consider the portrayal of Zhao Feiyan as a jealous woman in texts of different dates.

Women have often responded both to the historical figure of Empress Zhao and to reading *The Scandalous Tale* in a way that was different to men. There are actually relatively few literary works by women that take Zhao Feiyan as their subject; in fact for both men and women it seems that the character of her rival, Ban Jieyu, was significantly more appealing. This was not least because the latter was in a position to control her own image through the writings that she herself produced. The survival of a number of major works by the Ban family in general, and Ban Jieyu in particular, would ensure that she was regarded in a very positive light by later generations of literati, and she continues to be highly thought of as a virtuous woman right up to the present day. By contrast, it appears that Empress Zhao was too controversial a character and her behavior considered too unfeminine to appeal much to women as a topic for their own literary endeavors. It is therefore only in the Qing dynasty that women would begin to write about their understanding of Zhao Feiyan—though generally in a strongly negative light—and describe their readings of *The Scandalous Tale*. Study of these texts allows us to explore the interpretations made by women at the end of the imperial era of the life of a Han dynasty empress who was accused not just of heinous crimes, but of offenses that contravened every gender and social norm within a highly patriarchal society.

Zhao Feiyan: A Jealous Woman?

Throughout the imperial era, sexual jealousy was presented as a gendered emotion particularly associated with women.[4] *Du* was defined as the emotion of sexual jealousy directed against the other women with whom one shared a husband. When the term *du* was applied to men, it was also a pejorative term, denoting the jealousy and envy that male officials experienced with respect to their more successful colleagues.[5] The association between women and sexual jealousy was already being made long before the unification of China; since from the Warring States era onward, numerous ancient texts stressed that women were jealous by nature, that they were prone to react irrationally and violently because of this, and that men did not experience this kind of emotion in the same way. Indeed, the belief that men were incapable of feeling sexual jealousy—that is, a feeling of anger and resentment directed against women—eventually resulted in the development of a specific gendered term for male sexual jealousy, which denotes the intense negative emotions husbands directed against the male lovers with whom they shared their wives.[6] Furthermore, from at least the time of the Han dynasty, women could be divorced for showing sexual jealousy—this was one of the "seven departures" (*qichu* or *qiqu*), or seven legally sanctioned reasons for divorce.[7] This would significantly reinforce the widespread belief that only women experienced jealousy.

In spite of the strongly negative connotations of jealousy, like many other emotional states, it was routinely exposed in public; in other words, it was important that this display had an audience.[8] By making a show of sexual jealousy, women were attempting to legitimize their complaints, or at least achieve recognition that a problem existed, which might subsequently turn events in their favor. However, from the very earliest references to jealousy found in Chinese literature, there is also a clear ambiguity in the way that this emotion is portrayed, given that a woman's sensible advice about the problems caused by a concubine or junior wife could easily be dismissed as merely the result of her being jealous. Thus accounts of this emotion in Chinese literature have a double edge—the difference between the much-lauded "good wife" (*xianfu*) and her polar opposite, the "jealous wife" (*dufu*), could sometimes be very small indeed.

This analysis will focus on the representation of jealousy in the life of Zhao Feiyan in two texts: *History of the Han Dynasty* and *The Scandalous Tale*. In *History of the Han Dynasty*, as in Han dynasty literature generally, women were understood to be the only ones to suffer from sexual jealousy, but it is nevertheless portrayed as an individual character trait. Since it was thought to be highly pejorative, actions that might be understood to be "jealous" in other circumstances were unlikely to be described this way unless the authors of the text wished to stress the villainy of the woman concerned. As a result, only a few women in the Rear Palace are described as jealous in *History of the Han Dynasty*, one of whom was Zhao Feiyan. By the time *The Scandalous Tale* was written in the late Tang, attitudes toward jealousy had been transformed. From at least the time of the collapse of the Han dynasty onward, this emotion had come to be understood as a universal trait among women. With this came the belief that it was entirely normal and natural, and should not be problematized. This kind of normalization can be seen even in situations where pathological traits or extreme violence were concerned: such behavior was regrettable but understandable. The portrayal of jealousy in *The Scandalous Tale* should be understood in this historical context: since all women were thought to be jealous, it is not surprising that Empress Zhao should be so too. What might be more concerning is that her emotional display is provoked not by her husband, Emperor Cheng, but by her lover, Yan Chifeng, whom she is horrified and upset to discover she has been sharing with her sister. Therefore, both of these important representations of Zhao Feiyan describe her as jealous, but what they mean by that are entirely different things.

Jealousy in *History of the Han Dynasty*

In *History of the Han Dynasty* only a very small number of women are described as jealous. It is understood as an individual failing, and regardless of whether jealousy per se was a character trait possessed by many women, it is clear from context that this term was only applied when her behavior was seen as threatening dynastic or governmental security. The same logic seems to apply to jealous or envious men: this is only mentioned when their behavior damages the institutions of the regime—hence terms like "jealous of the intelligent and envious of the wise" (*duxian jineng*) indicated that the personality of a monarch was dangerously unsuitable for his position.[9] Only ten women mentioned in *History of the Han Dynasty* are described as jealous: Empress Lü; Queen Lü, the wife of Liu You, King You of Zhao; Xu Lai and Consort Jue Ji, the second wife and the consort of Liu Ci, king of Hengshan (d. 122 BCE), respectively; Consort Li, a junior wife of Emperor Jing; Empress Chen, the first wife of Emperor Wu, and her mother, Senior Princess Liu Piao (d. 116 BCE); the unnamed wife of Liu Shun, King Xian of Changshan (d. 114 BCE); and Zhao Feiyan and her sister, Zhao Zhaoyi.[10] In addition, *History of the Han Dynasty* also mentions an innocent woman suspected of a murder motivated by jealousy: the wife of a senior government official, Wei Xiang (d. 59 BCE), was wrongly accused of killing a maid in her household by another official, named Zhao Guanghan (d. 67 BCE).[11] This example does not fit the general pattern of jealousy being invoked only when the behavior of female members of the imperial house threatens the security of the regime, and hence it is somewhat surprising to see the term being used.

History of the Han Dynasty can be usefully compared with *Records of the Grand Historian* and *History of the Later Han Dynasty* (Hou Hanshu) to gain an impression of the frequency with which women were said to be jealous in Han dynastic histories. In *Records of the Grand Historian*, which documents the reigns of the first five Han emperors (including Empress Lü), there are references to nine jealous women: Empress Lü; Queen Lü; Xu Lai and Consort Que; Consort Li; Empress Chen and her mother; the consort of King Xian of Changshan; and a woman named Yijun, the wife of Shi Zihui, Marquis of Jiangling.[12] All but the last of these are also mentioned in *History of the Han Dynasty*, which only adds two additional jealous women: Zhao Feiyan and her sister. Meanwhile, in *History of the Later Han Dynasty*, only four women are described as jealous: Empress Yin (d. ca. 102 CE) is said to have been jealous (*duji*) of Deng Guiren (another of Emperor He's senior consorts, who was subsequently appointed as his second empress), which resulted in her being deposed; Empress Yan Ji (d. 126 CE) is said to have monopolized imperial favor and been jealous (*zhuanfang duji*), so that when she discovered that a palace slave was pregnant, she waited until after the woman gave birth and then poisoned her; and the deposition of Empress Fu Shou—a purely political move—was justified by her supposedly jealous nature. In addition, Liu Shou, Princess of Liyi (d. 59 CE), a daughter of Emperor Guangwu and wife of Yin Feng (d. 59 CE), is described in *History of the Later Han Dynasty* as being "arrogant and jealous" (*jiaodu*); the violent marriage between this ill-matched pair ended in murder.[13] This text also mentions one woman, Empress Song, who is said to have been a victim of malicious and jealous gossip (*chandu zhi shuo*).[14] Given the strong political associations of the term, it is not surprising that *History of the Later Han Dynasty* makes no reference to jealousy on the part of women outside the imperial house except in the most general of terms.

In *History of the Han Dynasty*, the female relatives of Emperor Cheng are recorded in a detail not granted to any other women in this official history of the dynasty. By far the most positive portrayal is accorded to Ban Jieyu, the great-aunt of the main author of the text. She is described as a person of exceptionally virtuous behavior, who engages in displays of overt non-jealousy—in particular she is said to have presented one of her own maids, a woman named Li Ping, to Emperor Cheng, in the hope that she would get pregnant by him. That not everyone viewed this as an entirely good thing can be seen from Liu Xiang's horror that a woman of such low status could be appointed to the rank of *jieyu*—the relevant passage is translated in chapter 3. However, by choosing which other women would be presented to the emperor, Ban Jieyu retained some control over his sexuality. Although her decision to act in this way may have been motivated by a desire to affirm her own position, Ban Jieyu is presented in *History of the Han Dynasty* as a model of feminine behavior, as other women who encouraged their spouses to produce children with concubines or junior consorts would be throughout the imperial era. This idealization stands in contrast to the treatment of the other important female figures in Emperor Cheng's life, including his mother, Dowager Empress Wang Zhengjun; his father's two most favored consorts, the former Fu Zhaoyi and Feng Zhaoyi (both raised on Emperor Cheng's accession to the title of dowager queen); his first wife, Empress Xu; and so on. Naturally, out of all of these women, Empress Zhao Feiyan and her sister, Zhao Zhaoyi, are the only ones to be described as "arrogant and jealous" (*jiaodu*).[15] This reflects the understanding that the actions of the Zhao sisters were seriously imperiling the dynasty. *History of the Han Dynasty* reinforces the impression that Zhao Feiyan and Zhao Zhaoyi were seen as a malign influence upon the throne by repeated reference to evil omens:

> On Kuichou Day in the first month of the first year of the Yongshi reign era, the government icehouse caught fire. On Wuwu Day, the southern gate at the tomb of Empress Li caught fire. At this time, Zhao Feiyan was much favored. Since Empress Xu had been deposed, His Majesty wanted to appoint her [as empress], and so Heaven caused this omen to appear at the icehouse, just as in the fourth year of Emperor Hui.[16] Empress Li was the consort of Crown Prince Wei, but she died amid accusations of witchcraft and *gu* poisoning. When Emperor Xuan was established, he gave her this additional honorific title, but it was not ritually correct. Furthermore, Empress Li rose from very humble origins, just like Lady Zhao.[17] The Heavenly warning was as follows: a person of humble background and lacking in virtue cannot support the ancestral shrines and in the future sacrifices will be cut off—violence and evil will come to pass. In the sixth month on Bingyin Day, Empress Zhao was appointed. She and her younger sister were arrogant and jealous, and so they murdered the emperor's children and in the end both were executed.[18]

In the biography of Empress Zhao Feiyan given in *History of the Han Dynasty*, "jealousy" seems to refer to the fact that Emperor Cheng died without living offspring—a situation for which she was consistently blamed. It is not known why, in spite of an apparently vigorous sex life and numerous recorded births, all of Emperor Cheng's children should have died at a very young age, but this is a situation in which Empress Zhao was considered to be at fault. *History of the Han Dynasty* even records a children's song on this subject, reflecting the fact that such compositions were believed to be important omens of future events:

> Here is a swallow: how glossy is its tail!
> Young Master Zhang meets it in its prime.[19]
> Here is a wooden door, with bronze bosses and rings.[20]
> The swallow flies in, and pecks at the emperor's children.
> The emperor's children die; the swallow has pecked them
> to an early death![21]

As noted by *History of the Han Dynasty*, Empress Zhao enjoyed sixteen years at the very top of the hierarchy in the Han Rear Palace. Her execution occurred in 1 BCE, and she died alongside others, including Emperor Ai's widow, indicating that this was a political killing. Although at first glance it might seem that both women were executed for the crime of having failed to bear children for the imperial house, such would be a superficial view of the situation. Their deaths occurred at the time of a general purge of the political scene following the installation of Emperor Ping, indicating that they were punished for being identified with a faction opposed to Grand Dowager Empress Wang and the henceforth all-powerful Wang family.

Jealousy in *The Scandalous Tale of Zhao Feiyan*

By the time *The Scandalous Tale* was written in the late Tang dynasty, perceptions of jealousy had changed significantly. Jealousy continued to be regarded not only as an emotion natural and intrinsic to women, but was now viewed as a characteristic shared by all. As a result, it was redefined as a matter of personal self-respect and a very necessary adjunct to proper household management—a woman who did not show jealousy could not control her husband's sexual behavior. To cite but one example of this perception being articulated during the Age of Disunion, in 465, Liu Chang, king of Song (436–497), surrendered to the Northern Wei, and his daughter was subsequently selected to become the main wife of a member of the imperial house: Yuan Xiang, King Ping of Beihai (476–504). Lady Liu would display a total lack of jealousy toward her husband, who became notorious for his incestuous and illegal extramarital relationships, for which he was eventually punished by his mother. Yuan Xiang's mother was deeply irritated with Lady Liu for her failure to exert any control over her spouse and had her beaten several dozen strokes of the cane, stating: "You are a bride from a noble family, and in every way an appropriate match. What are you afraid of that you do not control your husband? Women are all jealous, so why should you be the only one that is not?"[22] In keeping with the impression that Lady Liu was an unusually submissive character, her response was to keep smiling as she accepted her punishment in silence. It is likely that many people in medieval China would have understood and agreed with Yuan Xiang's mother's attitude: Lady Liu was failing to manage her household properly and showing a serious lack of self-respect in not making any complaint about her husband's dreadful behavior. A lack of jealousy could have appalling consequences for the family as a whole, with unrestrained male sexuality leading to the formation of dangerous extramarital relationships, as well as blurring boundaries and hierarchies within the household.[23] In this reading, Lady Liu was guilty of risking the long-term interests of the family for the short-term gain of not having to confront her spouse.

Although medieval attitudes toward jealousy display some elements of continuity with earlier times, there were also important changes. During the Age of Disunion, elite women in the Northern Dynasties enjoyed considerable economic freedom and traditions of independent action that were enshrined in law. These privileges would be characterized by the disapproving as their "jealous and violent customs" (*duhan feng*), a term that also appears in modern scholarship on this subject.[24] Drawing on the terminology from Ban Zhao's *Admonitions for Women* (Nüjie), Yuan Xiaoyou (d. 551), a senior member of the Northern Wei imperial family who ended up serving the Northern Qi dynasty, turned the terms for an ideal woman's behavior on their head: "When parents marry off a daughter, they instruct her to be jealous; when female relatives meet, they always encourage each other to be jealous. Controlling their husbands has become a [sign of a] woman's virtue and jealousy has become women's work."[25] Although Yuan Xiaoyou did not regard this as a positive development, he blamed the behavior of elite men for provoking their wives' unhappy situation by taking multiple concubines. Jealousy was considered a defining characteristic of women in the Southern Dynasties too; this was thought to be a continuation of the decline in morality that had already set in during the Three Kingdoms period and Jin dynasty.[26] The Tang dynasty historian Fang Xuanling's (579–648) account of the behavior of elite women in the reign of Emperor Xiaomin of Jin (r. 313–316) is illuminating in the way it draws on the stereotype of contemporary women failing to achieve the virtue shown by those of earlier generations:

> As for the wives and daughters [of officials], whether it was getting properly dressed or making cloth, these were things only studied by slaves; they never learned women's work in the form of techniques for weaving silk or hemp, or the tasks of producing wine and food so that the whole family could eat together. Instead, they got married at the earliest opportunity and acted entirely according to their feelings, and therefore none of them felt ashamed at any slip in the form of an illicit sexual relationship or loss of chastity, nor

did they control the evil of jealousy. Their male relatives did not punish them, which meant that nobody else did either.[27]

Although there was a strong awareness of the fact that sexual jealousy on the part of the main wife would limit the number of children that emperors and other elite men were able to have, during the Age of Disunion it seems to have become generally accepted that this was a normal state of affairs. The importance of the main wife not being jealous for maximizing an elite man's opportunities to have sex with other women, and thus to produce more children, had long been advocated in literature; the locus classicus for this appears to be the preface to the ode "Grasshoppers" (Zhongsi) in *Book of Songs*: "If [queens and senior consorts] are not jealous, then children and grandchildren will be numerous."[28] By the Age of Disunion, when it was generally understood that all women were jealous, it was also widely accepted that there was not much point in complaining about it. This belief was emphasized by Emperor Xiaowen of Wei (r. 471–499), who said of his own Empress You (d. 499): "Women are jealous and defensive. Even monarchs cannot escape [this fact], let alone government officials and commoners!"[29] There were a few dissenting voices concerning this assessment: Liu Yu, Emperor Ming of Liu-Song (r. 465–472), commanded one of his ministers, Yu Tongzhi, to compile *Records of Jealous Wives* (Dufu ji) for the edification of his daughters in the hope of changing their behavior.[30] By all accounts, His Majesty was unsuccessful in his aim, though the surviving quotations from this text provide a fascinating insight into some very troubled Age of Disunion marriages. Meanwhile, Xiao Luan, Emperor Ming of Southern Qi (r. 494–498), ordered the punishment, even execution, of the wives of government officials for the crime of jealousy.[31] These are very unusual attempts by emperors to control behavior within private life. Not surprisingly, such efforts failed to have the slightest effect, given overwhelming popular agreement that women were naturally jealous. The challenge to patriarchy by women of this period even reached to the classics. *Records of Jealous Wives* gives a tale in which a wife refuses to accord *Book of Songs* its usual canonical authority, since she regards it as an expression of masculine oppression:

Lady Liu, the main wife of Grand Mentor Xie [Xie An, 320–385], did not allow her husband to have any other women. He very much enjoyed singing and music, and he also really wanted to have courtesans and concubines in his

> household. His brothers, sons, and nephews decided to communicate this wish. They went in a delegation to Lady Liu, to ask her to accept this. They mentioned how [the songs] "The Fish Hawk's Cry" [Guanju] and "Grasshoppers" spoke of the virtue of not being jealous.[32] Her ladyship knew that they were making fun of her. Then she asked who had selected these songs. They answered: "The Duke of Zhou." Lady [Liu] said: "The Duke of Zhou was a man, like you. If the Duchess of Zhou had compiled *Book of Songs*, it would not have been like this!"[33]

By the Tang dynasty, an enormous body of literature had been produced on the subject of women's jealousy. In addition to prescriptive texts that continued to stress the dangers of jealousy, and fictional representations of this emotion, a number of famous parables of its shocking effects were widely circulated. One such story was the particularly notorious tale of an aristocratic woman named Guo Huai (d. 296) in the Jin dynasty, whose murderously jealous reactions to her husband's behavior is supposed to have resulted in the deaths of their two sons.[34] Guo Huai was undoubtedly a genuine historical individual, and the early deaths of her two sons appear to be factual, but the truth of the tale of her jealous behavior is very much open to question.[35] Regardless of what actually happened, the image of Guo Huai as a wickedly cruel and jealous spouse was widely reported in medieval times, and this remains one of the most famous stories of female sexual jealousy in Chinese history right up to the present day. Tang dynasty accounts make it entirely clear that women continued to feel they had a right to be jealous, and that this was a private matter in which others had no authority—even the emperor could not control this emotional response. Where earlier medieval rulers like Emperor Ming of Southern Qi are said to have executed wives of officials for jealousy, by the Tang, emperors were reduced to merely threatening punishment. That some women were not prepared to accept imperial interference in their marriages can be seen in stories such as that of the wife of the Tang dynasty official Ren Gui (d. 629)—a tale that emphasizes that she felt jealousy to be a matter of proper self-respect. Here, the emotion is understood not merely as intrinsic, but also as an important aspect of a woman's ability to determine her own mode of life:

> In appreciation of his meritorious service, Emperor Taizong of Tang gave [Ren Gui] two maids. Gui bowed and thanked him, but did not dare to take

> them home. Emperor Taizong summoned his wife, and gave her wine, saying: "For a woman to be jealous means that she ought to be divorced. Either you must change your behavior and stop being jealous, in which case you do not have to drink this wine. Or you have to drink it." His wife said: "I cannot change my jealous ways, so I ask your permission to drink the wine." Then she drank it. When she arrived back home drunk, his wife said a final farewell to her family, but in fact it was not poison at all.[36]

When it comes to *The Scandalous Tale*, jealousy is concentrated in the relationship between the two sisters: Empress Zhao and Zhao Hede. The portrayal of Emperor Cheng's Rear Palace found in this novella excludes all mention of his numerous other consorts, and so narrows the focus upon the rivalry between the pair of them. In the early part of the novella, their jealousy seems to be expressed in material terms—the relationship between Empress Zhao and her husband crumbles early on thanks to sexual boredom on the part of Emperor Cheng, and Zhao Hede makes great efforts to ensure that he remains fascinated by her, while going out of her way to guarantee that her sister's position in the harem is never threatened. Therefore, the real climax of their jealousy comes over the sexual relationship that both women are pursuing with a palace slave named Yan Chifeng: Empress Zhao believes him to be her lover alone, an illusion that is shattered when she catches him sneaking out of the Junior Consort House. She responds by quarreling with her sister, though the incident ends with Zhao Hede apologizing to her twin. Subsequently, however, the quarrel does become known to the emperor, who (being far too frightened of his wife to question her directly) asks Zhao Hede what has happened. She is able to explain the whole thing away, assuring Emperor Cheng in disingenuous terms that she and her sister have been arguing over his sexual favors, and the incident concludes with the words "His Majesty believed this and was very pleased."[37]

The sensibilities shown by Emperor Cheng here are very much those of the Tang dynasty. First of all, in the Han dynasty, emperors and other members of the imperial house expressed their fear and terror of many things—having to do battle against a powerful enemy, encountering inauspicious omens, the prospect of losing popular support, and so on—but women were not included among them. Although such men may have had good reason to be afraid of the senior women in the Rear Palace, this is simply not recorded. By contrast, many later emperors—both in the Age of Disunion and during the Sui and

Tang dynasties—were comfortable with discussing the terror induced by their womenfolk. While they may not have been happy about being in such a situation, they were prepared to talk about it to others, and hence their feelings come to be recorded in a wide variety of sources, including the dynastic histories. As mentioned above, Emperor Xiaowen of the Northern Wei dynasty described his wife's jealousy as a fact of life; Xiao Yi, Emperor Yuan of Liang (r. 552–555), is said to have documented his anger at his main wife, Xu Zhaopei (d. 549), in his magnum opus *Master of the Golden Tower* (Jinlouzi); and Emperor Wen of Sui (r. 581–604) would say of Empress Dugu Jialuo (544–602): "I may be honored as the Son of Heaven, but I am still not free!"[38] Such frankness would have been unthinkable just a few centuries earlier.

Likewise, when it comes to the portrayal of jealousy in *The Scandalous Tale*, the situation is not one that could have been described this way prior to the end of the Han dynasty. There is no suggestion here that jealousy is in any way problematic; Emperor Cheng is very happy to be told that his wife is angry and upset about his sexual relationships with other women. Unlike the pejorative meanings attached to the term in the Han period, when *jealousy* was the word used to describe women's behavior that imperiled the dynasty, it was possible in a Tang representation of Emperor Cheng's life for him to be delighted at evidence of his wife's jealousy of her sister and to appreciate what he imagines is Empress Zhao's determination to monopolize his sexual attentions.[39] Although he apparently has no interest in rekindling his relationship with his main wife, Emperor Cheng views her feelings on this occasion as normal and natural, even flattering in the way that he is being treated as so desirable. The discussion of the concept of jealousy as it is articulated in two different accounts of the life of Empress Zhao Feiyan serves to demonstrate the extent to which it is impossible to escape from the iron grasp of stereotype. There are very few facts known about the life of Empress Zhao: she was a slave who was raised to eminence by her loving husband, Emperor Cheng, and having successfully presided over the transfer of the throne to Emperor Ai, she was forced to commit suicide when he died without heirs. This handful of facts has left plenty of room for the imaginative recreation of her biography, whether this is in historical works portraying her as a corrupt and greedy murderess or in more overtly fictional representations where she appears as a promiscuous woman, determined to provide her husband with an heir by any means, riven by jealousy of her more attractive younger sister, or wasting vast sums of money on luxurious living.

Women's Responses to Empress Zhao Feiyan

At present, the earliest surviving literary work written by a woman that describes her reaction to Zhao Feiyan is the piece titled "Rhapsody in Self-Commiseration" (Zidao fu) by Ban Jieyu.[40] Unlike some of the other writings attributed to this lady, the authenticity of this piece has never been called into question since it was included in the official history of the Han dynasty compiled by members of the Ban family. This piece is exceptional in that the writer had personal experience of dealing with Zhao Feiyan, and when accused of witchcraft by her, she barely escaped with her life. Nevertheless, if it is correct that the rhapsody was written during the lifetimes of Emperor Cheng and Empress Zhao, as implied by its placement within Ban Jieyu's biography, it is unsurprising that it approaches the subject of the collapse of her marriage extremely obliquely. Rather than complain about the emperor's fickleness or the problems caused by Empress Zhao's venomous hostility, she stresses the way in which she has learned from earlier female moral exemplars to be loyal and undemanding. Ban Jieyu mentions the distress caused by Emperor Cheng's absence from her life, but makes it clear that the favor she had already enjoyed was more than she deserves and that she is fully reconciled to her lot. The coda to the rhapsody encapsulates Ban Jieyu's strategy for not offending the emperor should her writings come to his attention, with the relevant section reading as follows:

> I lower my head and gaze at the palace steps,
> Remembering my lord's footprints there.
> I raise my head and look out upon the lofty rooftops,
> As tears course wildly down my cheeks.
> But on turning to look at my entourage, I calm my features,
> I pour a cup of wine, and thus dispel my sorrows.[41]

Nowhere in this rhapsody is there any direct reference to Zhao Feiyan, though the final line of the coda does make reference to the titles of two songs from *Book of Songs*, both of which are conventionally understood to refer to the malign influence of women on politics.[42] After Ban Jieyu died, there appears to be a long hiatus in women's writings about Empress Zhao; if any such texts were produced, they have not survived. Rather than writing about so controversial a female figure, poems written by women focus on the modest, well-educated, and virtuous Ban Jieyu herself, who was so viciously slandered by her wicked rival and who remained so self-controlled throughout all her trials and tribulations.[43] As a result of this kind of black-and-white moral evaluation of the two women, Empress Zhao appears only tangentially in the written tradition of early imperial-era China, and the situation does not improve much in the Song, Yuan, or Ming dynasties. Conventionally, Empress Zhao is reduced to a voice heard in the distance, as a succession of female poets bewailed the suffering inflicted on the neglected, innocent Ban Jieyu as she endured lonely years in a deserted palace. For example, in the poem "Changxin Palace" (Changxin gong) by the Southern Song-to-Yuan transition-era woman poet Zhang Yuniang (1250–1277), the evil influence of Zhao Feiyan upon the relationship between Ban Jieyu and Emperor Cheng is encapsulated in two couplets—in the first, Ban Jieyu withers away in the darkness, while in the second, Zhao Feiyan parties the night away in a blaze of light:

> The pearl blind keeps out the hazy moonlight,
> The fireflies drift to rest, settling against her embroidered skirts.
> West of the palace, the lamplight blazes,
> As the sound of singing and music rises from the Zhaoyang [Hall].[44]

A number of anthologies and studies of poetry by women from imperial-era China include a piece on Zhao Feiyan attributed to Empress Xiao Guanyin (1040–1075), which would appear to run counter to the prevailing trend. This empress, the cousin and main consort of Yelü Hongji, Emperor Daozong of Liao (r. 1055–1101), is described in her official biography as a very talented poet and songwriter.[45] In the past couple of decades, there has been much study of the works of Empress Xiao Guanyin, particularly by feminist scholars, and she is today frequently described as the greatest poet of the Liao dynasty.[46] The piece that Xiao Guanyin is supposed to have written about Zhao Feiyan is titled "Cherishing Antiquity" (Huaigu) and runs as follows:

> In the palace there were the finest of jewels from the Zhao family.
> In driving rain and scattered clouds,[47]
> They bewitched the ruler of the Han.
> The only one who knew the truth was the crescent moon
> That watched these flying birds enter the Zhaoyang [Hall].[48]

The reference to flying birds in the final line explicitly links this piece with the prophetic children's song recorded in *History of the Han Dynasty*—this poem thus implicitly criticizes the damage done by the Zhao sisters to the Han imperial house. The problem with this piece, as with the other writings ascribed to the authorship of Empress Xiao Guanyin, is the provenance. Every single poem and song lyric that is today attributed to her is derived from a Silk Pillow text: *An Account of Burned Pepper* (Fenjiao lu).[49] This text is attributed to a genuine historical individual—a Liao dynasty government official named Wang Ding (d. 1106)—but actually appears to date to the late Ming dynasty. Since *An Account of Burned Pepper* has all too often been regarded as a genuine text, the major problems with it are not well known. Leaving on one side the implausible plot and numerous anachronisms, there is no evidence this text was in existence prior to the late Ming dynasty: there are no earlier editions or manuscripts, nor is it quoted anywhere, nor is it discussed in literature.[50] This means that there is a five-century gap between the events described and the first references to the existence of this text. Furthermore, *An Account of Burned Pepper* cannot have been written prior to the publication of the official history of the dynasty in 1344, since it copies numerous errors from that text, including getting the name of the empress's father wrong. This is not a mistake that the putative author, a senior government official, could possibly have made, and the explanation put forward to account for this—that the text was originally correct but that it was later rewritten, introducing mistakes to bring it into line with the official history of the dynasty—is not persuasive.[51]

Hence, *An Account of Burned Pepper* is a Silk Pillow text that purports to offer an eyewitness account of the downfall and death of Empress Xiao Guanyin thanks to the machinations of a senior government official named Yelü Yixin (d. 1083). When quoted out of context, the poem about Zhao Feiyan appears relatively pedestrian; however, the plot of *An Account of Burned Pepper* hinges upon the interpretations made of this piece. The villainous Yelü Yixin accused Empress Xiao Guanyin of conducting an affair with a court musician named Zhao Weiyi (d. 1075), and her poem on Zhao Feiyan was twisted into providing evidence of her adultery.[52] It was this forced reading of her writings that induced the emperor to give orders for her to commit suicide: "Pointing to the empress's poem 'Cherishing Antiquity,' [Emperor Daozong] said: 'Here Her Majesty is criticizing Feiyan. . . .' [Zhang] Xiaojie [*jinshi* 1055] stepped forward and said: 'In fact [the wording] shows the affection that the empress felt for Zhao Weiyi.'[53] 'What do you mean?' the emperor asked. Xiaojie said: '"In the palace there were the finest of jewels from the *Zhao* family." . . . "The only one [*wei . . . yi*] who knew the truth was the crescent moon"'—these two lines contain the three characters of Zhao Weiyi's name."[54]

An Account of Burned Pepper is a Silk Pillow text, but also a polemic against education for women. This is made quite explicit in the conclusion, when the author states: "There are three reasons why Empress Yide [Xiao Guanyin] suffered such disaster. These are her love of music, the fact that she could compose poetry, and that she was interested in reading."[55] To the author of *An Account of Burned Pepper*, being guilty of being educated seems to have been almost as heinous a crime for a woman as being guilty of adultery. The empress proves to be unable to defend herself in a literary inquisition that turns upon the fact that her writings are read autobiographically. The persecution of Empress Xiao Guanyin, as described in *An Account of Burned Pepper*, represents a nadir of poetry reading, which posits that there is no difference between the poet and the voice in which she writes, and allows allusion and wordplay to be used as evidence of evildoing. On the other hand, this account serves to illustrate exactly why women chose not to write about controversial or sexually explicit topics—far too many readers used this as an opportunity to regard them as promiscuous, wonton, or wicked, treating them as if they were morally compromised by the subjects they wrote on. Interesting though it would be to have a poem by a Liao dynasty empress condemning Zhao Feiyan, particularly one composed in such dramatic circumstances, this piece was almost certainly written by a man. This fits with the general trend observable in anthologies and compilations of writings by women: literary works about Zhao Feiyan only began to be produced during the course of the Qing dynasty by female poets confident enough to proclaim their familiarity not only with historical accounts of her life, but also with sexually explicit writings like *The Scandalous Tale.*

Qing Women's Poetic Responses to *The Scandalous Tale of Zhao Feiyan*

Citations from *The Scandalous Tale* by men began to appear in late Tang dynasty literature, and by the time of the Song dynasty, not only were poets engaged in writing of their reactions to reading this book, but a number of expressions derived from this work had already entered the Chinese language. However, the first significant responses to this text by women were only produced in the Qing dynasty. The earliest poem by a woman that makes explicit reference to *The Scandalous Tale* is the piece titled "Flying Swallow" (Feiyan) by Yun Zhu (1771–1833), which was incorporated into her collection *Poetry Drafts from the Red Fragrant Mansion* (Hongxiangguan shicao). In recent years, Yun Zhu, the daughter of a distinguished scholarly family from Changzhou in Jiangsu Province, has been the subject of a great deal of academic research thanks to her talent as both a painter and a poet, and because of her unusual position as the wife of a Manchu aristocrat, Wanyan Tinglu (d. 1820). Such an exceptional intermarriage between a woman from a Chinese literati family and a member of the Manchu ruling elite gave her a special position in her own time, and the sensibilities shown in her writings have continued to interest scholars right up to the present day.[56] However, the multicultural background in which Yun Zhu lived is not relevant to understanding her poem on Zhao Feiyan. What is remarkable about this poem is that it represents the fusion between a very conventional condemnation of the behavior of the empress and a remarkable statement of feminine appreciation of the source of Zhao Feiyan's power: her seductive beauty and her skill in the performing arts. The second line underscores the idea that women could also admire and enjoy the loveliness that bewitched the emperor:

> This lovely lady moves with ease, dancing as if floating,
> Her fine skin and elegant deportment make me love her too.
> If only it had been known that the imperial offspring would
> be pecked by this sparrow!
> How sad someone was "restraining the immortal" when her
> skirts were blown by the wind.[57]

Although the first couplet expresses some unusual positive impressions of Empress Zhao, the second couplet, by referring first to the song from *History of the Han Dynasty* and then to the incident in *The Scandalous Tale* in which her skirts were torn, cancels this out: the poet wishes that Zhao Feiyan had killed herself before she had the opportunity to murder His Majesty's children. The same incident from *The Scandalous Tale* would also serve to inspire other female poets. For example, Ji Lanyun (1793–1848) included a poem titled "Zhao Feiyan's Restraining the Immortal Skirts" (Zhao Feiyan liuxian qun) in her *Collected Writings from the Chu Orchid Garden Belvedere* (Chuwan'ge ji). This allusive poem seems to suggest that Empress Zhao had no wish to die when she appeared to attempt suicide; she was just playing on the emperor's feelings, and thus ultimately succeeded in triumphing over her sister:

> On the banks of the Taiyi Pool, it did not appear she was about to die,
> As the wind plucked at her emerald sleeves, she wanted immortality!
> Because someone grabbed hold of her skirts, they were called "Restraining the Immortal";
> In the end Hede would fail to match up to this delicate dancer.[58]

By far the most detailed response by a woman to the experience of reading *The Scandalous Tale* was produced by Li Shuyi (b. 1817), who wrote two poems on the Zhao sisters that were included in her collection *One Hundred Poems on Famous Beauties from the Hall of Shadows* (Shuyinglou mingshu baiyong). Each of these poems is prefaced by a reference to *The Scandalous Tale*. (It is worth noting that although very close in wording to *The Scandalous Tale* and attributed to this text, this introduction is not a quotation but a summary of one part of the story.) Indeed, this seems to have been a characteristic of this collection: a reference to some historical or literary text is used to introduce each of the one hundred women commemorated. The first of these poems, titled "Zhao Feiyan," runs as follows:

> The palace slave Yan Chifeng was having an affair with the empress and also with the *zhaoyi*. Just when Chifeng was leaving the Junior Consort House, the empress happened to come to visit. Thus the song "The Arrival of the Red Phoenix" was composed for him.
>
> The two sisters received great favor and were awarded jade hairpins;
> Both in their separate residences housed a miraculous creature.
> How laughable that [Emperor Cheng] himself created this jeweled tree,
> Which then provided a perch for a Red Phoenix.[59]

This particular piece plays upon the meaning of Yan Chifeng's name—as the "Red Phoenix" he is said to perch in the palace, where his presence is the source of much gratification to the empress and her sister. The emperor, meanwhile, is completely in the dark as to his real role within the palace walls, for all that he is luxuriously housed at imperial expense. Li Shuyi's second poem, titled "Zhao Hede," is also prefaced by a reference to the text of *The Scandalous Tale*. Here, the poet muses on the illusory nature of the satisfaction Emperor Cheng found in his relationship with Zhao Hede—his affection for her was utterly misplaced, since she would ultimately bring about his death. The last line alludes to the circumstances in which Emperor Cheng is said to have died, poisoned by an aphrodisiac. Li Shuyi seems to have anticipated that the audience for her poems would at least be familiar with the outline of the story given in *The Scandalous Tale*, and would be aware of the way the author of this text consistently plays with the way the emperor fails to understand what is going on around him:

> The empress sent her sister, Hede, to the emperor. The emperor was very pleased. By touching every part of her body, he discovered that she was in every way delightful. He called her body his "Realm of Soft Warmth." He said: "I plan to grow old in this realm; I simply cannot imitate Emperor Wu in his search for the Realm of White Clouds." He granted her the title of *zhaoyi*.

> In a fashionable hairdo, and fully bejeweled,
> She has her share of His Majesty's generosity at the Taiyi [Pool].
> Once he began to wander in this fairy realm, dreaming
> of a happy marriage,
> His Majesty was doomed not to live long.[60]

The final work by a Qing dynasty woman to be considered here is the poem titled "Zhao Feiyan" by Wang Renpei (d. 1891). Here the poet addresses an issue that is at the heart of all representations of Zhao Feiyan: her failure to behave as a proper empress should. Wang Renpei was clearly thinking of the delicate and beautiful dancer as a vicious murderess, since the wording of her poem makes reference to *History of the Han Dynasty*. It is this sense of almost unbelievable levels of transgressive behavior on the part of Empress Zhao and her sister, slaying innocent and defenseless infants to secure their own dominance of the Rear Palace, that informs Wang Renpei's poem:

> Her betrayals of the virtues of an empress were hard to believe,
> She seemed so sweet-natured and so fragile.

When the swallow pecked the imperial offspring, who helped her
in her wickedness?
How much she was hated: Zhao Zhaoyi![61]

These writings by women are in one sense not particularly original; they explore themes in the life of Empress Zhao that had been written about by men for hundreds if not thousands of years. However, in another sense, these poems are revolutionary, since for the first time in Chinese history, women in the late Qing decided that they could tackle the subject of such a controversial female figure in their own writings without this being seen as threatening their own moral values. Although the responses of Qing dynasty women to their readings about Zhao Feiyan were overwhelmingly negative, this is hardly surprising given that she was widely believed to be guilty of mass murder, malicious jealousy and venomous spite in her dealings with others, and gross promiscuity. Though some male poets and writers during the imperial era would explore Zhao Feiyan as a symbol of eroticism and sexuality without any overt negative moral evaluation, there appear to be no writings by women that follow this pattern. Nevertheless, the groundbreaking achievement of Qing dynasty female poets in exploring their feelings about such a transgressive figure should not be underestimated.

Conclusion

From the moment she was installed in Emperor Cheng's Rear Palace, Zhao Feiyan was a very notorious woman. With her rise from slave-entertainer to the rank of empress, speculation about what lay behind her meteoric ascent resulted in numerous salacious rumors. The subsequent allegations of murder and promiscuity only added to the initial stereotype informed by her circumstances, which emphasized that, like other entertainers, she was both manipulative and immoral, trained in the use duplicitous wiles, a practiced seductress whose words and deeds were calculated to seduce unwary men. Empress Zhao Feiyan has now been dead for over two millennia, but in another sense, she is very much alive today. Her story is one that has touched the public imagination in a way that seems timeless. There is an apparently insatiable appetite for retellings of her life story, ranging from more or less serious academic works to popular fiction, plays and operas, storytelling and poetry, as well as film and TV representations. Popular fascination with Zhao

Feiyan has survived twenty centuries of creative reinterpretation, as the tales told about her have moved from one genre to the next, with fresh perspectives being adduced, and prejudices aired, at every twist and turn.

The history of the genre here termed "Silk Pillows" is at present very unclear, but it is likely that *The Scandalous Tale* is one of the earliest texts to be produced. The influence of this novella has been great, but it has often been treated quite uncritically as a genuine Han dynasty text, and a private view into life within the Rear Palace. This means that *The Scandalous Tale* has not only influenced our perception of Empress Zhao's biography, but has also served to create a stereotype about the lives of palace women that has been accepted by hundreds of millions of people right up to the present day. However, for all that *The Scandalous Tale* has played a key role in establishing the image of the imperial harem as a site where beautiful women lie and scheme amid settings of unimaginable luxury, the author of this novella handles his material with unusual sophistication. From being a frivolous and vulgar slave, Zhao Feiyan metamorphoses into an imperial favorite, a neglected wife, and then a jealous lover, but her true feelings are hidden from the reader. This allows us to question any simplistic, black-and-white construction of personality. By silence, the author restores psychological complexity to the character of Empress Zhao, and thanks in large part to the mysterious qualities of its eponymous main protagonist, *The Scandalous Tale* resists easy categorization. Where many other writings purporting to tell the "true story" of life behind the palace walls have vanished into obscurity, *The Scandalous Tale* continues to appeal to readers more than a thousand years after it first appeared.

Concluding Remarks

THE SCANDALOUS TALE OF ZHAO FEIYAN IS OFTEN DESCRIBED AS an early work of erotic fiction, but such a designation does not do justice to the contents, since this is a text that is not really intended to be titillating. Instead, the focus of the sexually explicit sections is on the intricacies of human relationships, exploitation and boredom, provocation and deception. It is through his unrestrained sexual appetite that Emperor Cheng ruins his own health and eventually brings about his death; meanwhile, in the pursuit of attractiveness and the hope that through her beauty she will be able to keep the emperor's favors, Zhao Feiyan destroys her chances of having children and thus ensures that once the monarch dies, she will find herself helpless. Zhao Hede attempts to fulfill his majesty's every desire, even those he has not articulated to himself, in order that she might be able to manipulate the emperor, but in the end, she pays for this with her life. The men and women of this novella turn out to be tormented by desires that are impossible to achieve: for sexual prowess in failing health, for children when infertile, for dominance within the dangerous and complex realm of the Han dynasty Rear Palace, when the slightest mistake can be fatal.

Instead of considering this text exclusively in the light of the parts of the narrative concerned with sexuality, it is perhaps more useful to think of *The Scandalous Tale* as a work of palace literature, in the Silk Pillow tradition. The focus of the narrative is on the characters of the women who reside in the Rear Palace; some are the consorts of the emperor, others are his servants, women officials who served the dynasty within the great walls of the palaces at Chang'an. It is these women who surround Emperor Cheng, ostensibly doing his every bidding, while in fact they pursue their own ambitions—this web of conflicting desires is concealed by the power imbalance between the Son of Heaven and the women around him, which means that they cannot openly assert their own wishes, and it is also affected by the circumstances of incredible luxury in which these people live. With every material desire more than satisfied, housed in the most beautiful and luxurious residences, dressed in the most lavish of clothing, the women are focused on the most fundamental of human needs: stability and security, affection and honesty from those around them. In the world of *The Scandalous Tale*, the Han palace is a place where women can only rely upon each other, but any trust vested in these relationships is often misplaced, as they are forced into competition with one another for the emperor's favors. This dark image of the imperial harem in the time of Emperor Cheng has proved enormously influential, not only on representations of the Han Rear Palace, but on the Rear Palace in every dynasty in Chinese history since then. For more than a thousand years, our image of the lives of consorts and concubines in the palaces of Chinese emperors has reflected the travails of Zhao Feiyan and Zhao Hede, trying to survive in the cutthroat world of the harem of Emperor Cheng.

APPENDIX ONE

Offices in the Han Dynasty Rear Palace

Women's ranks from the Western Han dynasty Rear Palace, shown against men's ranks and salaries where known.

WOMAN'S RANK	MAN'S RANK	SALARY (IN *DAN* OF GRAIN)
zhaoyi (21) "lady of bright deportment"	*zhuhouwang* (21) "king"	10,000
jieyu (20) "lady of handsome fairness"	*liehou* (20) "adjunct marquis"	
xing'e (19) "lady of graceful beauty"	*guanneihou* (19) "marquis within the passes"	a full 2,000
ronghua (18) "lady of lovely countenance"	*dashangzao* (16) "senior imperial provider"	exactly 2,000
meiren (17) "beauty"	*shaoshangzao* (15) "junior imperial provider"	less than 2,000
bazi (16) "consort of the eighth rank"	*zhonggeng* (13) "head of the middle watch"	1,000
chongyi (15) "lady of complete deportment"	*zuogeng* (12) "head of the left watch"	

WOMAN'S RANK	MAN'S RANK	SALARY (IN *DAN* OF GRAIN)
qizi (14) "consort of the seventh rank"	*youshuzhang* (11) "chief of the right host"	800
liangren (13) "virtuous lady"	*zuoshuzhang* (10) "chief of the left host"	
changshi (12) "senior palace maid"	*wudafu* (9) "grand master"	600
shaoshi (11) "junior palace maid"	*gongsheng* (8) "master of chariots"	400
wuguan (10) "all-purpose maid"		300
shunchang (9) "lady of obedient constancy"		200
wujuan (8) "lady without impurity"		100
gonghe (7) "lady of reverent gentleness"		
yuling (6) "lady of pleasing spirit"		
baolin (5) "lady of the precious bevy"		
liangshi (4) "maid of virtuous employment"		
yezhe (3) "lady of night attendance"		
shangjiarenzi (2) "senior woman of the household"		less than 100
zhongjiarenzi (1) "ordinary woman of the household"		

APPENDIX TWO

Chinese Text of The Scandalous Tale of Zhao Feiyan

The translation given in chapter 2 is based upon a variorum edition of the text that has been prepared specifically for this publication. The best readily available edition is that given in *The Complete Collection of Books from Various Collectanea* (Congshu jicheng), which collates three different versions of the text: that from the collection *Fiction from the Gu Family Library* (Gushi wenfang xiaoshuo), *The Collectanea of Literature from the Han and Wei Dynasties* (Han-Wei congshu), and *Secret Books from Longwei* (Longwei mishu). However, since *The Complete Collection of Books from Various Collectanea* edition does not indicate textual variants, the three texts have been collated again. The base edition was the version of the text given in *Fiction from the Gu Family Library*, published in Changzhou in 1522, from the collection of the National Central Library in Taipei, Taiwan.[1] In the Chinese text below, 【HW】 indicates *The Collectanea of Literature from the Han and Wei Dynasties* compiled during the reign of Emperor Wanli of the Ming dynasty (r. 1573–1619) by Cheng Rong (fl. 1590s), and 【LW】 the recension given in *Secret Books from Longwei*, a compilation produced by Ma Junliang in 1794.[2] In addition to that, a number of other different editions of the text were consulted: 【SF】 indicates a variant reading derived from *Stories from the Suburbs* (Shuofu), a collection compiled by Tao Zongyi; 【JX】 the recension published in the compilation *Early Fiction: Han, Wei, and Six Dynasties* (Jiu xiaoshuo: Han Wei Liuchao); 【WC】 is the compilation *Overview of Fiction from Five*

Dynasties (Wuchao xiaoshu daguan); 【BJ】 is the collection titled *Overview of Occasional Writings and Fiction* (Biji xiaoshuo daguan); and 【WS】 indicates the Wu family Qing dynasty manuscript in the collection of the National Library of China.[3] Amendments to the text are indicated in square brackets: [. . .]. The textual history of *The Scandalous Tale of Zhao Feiyan* is considered in detail in chapter 3.

趙飛燕外傳

趙后飛燕, 父馮萬金, 祖大力【HW, LW, and SF 九】. 工理樂器. 事江都王協律舍人. 萬金不肯傳家業, 編【WS 徧】習【WS 集】 樂聲, 亡【WS 七】章【WS 篇】曲. 任爲繁手哀聲, 自號凡靡之樂. 聞者心動焉. 江都王孫女姑蘇【WS adds the character 郡】主, 嫁江都中尉趙曼. 曼幸萬金; 食不同器不飽. 萬金得通趙主. 主有娠. 曼性暴妬, 且早有私病, 不近婦人. 主恐, 稱疾居王宮. 一產二女. 歸之萬金. 長曰宜主, 次曰合德. 然皆冒姓趙.

宜主纫【HW, LW, and SF 幼】聰悟. 家有彭祖方【HW, LW, SF, JX, WC, and WS 分】脈之書, 善行氣術. 長而纖便輕細, 舉止翩然. 人謂之飛燕. 合德膏滑, 出浴不濡, 善音辭, 輕緩可聽. 二人皆出世色. 萬金死, 馮氏家敗. 飛燕妹【WS 姉】[姊]弟流轉至長安. 於時人稱趙主子, 或云曼之他子. 與陽阿主家令趙臨共里巷, 託附臨. 屢爲組文刺繡, 獻臨. 臨愧【WS 悅】 受【WS 愛】之. 居臨家, 稱臨女. 臨常有女事宮省, 被病歸死. 飛燕或稱死者.

飛燕妹【WS 姉】[姊]弟, 事陽阿主家, 爲舍直. 嘗竊傚歌舞, 積思精切. 聽至終日, 不得食. 待直貲服疏苦. 財且顓事膏沐澡粉, 其費亡所愛. 共直者指爲愚人. 飛燕通隣羽林射鳥者. 飛燕貧, 與合德共被. 夜雪, 期射鳥者於舍傍. 飛燕露立, 閉息順氣, 體溫舒亡疹粟. 射鳥者異之, 以爲神仙. 飛燕緣主家大人入宮, 召幸. 其姑妹樊嫕爲丞 [承] 光司帑者, 故識飛燕與射鳥兒事, 爲之寒心.

及幸, 飛燕瞑目牢握, 涕交頤下. 戰栗不迎帝. 帝擁飛燕三夕, 不能接. 略無譴意. 宮中素幸者從容問帝. 帝曰: “豐若有餘, 柔若無骨. 遷延謙畏, 若遠若近, 禮義 [儀] 人也. 寧於曹婢脅肩者比邪【JX and WS 耶】!” 既幸, 流丹浹藉. 嫕私語飛燕曰: “射鳥者不近女邪 【JX and WS 耶】?” 飛燕曰: “吾內視三日, 肉肌盈實矣. 帝體洪壯, 創吾甚焉.” 飛燕自此特幸後宮, 號趙皇后.

帝居鴛【WS 未】鴦【WS 央】殿便房. 省帝【WS omits this character】簿. 嫕上簿. 嫕因進言飛燕有女弟合德, 美容體, 性醇粹可信, 不與飛燕比. 帝即令舍人呂延福, 以百寶鳳毛步【JX 玉】輦迎合德. 合德謝曰: "非貴人姊召, 不敢行. 願斬首以報宮中." 延福還奏. 嫕爲帝取后五采組文手藉爲符, 以召合德. 合德新沐, 膏九曲沈水香. 爲卷髮, 號新髻. 爲薄眉, 號遠山黛. 施小朱, 號慵來粧. 衣故短, 繡裙小袖, 李文襪. 帝御雲光殿帳. 使樊嫕進合德. 合德曰: "貴人姊虐妬【WC 妒】, 不難滅恩. 受恥不愛死. 非姊教, 願以身易恥." 不望旋踵, 音詞舒閑清切. 左右嗟賞之嘖嘖. 帝乃歸合德.

宣帝時披香博士淖方成. 白髮教授宮中, 號淖夫人. 在帝後, 唾曰: "此禍水也. 滅火必矣." 帝用樊嫕計, 爲后別開遠條館. 賜紫茸雲氣帳, 文玉几, 赤金九層博山緣【WS 爐】. 合嫕諷后曰: "上久亡子, 宮中不思千萬歲計邪【JX and WS 耶】? 何不時進上, 求有子?" 后德嫕計, 是夜進合德. 帝大悅. 以輔屬体【HW, LW, SF, and JX 體】. 無所不靡. 謂爲溫柔鄉. 謂嫕曰: "吾老是鄉矣. 不能效武皇帝求白雲鄉也." 嫕呼萬歲. 賀曰: "陛下真得仙者." 上立賜嫕鮫文萬金錦二十四疋【LW and WS 匹】.

合德尤幸, 號爲趙婕【WS 倢】妤【WS 伃】. 婕【WS 倢】妤【WS 伃】事后, 常爲兒拜. 后於婕【WS 倢】妤【WS 伃】坐. 后誤唾婕【WS 倢】妤【WS 伃】褏【WC 袖】. 婕【WS 倢】妤【WS 伃】曰: "姊唾染人紺褏【WC 袖】, 正似石上華. 假令尚方爲之, 未必能若此衣之華, 以爲石華廣袖." 后在遠條館, 多通侍郎宮奴多子者. 婕【WS 倢】妤【WS 伃】傾心翊護. 常謂帝曰: "姊性剛, 或爲人搆陷, 則趙氏無種矣." 每泣下悽惻. 以故白后姦狀者, 帝輒殺之. 侍郎宮奴, 鮮絝蘊香, 恣縱棲息遠條館. 無敢言者. 后終無子.

后浴五蘊七香湯, 踞通香沉水坐, 燎【WC, SF, and JX 潦】降神百蘊香. 婕【WS 倢】妤【WS 伃】浴荳蔻湯, 傅露華百英粉. 帝常私語樊嫕曰: "后雖有異香, 不若婕【WS 倢】妤【WS 伃】體自香也." 江都易王故姬李陽華, 其姑爲馮大力【SF 刀】妻. 陽華老, 歸馮氏. 后姊弟母事陽華. 陽華善賁飾, 常教后九迴沉水香澤, 雄麝臍内息肌丸. 婕【WS 倢】妤【WS 伃】亦内息肌丸. 常試若爲婦者月事益薄. 他日后言於承光司劑者上官嫵. 撫膺曰: "若如是, 安能有子乎?" 教【JX omits this character】后煮美花滌之. 終不能驗【WS 娠】.

真臘【JX 獵】夷獻萬年蛤, 不夜光珠. 彩皆若月, 照人亡妍醜, 皆美艷【BJ, LW, JX, WC, and WS 豔】. 帝以蛤賜后, 以珠賜婕【WS 倢】妤【WS 伃】.

后以蛤粧五成金霞帳. 帳中常若滿月. 久之, 帝謂婕【WS 倢】好【WS 伃】曰: "吾晝視后, 不若夜視之美. 每旦令人忽忽如失." 婕【WS 倢】好【WS 伃】聞之, 即以珠號爲枕前不夜光珠, 爲后壽, 終不爲后道帝言.

始加大號. 婕【WS 倢】好【WS 伃】揍書於后曰: "天地交暢, 貴人姊及此令吉. 光登正位, 爲先人休, 不堪喜豫. 謹奏上二十六物以賀: 金屑組文茵一鋪. 沉水香蓮心椀一面. 五色同心大結一盤. 鴛央【HW, LW, SF, and WS 鴦】萬金錦一疋【LW 匹】. 玻璃屏風一張. 枕前不夜珠一枚. 含香綠毛狸藉一鋪. 通香虎皮檀象一座. 龍香握魚二首. 獨搖寶蓮一鋪. 七出菱花鏡一奩. 精金彄環四指. 若亡絳綃單衣一襲. 香文羅手藉三幅. 七回【BJ, JX, WC, and WS 面】光雄肪髮澤一盎. 紫金被褥香爐三枚. 文犀辟毒箸二雙. 碧玉膏奩一合. 使侍兒郭語瓊拜上." 后報以雲錦五色帳, 以沉水香玉壺. 婕【WS 倢】好【WS 伃】泣怨帝曰: "非姊賜, 我死不知此器." 帝謝之. 詔益州, 留三年輸爲婕【WS 倢】好【WS 伃】作七成錦帳, 以沉水香飾.

婕【WS 倢】好【WS 伃】接帝於太液池, 作千人舟, 號合宮之舟. 池中起爲瀛洲榭. 高四十尺. 帝御流波文縠無縫衫, 后衣南越所貢雲英紫裙碧瓊輕綃. 廣榭上. 后歌舞歸風送遠之曲, 帝以文犀簪擊玉甌. 令后所愛侍郎馮無方吹笙以倚后歌. 中流歌酣. 風大起. 后順風揚音. 無方長噏細嫋, 與相屬. 后裙髀, 曰: "顧我! 顧我!" 后揚袖, 曰: "仙乎! 仙乎! 去故而就新, 寧忘懷乎!" 帝曰: "無方爲我持后." 無方捨吹持后履. 久【WS 留】之, 風霽. 后泣曰: "帝恩我, 使我仙去不待【LW, SF, WS, and WC 得】." 悵然曼嘯, 泣數行下. 帝益愧愛后, 賜無方千萬, 入后房闥. 他日宮妹幸者, 或襞裙爲紐【HW, LW, and SF 縐】【JX 絲】. 號曰留仙裙.

婕【WS 倢】好【WS 伃】益貴幸, 號昭儀. 求近遠條館. 帝作少嬪館; 爲露華殿, 含風殿, 傳昌殿, 求安殿, 皆爲前殿. 後殿又爲溫室, 凝缸室, 浴蘭室. 曲房連檻, 飾黃金白玉, 以璧爲表裏. 千變萬狀, 連遠條館, 號通仙門. 后貴寵, 益思放蕩. 使人博求術士, 求匪安劫老之方. 時西南北波夷致貢. 其使者舉茹一飯【LW 飲】, 晝夜不臥偃. 典屬國上其狀. 屢有光怪. 后聞之. 問何如術. 夷人曰: "吾術天地平, 生死齊, 出入有無, 變化萬象, 而卒不化." 后令樊嫕弟子不周遺千金. 夷人曰: "學吾術者, 要不淫與謾言." 后遂不報. 他日樊嫕侍后浴, 語甚讙. 后爲樊嫕道夷言. 嫕抵掌曰: "憶在江都時, 陽華李姑, 畜鬬鴨水池上. 苦獺囓鴨. 時下朱里芮姥者, 求捕獺狸獻. 姥謂姑曰: '是狸不他食, 當飯以鴨.' 姑怒, 絞其狸. 今夷術真似如此也." 后大笑曰: "臭夷何足汙吾絞乎?"

后所通宮奴燕赤鳳者, 雄捷能超觀閣. 兼通昭儀. 赤鳳始出少嬪館, 后適來幸. 時十月五日, 宮中故事, 上靈安廟. 是日吹塤擊鼓, 連臂踏地歌赤鳳來曲. 后謂昭儀曰: "赤鳳爲誰來?" 昭儀曰: "赤鳳自爲姊來; 寧爲他人乎?" 后怒. 以杯抵昭儀裙曰: "鼠子能囓人乎?" 昭儀曰: "穿其衣, 見其私, 足矣. 安能嚙人乎?" 昭儀素卑事后, 不虞見答之暴, 熟視不復言. 樊嫕脫簪, 叩頭出血. 扶昭儀爲拜后. 昭儀拜. 乃泣曰: "姊寧忘共被夜長, 苦寒不成寐. 使合德雍姊背邪【JX and WS 耶】. 今日垂得貴, 皆勝人, 且無外搏. 我姊弟其忍内相搏乎?" 后亦泣. 持昭儀手, 抽紫玉九鶵釵, 爲昭儀簪髻. 乃罷. 帝微聞其事, 畏后不敢問. 以問昭儀. 昭儀曰: "后妬【SF, JX, and WC 妒】我尒【BJ, HW, LW, SF, JX, WC, and WS 爾】. 以漢家火德, 故以帝爲赤龍鳳." 帝信之. 大悅.

帝嘗蚤獵, 觸雪得疾, 陰緩弱不能壯發. 每持昭儀足, 不勝至欲, 輒暴起. 昭儀常轉側. 帝不能常持其足. 樊嫕謂昭儀曰: "上餌方士大丹, 求盛大, 不能得. 得貴人足一持, 暢動, 此天與貴妃大福. 寧轉側俾帝就邪【JX and WS 耶】?" 昭儀曰: "幸轉側不就, 尚能留帝欲. 亦如姊教帝持, 則厭去矣. 安能復動乎?" 后驕逸, 體微病, 輒不自飲食, 須帝持匕箸. 藥有苦口者, 非帝爲含吐, 不下咽.

昭儀夜入浴蘭室, 膚體光發占燈燭. 帝從幃中竊望之. 侍兒以白昭儀. 昭儀覽巾, 使徹燭. 他日, 帝約賜侍兒黃金, 使無得言. 私婢不豫約中. 出幃值帝, 即入白昭儀. 昭儀遽隱辟. 自是帝從蘭室幃中窺昭儀, 多袖金, 逢侍兒私婢, 輒牽止賜之. 侍兒貪帝金, 一出一入不絕. 帝使夜從帑益至百餘金.

帝病緩弱, 大醫萬方不能救, 求奇藥, 嘗得昚卹膠. 遺昭儀. 昭儀輒進帝, 一丸一幸. 一夕, 昭儀醉, 進七丸. 帝昏夜擁昭儀, 居九成帳, 笑吃吃不絕. 抵明, 帝起御衣. 陰精流輸不禁. 有頃絕倒. 褰衣視帝, 餘精出湧, 霑汙被內. 須更【LW, SF, WC, and WS 臾】帝崩. 宮人以白太后. 太后使理昭儀. 昭儀曰: "吾持人主如嬰兒, 寵傾天下. 安能斂手掖庭令, 爭帷帳之事乎?" 乃拊膺呼曰: "帝何往乎?" 遂歐血而死.

伶玄自序

伶玄字子于潞水人, 學無不通, 知音善屬文, 簡率尚真樸, 無所矜式, 揚雄獨知之. 然雄貪名矯激, 子于謝不與交, 雄深慊毀之. 子于由司空小吏, 歷三署刺守州郡, 爲淮南相, 人有風情. 哀帝時, 子于老休, 買妾樊通德, 通德嫕之弟子, 不周之子也. 有才色, 知書, 慕司馬遷史記, 頗能言趙飛燕姊弟故事. 子于閑居命言, 慶慶不倦. 子于語通德曰: "斯人俱灰滅矣. 當時疲精力, 馳騖嗜欲, 蠱惑之事, 寧知終歸荒田野草乎?" 通德占袖, 顧視燭影, 以手拥髻, 凄然泣下, 不勝其悲, 子于亦然. 通德奏子于曰: "夫淫於色, 非慧男子不至也. 慧則通, 通則流, 流則不得其防, 則百物變態, 爲溝爲壑, 無所不往焉. 禮義[儀]成敗之說, 不能止其流, 惟感之以盛衰奄忽之變, 可以防其壞. 今婢子所道趙后姊弟事, 盛之至也. 主君悵然有荒田野草之悲, 衰之至也. 婢子拊形屬影, 識夫盛之不可留, 衰之不可推, 俄然相緣奄忽. 雖婕妤聞此, 不少遺乎? 幸主君著其傳, 使婢子執研削道所記." 於是撰趙后別傳. 子于爲河東都尉, 班躅爲決曹, 得幸太守, 多所取受. 子于召躅, 數其罪而捽辱之. 躅從兄子彪, 續司馬史記, 絀子于, 無所收錄.

桓譚

王莽時茂陵卞理者, 不仕以夏侯尚書授. 時更始二年, 赤眉過茂陵, 卞理棄圖書隱山. 劉恭入其廬獲金縢漆匱. 發之, 乃得玄書. 建武二年, 賈子翊以書示予曰: "卞理之琴師玄云也."

荀勖

右伶玄趙后傳, 竹簡磨滅, 文義交錯, 不可具曉. 謹與臣勖書同校定相證, 別刪去其不可詳者,合爲一篇. 其趙后樊嫕無所終, 疑玄之闕文也.

GLOSSARY OF CHINESE CHARACTERS

An Lushan 安祿山 (ca. 703–757)

Bai Juyi 白居易 (772–846)
"Baihua" 白華
Baiyun Xiang 白雲鄉
Ban Biao 班彪 (3–54 CE)
Ban Gu 班固 (32–92 CE)
Ban Jieyu 班婕妤 (d. 6 BCE)
"Ban Jieyu zan" 班婕妤贊
Ban Zhao 班昭 (45–ca. 116 CE)
baolin 保林
Baopuzi 抱樸子
Baoshi 暴室
bazi 八子
"Bi Hong'er shi" 比紅兒詩
biezhuan 別傳
Biji xiaoshuo daguan 筆記小說大觀
Bimen 璧門
Borjigit Bumbutai (Empress) 博爾濟吉特. 布木布泰 (1613–1688)

Cai Zhi 蔡質
Cao Cao 曹操 (155–220)
Cao Gong 曹宮
chandu zhi shuo 讒妒之說
Changcheng, Lord of 昌成君
"Changhen ge" 長恨歌
Changhen zhuan 長恨傳
changshi 長使
"Changxin gong" 長信宮
Chao Gongwu 晁公武 (1105–1180)
chen 臣
Chen, Empress 陳皇后 (d. ca. 110 BCE)
Chen Hong 陳鴻 (fl. 805 CE)
Chen Jinfeng (Empress) 陳金鳳 (d. 935 CE)
Chen Xuanyou 陳玄祐 (fl. 779 CE)
Chen Zhensun 陳振孫 (1179–1262)
Cheng, Lady 程姬
Cheng Dachang 程大昌 (1123–1195)
Cheng Rong 程榮 (fl. 1590s)
Chengyang, Marquis of 成陽侯
chenqie 臣妾
"Chifeng lai qu" 赤鳳來曲
chijin 赤金
chongyi 充依
Choumiu fengzhen yuanbei 綢繆鳳枕鴛被
chuanqi 傳奇
chuanqi zhi shou 傳奇之首
Chunyu Chang 淳于長
Chuwan'ge ji 楚畹閣集

Cixi, Dowager Empress 慈禧太后 (1835–1908)
congshu 叢書
Congshu jicheng 叢書集成
Cui Hao 崔顥 (704–754)

da sima cheji jiangjun Ping'en hou 大司馬車騎將軍平恩侯
Daming 大命
dan 石
dashangzao 大上造
Da-Song Xuanhe yishi 大宋宣和遺事
Daye shiyi ji 大業拾遺記
Deng Sui (Empress) 鄧綏 (d. 121 CE)
deng Yingzhou 登瀛洲
Di ju Weiyangdian bianfang 帝居未央殿便房
Di ju Yuanyangdian bianfang 帝居鴛鴦殿便房
Di ling zuoyou chi qi qun 帝令左右持其裙
dian 簟
du 妒
"Du *Zhao Feiyan waizhuan* zashi" 讀趙飛燕外傳雜詩
Duan Chengshi 段成式 (ca. 803–863)
dufu 妒婦
Dufu ji 妒婦記
Dugu Jialuo (Empress) 獨孤伽羅 (544–602)
duhan feng 妬悍風
duji 妒忌
duxian jineng 妒賢嫉能
Duyang zabian 杜陽雜編

Eyi, Princess 鄂邑公主 (d. 80 BCE)

Famensi 法門寺
Fan Tongde 樊通德
Fan Yannian 樊延年
Fan Yi 樊嫕
Fang Xuanling 房玄齡 (579–648)
"Feiyan" 飛燕
"Feiyan pian" 飛燕篇
Feiyan shi liutiao 飛燕事六條
Feiyan waizhuan 飛燕外傳
Feng, Lady 馮氏
Feng Wanjin 馮萬金
Feng Wufang 馮無方
Feng Zhaoyi 馮昭儀 (d. 6 BCE)
Feng Zhi 馮贄 (fl. ninth century CE)
Fengxiang Commandery 鳳翔郡
Fenjiao lu 焚椒錄
Fu Chang 傅暢 (d. 330 CE)
Fu Qian 服虔 (ca. 125–195)
Fu Shou (Empress) 伏壽 (d. 214 CE)
Fu yan renshi, ze shangfa buxin 婦言人事, 則賞罰不信
Fu Zhaoyi 傅昭儀 (d. 3 BCE)
Funan 扶南
furen 夫人

Gan Bao 干寶 (286–336)
Gaomei 高禖
"Gaotang fu" 高唐賦
Ge Hong 葛洪 (283–363)
Genji monogatari 源氏物語
gong 公
gong ci 宮詞
gong yuan 宮怨
gonghe 共和
gongnü 宮女
gongren 宮人
gongsheng公乘
gongyang shengzhong 共養省中
Gu Yuanqing 顧元慶 (1487–1565)
Guanfu ji 關輔記
"Guanju" 關雎
guanneihou 關内侯
Guanzhong ji 關中記
Guanzi 管子
Guhuantang 古歡堂
guifei 貴妃
Guigong 桂宮
guiren 貴人
Guliang zhuan 穀梁傳
Guo Huai 郭槐 (d. 296 CE)
Guo Shufei 郭淑妃 (d. after 878 CE)

Guo Xian 虢縣
Guomu 國母
Gushi wenfang xiaoshuo 顧氏文房小說

Han, Emperor Ai of 漢哀帝 (r. 7–1 BCE)
Han, Emperor Cheng of 漢成帝 (r. 32–7 BCE)
Han, Emperor Gengshi of 漢更始帝 (r. 23–25 CE)
Han, Emperor Guangwu 漢光武帝 (r. 25–57 CE)
Han, Emperor He of 漢和帝 (r. 88–105 CE)
Han, Emperor Huan of 漢桓帝 (r. 146–168 CE)
Han, Emperor Hui of 漢惠帝 (r. 195–188 BCE)
Han, Emperor Jing of 漢景帝 (r. 157–141 BCE)
Han, Emperor Ling of 漢靈帝 (r. 168–189 CE)
Han, Emperor Ming of 漢明帝 (r. 58–75 CE)
Han, Emperor Ping of 漢平帝 (r. 1 BCE–5 CE)
Han, Emperor Shun of 漢順帝 (r. 125–144 CE)
Han, Emperor Wu of 漢武帝 (r. 141–87 BCE)
Han, Emperor Xuan of 漢宣帝 (r. 73–49 BCE)
Han, Emperor Yuan of 漢元帝 (r. 48–33 BCE)
Han, Emperor Zhao of 漢昭帝 (r. 86–74 BCE)
"Han Chengdi fu shenxujiao" 漢成帝服慎恤膠
Han Chengdi neizhuan 漢成帝內傳
Han Feizi 韓非子
Han jiuyi 漢舊儀
Han Wo 韓偓 (842/844–ca. 923)
Han zashi mixin 漢雜事秘辛
"Handan gongren yuan" 邯鄲宮人怨
Hangong chunse 漢宮春色
Hanguan jiuyi 漢官舊儀
Hanguan yi 漢官儀
Hanshu 漢書
Han-Wei congshu 漢魏叢書
hanxiang 含香
Hao geng gai jiu yue Yi 好更改舊曰易
haojie 豪傑
He Fani (Empress) 何法倪 (339–404)
"He jieyu yuan" 和婕妤怨
He Zhu 賀鑄 (1052–1125)
Hehuan yuandang 合懽圓璫
Hejian 河間
Hepu 合浦
"Hong bajiao fu" 紅芭蕉賦
Hong Mai 洪邁 (1123–1202)
Hongxiangguan shicao 紅香館詩草
hou 侯
Hou, Consort 侯夫人
Hou Hanshu 後漢書
Hougong 後宮
Hu Yinglin 胡應麟 (1551–1602)
"Huai ji Zhou Yuanweng shishou" 懷寄周元翁十首
"Huaigu" 懷古
Huainan xiang 淮南相
Huan Tan 桓譚 (ca. 43 BCE–28 CE)
huang taihou 皇太后
Huangdu Fengyue Zhuren 皇都風月主人
huanghou 皇后
huanghou zhi bi guowang 皇后秩比國王
Huangtu 黃圖
Huhanye 呼韓邪 (d. 31 BCE)
hujing 狐精
Huo 霍
Huo Chengjun (Empress) 霍成君 (d. 54 BCE)

Inmok, Queen 仁穆王后 (1584–1632)

Ji Commandery 汲郡
Ji Lanyun 季蘭韻 (1793–1848)

Jia Nanfeng (Empress) 賈南風 (257–300)
Jiangdu, king of 江都王
jiaodu 驕妒
Jiaofang 椒房
"Jiaoliao" 椒聊
jieyu 婕妤
"Jihuan pin" 髻環品
Jiliu xiajian, buyi shangjie shenggong 妓流下賤, 不宜上接聖躬
Jin, Emperor Hui of 晉惠帝 (r. 290–301, 301–307)
Jin, Emperor Mu of 晉穆帝 (r. 344–361)
Jin, Emperor Wu of 晉武帝 (r. 265–290)
Jin, Emperor Xiaomin of 晉孝愍帝 (r. 313–316)
Jin zhugong zan 晉諸公贊
Jinfeng waizhuan 金鳳外傳
Jinlouzi 金樓子
Jinpingmei 金瓶梅
"Jinteng" 金縢
Jiu Tangshu 舊唐書
Jiu xiaoshuo: Han Wei Liuchao 舊小說: 漢魏六朝
jiuhua 九華
jiuqing 九卿
Jiuzhou chunqiu 九州春秋
jiuzi 九子
juan 卷
jue 爵
Jue Ji, Consort 厥姬
jun 君

Kaiyuan Tianbao yishi 開元天寶遺事
ke 科
Kuang Heng 匡衡 (fl. 50–33 BCE)
Kyech'uk ilgi 癸丑日記

Leishuo 類說
li 理 (restraint)
li 禮 (ritual)
Li, Consort (of Emperor Jing of Han) 栗夫人
Li, Consort (of Emperor Wu of Han) 李夫人
Li Mao, King of Shou 壽王李瑁 (d. 775 CE)
Li Ping 李平
Li Shangyin 李商隱 (813–858)
Li Shishi 李師師
Li Shishi waizhuan 李師師外傳
Li Shuyi 李淑儀 (b. 1817 CE)
Li Yannian 李延年 (d. 87 BCE)
Liang, Emperor Wu of 梁武帝 (r. 502–549)
Liang Na (Empress) 梁妠 (116–150)
Liang Nüying (Empress) 梁女瑩 (d. 159 CE)
liangren 良人
liangshi 良使
liao 聊
liehou 列侯
Lienü zhuan 列女傳
Liexian zhuan 列仙傳
"Lihun ji" 離魂記
Lin kui shou zhi 臨愧受之
Lin yue ai zhi 臨悅愛之
Lin Yuhong 林于弘
Lin Yutang 林語堂
Ling Xuan 伶玄
Ling Xuan zixu 伶玄自叙 (Ling Xuan's authorial postface)
Ling Xuan zixu 伶玄自序 (Ling Xuan's authorial preface)
Liu, Lady 劉氏
Liu An, King of Huainan 淮南王劉安 (r. 173–122 BCE)
Liu Bi, King of Wu 吳王劉濞 (r. 194–154 BCE)
Liu Chang, King of Song 宋王劉昶 (436–497)
Liu Ci, King of Hengshan 衡山王劉賜 (d. 122 BCE)
Liu Fei, King of Jiangdu 劉非 (168–128 BCE)
Liu Fu 劉輔
Liu Jian, King of Jiangdu 劉建 (r. 127–121 BCE)
Liu Jun, Emperor Xiaowu of the Liu-Song

dynasty 劉宋孝武帝劉駿 (r. 453–464)
Liu Lingxian 劉令嫻 (fl. 525 CE)
Liu Pengzu, King of Zhao 趙王劉彭祖 (r. 152–92 BCE)
Liu Penzi 劉盆子 (b. 10 CE)
Liu Piao, Senior Princess 上公主劉嫖 (d. 116 BCE)
Liu Shou, Princess of Liyi 酈邑公主劉綬 (d. 59 CE)
Liu Shun, King Xian of Changshan 常山憲王劉舜 (d. 114 BCE)
Liu Xiang 劉向 (77–6 BCE)
Liu Xiaobiao 劉孝標 (462–521)
Liu Xijun 劉細君 (d. 101 BCE)
Liu Xin 劉歆 (d. 23 CE)
Liu Xiu 劉休
Liu Yong 柳永 (987–1053)
Liu You, King You of Zhao 趙幽王劉右
Liu Yu, Emperor Ming of the Liu-Song dynasty 宋明帝劉彧 (r. 465–472 CE)
Liu Zhan 劉膽 (d. 874 CE)
Liuxian Qun 留仙裙
Longwei mishu 龍威秘書
Longyu, Dowager Empress 隆裕太后 (1868–1913)
Lü, Empress 呂皇后 (d. 180 BCE)
Lü, Queen 呂王后
Lu Xian 潞縣
Lüchuang xinhua 綠窗新話
luli 露立
lun 輪
luo 羅
Luo Qiu 羅虬 (fl. 874 CE)
Lushui 潞水
"Lüyi" 綠衣 (Green Robes)
"Lüyi" 綠意 (Greens of Spring)
Lüzhu zhuan 綠珠傳

Ma, Empress 馬皇后 (40–79)
Ma Chun 馬純 (fl. 1160s CE)
Ma Junliang 馬俊良
Ma Ruichen 馬瑞辰 (1782–1853)
mao 媢
Mei Fei zhuan 梅妃傳
meiren 美人
"Meiren fu" 美人賦
meise ru wang yuan shan 眉色如望遠山
Mi Bazi 羋八子 (d. 265 BCE)
Miao Changyan 苗昌言 (*jinshi* 1142)
Milou ji 迷樓記
Min, Emperor Huizong of 閩惠宗 (r. 933–935)
Ming, Emperor Wanli of 明萬曆 (r. 1573–1619)
Ming Fei 明妃
Mingci, Marquis of 鳴雌侯
Mu Tianzi zhuan 穆天子傳
mu yi 母儀
mu yi Tianxia 母儀天下
Mu yi zi gui 母以子貴
mulin Tianxia 母臨天下
mulin wanguo 母臨萬國
Murong Xi, Emperor Zhaowen of Later Yan 後燕昭文帝慕容熙 (r. 401–407)

Nanyue 南越
Nü Ji 女几
Nü Wan 女丸
Nüjie 女誡
nüshi 女使

On Shionoya 鹽谷溫 (1878–1962)

pei 配
Pengzu jing 彭祖經
Pengzu yangxing 彭祖養性
pian 篇
Pixiang Dian 披香殿

Qi zhou 歧州
Qiangong 前宮
qibao 七寶
qichu 七出
Qidong yeren 齊東野人
Qin, King Xiaowen of 秦孝文王 (r. 250 BCE)

Qin, King Zhaoxiang of 秦昭襄王 (r. 306–251 BCE)
Qin Chun 秦醇
Qing Anshi 慶安世
qingmu 青木
qiqu 七去
qiu 莍
Qiu Ying 仇英 (1494?–1552)
qizi 七子
Qu Songman 屈頌滿 (1792–1815)
"Quanxiu" 權修

Ren Gui 任瓌 (d. 629 CE)
"Renshi zhuan" 任氏傳
Rong Yanyuan 榮彥遠
ronghua 傛華
Runan, king of 汝南王
ruoti fengji 弱骨豐肌
Ruyijun zhuan 如意君傳

Sanfu huangtu 三輔黃圖
Shang 上
Shangguan, Empress 上官皇后 (d. 37 BCE)
Shangguan Wu 上官嫵
shangjiarenzi 上家人子
Shangshu 尚書
shaoshangzao 少上造
shaoshi 少使
Shen Jiji 沈既濟 (ca. 750–ca. 797)
Shi Zihui, Marquis of Jiangling 將陵侯史子回
Shiguo chunqiu 十國春秋
Shiji 史記
Shijing 詩經
Shishuo xinyu 世說新語
Shiyi ji 拾遺記
Shuihu zhuan 水滸傳
Shuijing zhu 水經注
Shun 舜
shunchang 順常
Shuofu 說郛
Shuyinglou mingshu baiyong 疏影樓名姝百詠

Sima Qian 司馬遷 (ca. 145–86 BCE)
Sima Xiangru 司馬相如 (ca. 179–117 BCE)
siyi 司帟
Song, Emperor Huizong of 宋徽宗 (r. 1110–1126)
Song, Empress 宋皇后 (d. 178 CE)
Song Yu 宋玉 (fl. 298–263 BCE)
Songshu 宋書
Soushen ji 搜神記
Su E 蘇鄂 (*jinshi* 886)
Su Shi 蘇軾 (1037–1101)
Sui, Emperor Wen of 隋文帝 (r. 581–604)
Sui, Emperor Yang of 隋煬帝 (r. 604–618)
Sui Yangdi yanshi 隋煬帝艷史
Suishu 隋書
Sui-Tang yanyi 隋唐演義
Sun Quan, Emperor Da of Wu 吳大帝孫權 (r. 229–252)
Sun Xingyan 孫星衍 (1753–1818)
Sunü jing 素女經

taihuang taihou 太皇太后
Taiyi Pool 太液池
Tang, Dowager Queen (formerly Tang Bazi) 唐太后
Tang, Emperor Gaozong of 唐高宗 (r. 649–683)
Tang, Emperor Taizong of 唐太宗 (r. 626–649)
Tang, Emperor Xuanzong of 唐玄宗 (r. 721–756)
Tang, Emperor Yizong of 唐懿宗 (r. 859–873)
Tang Bazi 唐八子
Tangyi 堂邑
Tao Zongyi 陶宗儀 (1329–1410)
Taozhu xinlu 陶朱新錄
Tian E 田娥
Tianmen 天門
Tianming 天命
Tianzi 天子

Tianzi zuo min fumu, yiwei Tianxia wang 天子作民父母, 以爲天下王
Ting zhumu zhi ling, nüzi yong guo . . . ke wang ye 聽主母之令, 女子用國 . . . 可亡也
"Tongchang gongzhu waizhuan" 同昌公主外傳
tongxiang 通香
tongxiang hupi tanxiang yi zuo 通香虎皮檀象一座

"Waiqi zhuan" 外戚傳
waizhuan 外傳
Wang Ding 王鼎 (d. 1106 CE)
Wang Han 王翰 (fl. early eighth century CE)
Wang Jia 王嘉 (d. 390 CE)
Wang Jian 王建 (ca. 751–ca. 830)
Wang Renpei 王紉佩 (d. 1891 CE)
Wang Renyu 王仁裕 (880–956)
Wang Shizhen 王世貞 (1526–1590)
Wang Yunxiu 王韞秀 (d. 777 CE)
Wang Zhaoyun 王朝雲 (1062–1095)
Wang Zhengjun, Dowager Empress 王政君 (71 BCE–13 CE)
"Wang Zinian *Shiyi ji*" 王子年拾遺記
"Wangzheng" 亡徵
Wanyan Tinglu 完顏廷璐 (d. 1820 CE)
Wei 尾
Wei, Emperor Xiaowen of 魏孝文帝 (r. 471–499)
Wei, Princess Wenyi of the State of 衛國文懿公主 (849–870)
Wei Baoheng 韋保衡 (d. 873 CE)
Wei Hong 衛宏 (fl. 25–57 CE)
wei Jiaofang 爲椒房
Wei Qing 衛青 (d. 106 BCE)
wei Tianxia mu 爲天下母
Wei Xiang 魏相 (d. 59 BCE)
Wei Zhao 韋昭 (201–273)
Wei Zifu (Empress) 衛子夫 (d. 91 BCE)
Weiyang, Palace 未央宮
Weizhi 魏志
Wen Zhengming 文徵明 (1470–1559)
Wenrou Xiang 溫柔鄉
Wu 吳
Wu Jun 吳均 (469–520)
Wu Renchen 吳任臣 (ca. 1628–ca. 1689)
Wu Zetian, Emperor 武則天 (r. 690–705)
Wuchao xiaoshuo daguan 五朝小說大觀
wudafu 五大夫
wuguan 五官
wujuan 無涓
wuming 五明
Wusun, king of 烏孫王
wuzhu 巫祝

"Xia" 夏
Xiahou Sheng 夏侯勝
Xian, Lady 顯 (d. 66 BCE)
xianfu 賢婦
Xiang Yu 項羽 (232–202 BCE)
Xiao, Empress 蕭皇后 (d. 648 CE)
Xiao Ben 蕭賁 (d. 549 CE)
Xiao Fei 蕭妃
Xiao Guanyin (Empress) 蕭觀音 (1040–1075)
Xiao Luan, Emperor Ming of Southern Qi 南齊明帝蕭鸞 (r. 494–498)
Xiao Qi 蕭綺
Xiao Yi, Emperor Yuan of Liang 梁元帝蕭繹 (r. 552–555)
Xiaocheng, Empress (Zhao Feiyan) 孝成皇后 (d. 1 BCE)
Xiaocheng Zhao huanghou zhuan 孝成趙皇后傳
Xiaojun 小君
Xiaoyao gong 逍遙宮
"Xidu fu" 西都賦
Xie An 謝安 (320–385)
xielü duwei 協律都尉
xielü sheren 協律舍人
"Xijing fu" 西京賦
Xijing zaji 西京雜記
Ximen Qing 西門慶
Xin Tangshu 新唐書
xing 幸

xing'e 娙娥
xiongluqi 雄麝臍
Xu, Empress 許皇后 (d. 8 BCE)
Xu Fu 許負
Xu Jia 許嘉
Xu Lai 徐來
Xu Lienü zhuan 續列女傳
Xu Meiren 許美人
Xu Mi 許孃
Xu Pingjun (Empress) 許平君 (89–71 BCE)
Xu Tong 徐熥 (1561–1599)
Xu Yong 許永
Xu Zhaopei 徐昭佩 (d. 549 CE)
Xuan, Dowager Queen (formerly Mi Bazi) 宣太后
Xue Zong 薛綜 (d. 243 CE)
Xun Xu 荀勖 (d. 289 CE)

Yan Chifeng 燕赤鳳
Yan Ji (Empress) 閻姬 (d. 126 CE)
Yan Shigu 顏師古 (581–645)
yang 養
Yang Shen 楊慎 (1488–1559)
Yang Taizhen waizhuan 楊太真外傳
Yang Xiong 楊雄 (52 BCE–18 CE)
Yang'a, Princess of 陽阿公主
yanjing 燕精
Yanyansheng 艷艷生
Yanyi bian 艷異編
Yao Mian 姚勉 (1216–1262)
Yelü Hongji, Emperor Daozong of Liao 遼道宗耶律洪基 (r. 1055–1101)
Yelü Yixin 耶律乙辛 (d. 1083 CE)
yemingzhu 夜明珠
yeshi 野史
Yeting 掖庭
yezhe 夜者
Yi 易
yi shou yong ji 以手拥髻
Yi Zhoushu 逸周書
Yijun 宜君
yin 淫
Yin, Empress 陰皇后 (d. ca. 102 CE)
Yin Feng 陰豐 (d. 59 CE)
Yin Lihua (Empress) 陰麗華 (5–64 CE)
yinfu 淫婦
Ying Shao 應劭 (140–206)
Yizhu 宜主
"Yongyu" 詠浴
You, Empress 幽皇后 (d. 499 CE)
you beng 幽崩
you si 憂死
youshuzhang 右庶長
Yu Fei meishi 玉妃媚史
Yu Tongzhi 虞通之
Yu Xin 庾信 (513–581)
Yuan, Emperor Huizong of 元惠宗 (r. 1333–1368)
Yuan, Emperor Wuzong of 元武宗 (r. 1307–1311)
Yuan Shao 袁紹 (d. 202 CE)
Yuan Shu 袁術 (d. 199 CE)
Yuan Xiang, King Ping of Beihai 北海平王元詳 (476–504)
Yuan Xiaoyou 元孝友 (d. 551 CE)
Yuan Zai 元載 (713–777)
Yuanshi yeting ji 元氏掖庭記
Yuantiao Guan 遠條館
Yuanyang Dian 鴛鴦殿
"Yuchi bei" 尉遲杯
Yue Shi 樂史 (930–1007)
Yulin 羽林
yuling 娛靈
Yun Zhu 惲珠 (1771–1833)
Yunxian zaji 雲仙雜記
yunyu 雲雨
yuyun 雨雲

zai Jiaofang 在椒房
"Zan Zhao Zhige suozang si meiren hua" 贊趙直閣所藏四美人畫
Zeng Zao 曾慥 (d. 1155/1164)
Zhang, Empress 張皇后 (d. 163 BCE)
Zhang Fang, Marquis of Fuping 富平侯張放
Zhang Heng 張衡 (78–139)
Zhang Jianzhi 張柬之 (625–706)

Zhang Nie 張嵲 (1096–1148)
Zhang Puhui 張普惠 (467–525)
Zhang Xiaojie 張孝杰 (*jinshi* 1055)
Zhang Yan 張炎 (1248–1320?)
Zhang Yuniang 張玉娘 (1250–1277)
Zhao "Feiyan" 趙飛燕 (d. 1 BCE)
Zhao Feiyan biezhuan 趙飛燕別傳
Zhao Feiyan Hede biezhuan 趙飛燕合德別傳
"Zhao Feiyan liuxian qun" 趙飛燕留仙裙
"Zhao Feiyan sitong Chifeng" 趙飛燕私通赤鳳
Zhao Feiyan waizhuan 趙飛燕外傳
"*Zhao Feiyan waizhuan* chengshu ji banben chuancheng bijiao yanjiu" 趙飛燕外傳成書及版本傳承比較研究
Zhao Guanghan 趙廣漢 (d. 67 BCE)
Zhao Hede 趙合德
Zhao Hede you Xinchouji 趙合德有欣愁髻
Zhao Lin 趙臨
Zhao Weiyi 趙惟一 (d. 1075 CE)
Zhao "Zhaoyi" 趙昭儀 (d. 7 BCE)
Zhaohou waizhuan 趙后外傳
Zhaohou yishi 趙后遺事
Zhaoyang Dian 昭陽殿
Zhaoyang qushi 昭陽趣史
Zhaoyang yanshi 昭陽艷史
zhaoyi 昭儀
Zheng, Empress 鄭皇后 (1079–1139)
zheng yue 正樂
Zhenla 真臘
zhi 治
zhiguai 志怪
Zhishi 織室
zhiwen 治問
Zhizhai shulu jieti 直齋書錄解題
Zhong buneng shen 終不能娠
zhonggeng 中更
Zhongguo Jiben Guji Ku 中國基本古籍庫
Zhongguo jinhui xiaoshuo baibu 中國禁毀小說百部
zhongjiarenzi 中家人子
"Zhongsi" 螽斯
zhongwei 中尉
Zhou, Duke of 周公
zhu 誅
zhuanfang duji 專房妒忌
Zhuangzi 莊子
zhuhouwang 諸侯王
Zhuo Wenjun 卓文君
Zhuozhang, River 濁漳水
Zhushu jinian 竹書紀年
"Zidao fu" 自悼賦
ziluo 紫羅
Zuo Fen 左芬 (ca. 255–300)
zuogeng 左更
zuoshuzhang 左庶長

NOTES

INTRODUCTION

1 In addition to references in historical works, the Pepper Chamber is mentioned in Han dynasty literature, such as "Rhapsody on the Western Capital" (Xidu fu) by Ban Gu (32–92 CE); see *Wenxuan*, 5. For an overview of the literary evidence about this building, see Chen Caixun and Lü Jingfen, "Shuo Jiaofang."

2 *Hou Hanshu*, 56:1832 and 63:2075, respectively.

3 *Sanfu huangtu jiaoshi*, 163. The historicity of the account given in *Yellow Plans of the Three Capital Regions* is demonstrated by the archaeological excavations that have been carried out within the Weiyang Palace complex. Although the form of the buildings is quite different, the layout of the imperial apartments in the Han dynasty, including the Pepper Chamber, followed Qin dynasty norms; see Liu Qingzhu, "Han Chang'ancheng de kaogu faxian," 10.

4 The reference here to *Book of Songs* quotes the first line in the first verse of a song titled "Pepper Husks" (Jiaoliao):

> The fruit of the pepper plant grow lushly and fill a *sheng*-measure.
> That young man is handsome and great beyond compare.
> Oh, how lovely is the pepper plant, and how luxuriant its shoots!

See *Mao Shi zhengyi*, 385–87 ["Jiaoliao"]. This translation of the title of the song follows the reading suggested by the Qing dynasty scholar Ma Ruichen (1782–1853), that the character *liao* should be understood as a variant for *qiu*, meaning the husk of a Sichuan peppercorn; see Ma Ruichen, *Mao Shi zhuanjian tongshi*, 343 ["Jiaoliao"].

5 *Hanguan yi*, 174. All translations included in this book are my own, unless otherwise noted.

6 Traditionally, Chinese scholars have indeed made this assumption; see, for example, Wang Yinglin, *Yuhai*, 156:16a–16b.

7 Xue Ruisheng, *Yuezhang ji jiaozhu*, 64. For an alternative translation of the whole song, see Lam, "A Reconsideration of Liu Yong," 14–15.

8 The interpretation of these texts given here is strongly influenced by Darnton, *The Forbidden Best-Sellers of Pre-revolutionary France* and *The Corpus of Clandestine Literature in France*. His contention that erotic writings that allow women agency and self-determination are intrinsically radical, even if they contain no other overt political message, provides an important way to understand Chinese literature of this kind.

9 See, for example, Love, *English Clandestine Satire*; Rabb, *Satire and Secrecy in English Literature*; and Kaplan, *The Culture of Slander in Early Modern England*.

10 Some five thousand *mazarinades* survive to the present day; see Carrier, *Les mazarinades*, vol. 1, *La conquête de l'opinion*, and vol. 2, *Les hommes du livre*. See also Jouhaud, *Mazarinades*. Although numerous satirical writings aimed at Madame de Pompadour are known to have been produced, these have not been the subject of any focused academic research.

11 The studies published in the Palgrave Macmillan series Queenship and Power have been particularly useful for understanding the forces influencing representations of Zhao Feiyan and other Chinese empresses; in addition, writings on the harem from other cultures provide a useful comparison; see, for example, Booth, *Harem Histories*; Peirce, *The Imperial Harem*; and Gupta, *Mahal*.

12 Exactly how this control of information was achieved is not clear. An interesting comparison can be made with the Tokugawa shoguns' Rear Palace in the period from 1600 to 1868: staffed entirely by literate women, they all signed confidentiality agreements when they first entered service. Furthermore, high-ranking palace women with access to privileged information were contractually obliged to serve the regime for life; see Seigle and Chance, Ōoku, 26–28.

CHAPTER ONE: THE EMPRESS IN THE PEPPER CHAMBER

1 *Guanzi jiaozhu*, 53 ["Quanxiu"].

2 *Han Feizi jishi*, 269 ["Wangzheng"].

3 *Chunqiu Gongyang zhuan zhushu*, 13 [Yin 1]; and *Chunqiu fanlu yizheng*, 273 ["Guande"].

4 This reason extends the argument found in McMahon, *Women Shall Not Rule*, 37–38. For a discussion of the role of mother and stepmother regents in establishing the authority of their offspring, see Woodacre and Fleiner, *Royal Mothers and Their Ruling Children*.

5 *Shiji*, 49:1967–86; *Hanshu*, 97A–97B:3933–4012.

6 *Hou Hanshu*, 10A–10B:397–466. According to the official history of the Eastern Han dynasty, of fifteen empresses, only five died by violence (*you si* or *you beng*). However, unlike in the Western Han dynasty, when senior palace women seem

to have been imprisoned and died at a wide variety of locations, in the Eastern Han dynasty the deaths of empresses were concentrated in the "Drying Room" (Baoshi), an area within the Rear Palace otherwise used for processing textiles.

7 The origins of this term are extremely obscure and it has been the subject of no academic research, in spite of the importance of this concept within East Asian political history. The title of "Mother of the Country" (Guomu) is not found in ancient Chinese philosophy and seems to have developed only in the post–Han dynasty period. One of the earliest surviving references to the importance of an empress as "Mother of the Country" is found in the biography of Zhang Puhui (467–525), a man with a considerable interest in the social roles played by elite women, in the official history of the Wei dynasty; see *Weishu*, 78:1731. By the Tang dynasty, certain rituals (particularly those related to sericulture) had become strongly associated with the role of "Mother of the Country"; see *Jiu Tangshu*, 51:2173.

8 The term *mu yi* was also used to express the ideal relationship between a mother and her children. The locus classicus of this meaning is thought to be the chapter on maternal role models in *Biographies of Exemplary Women* (Lienü zhuan) by the scholar Liu Xiang (77–6 BCE); see *Lienü zhuan buzhu*, 1–46 ["Mu yi"].

9 For women outside the Rear Palace, social motherhood was invested in the principal wife, at the expense of biological mothers; see Bray, *Technology and Gender*, 353. Within the palace, biological mothers would normally retain custody of their children, but the empress might nevertheless claim motherhood over the heir to the throne.

10 *Hanshu*, 97A:3966.

11 *Hanshu*, 27A:1322.

12 *Shangshu zhengyi*, 112 ["Hongfan"]. The same idea is also mentioned in other texts; see, for example, *Mozi xiangu*, 60 ["Shangxian zhong"]; and *Yi Zhoushu huijiao jizhu*, 9:1067 ["Rui Liangfu jie"].

13 Many ancient bronzes record that the Son of Heaven was a standard Zhou dynasty designation for the monarch; see, for example, Shirakawa Shizuka, *Kinbun tsūshaku*, 11:273 ["Qiu Wei *gui*"] and 15:335 ["Shi Qiang *pan*"].

14 Loewe, *The Men Who Governed Han China*, 372, and *The Government of the Qin and Han Empires*, 11, 135. A similar position with respect to the position of the emperor and the state apparatus is also set out in Liu Zehua, Wang Maohe, and Wang Lanzhong, *Zhuanzhi quanli yu Zhongguo shehui*, 18; and Wan Changhua and Zhao Xingbin, *Qin-Han yilai jizeng xingzheng yanjiu*, 11–81.

15 Schwartz, "The Primacy of Political Order in East Asian Societies," argues that the Han emperor was not just the embodiment of political authority, but the focus of the spiritual-ethical authority of the entire society. The religious role of the monarch is described in Ching, "Son of Heaven." For a discussion of the ceremonial role of the Son of Heaven in rituals in which he "matched" (*pei*) Heaven, see Owen, "Reproduction in the *Shijing*," 305, 308.

16 Pines, "Subversion Unearthed," 161–64; and Allan, "Not the *Lun yu*."

17 *Liji zhengyi*, 1624 ["Hunyi"].

18 These rituals are described in *Lüshi chunqiu xin jiaoshi*, 64 ["Zhongchun"]; and *Liji zhengyi*, 474–75 ["Yueling"]. For a discussion of this fertility ceremony, see Bodde, *Festivals in Classical China*, 243–61.

19 These ceremonies are mentioned in *Hanshu*, 98:4030; and *Hanyi*, 218–19. See also Bodde, *Festivals in Classical China*, 263–72.

20 The terms in which Empress Song's transformation of the empire is described are identical to those employed elsewhere to describe the beneficent influence of the rule of the sage kings; see, for example, *Fengsu tongyi jiaozhu*, 10 ["Huangba"].

21 *Hou Hanshu*, 10B:448–49.

22 The Mandate of Heaven (Tianming or Daming) is also mentioned in a number of early bronze inscriptions; see, for example, Shirakawa Shizuka, *Kinbun tsūshaku*, 145:282 ["Guaibo *gui*"] and 30:647 ["Maogong *ding*"]. For studies of early articulations concerning the Mandate of Heaven, see, for example, Luo Xinhui, "Zhoudai tianming guannian de fazhan yu shanbian"; and Deng Peiling, *Tianming, guishen yu zhudao*, 30–48.

23 See *Hanshu*, 97A:3948 and 3968, respectively. The connection between the position of the empress and the Mandate of Heaven is discussed in Loewe, *The Men Who Governed Han China*, 438–51.

24 *Hou Hanshu*, 10B:454.

25 For a Han dynasty articulation of this idea, preserved in a memorial to the throne by Kuang Heng (fl. 50–33 BCE), see *Hanshu*, 81:3382.

26 *Chunqiu Guliang jingzhuan buzhu*, 195 [Zhuang 22].

27 Later dynasties used quite different principles from the Han for selecting an empress; see, for example, Cutter and Cromwell, *Empresses and Consorts*, for a detailed study of the principles underlying the appointment of empresses during the Three Kingdoms period (220–280 CE).

28 Exogamy might nevertheless result in close patterns of intermarriage through cross-cousin alliances; see K. C. Chang, *Art, Myth, and Ritual*, 30–32. Clan name exogamy continued to be extolled as normative marriage practice throughout the Han dynasty and beyond; see, for example, *Baihu tong shuzheng*, 477 ["Jiaqu"].

29 This idea is considered in Laynesmith, *The Last Medieval Queens*, 48–49.

30 *Hanshu*, 97A:3965.

31 Empress Wei Zifu's official biographies are given in *Shiji*, 49:1978–80; and *Hanshu*, 97A:3949–50. For studies of the witchcraft allegations that brought about her downfall, see Loewe, *Crisis and Conflict in Han China*, 37–90; and Liang Cai, *Witchcraft and the Rise of the First Confucian Empire*.

32 As a result of these complaints, Empress Xu's father received the honorific title of Lord of Changcheng; see *Hanshu*, 97A:3965.

33 *Hanshu*, 97B:3996.

34 This analysis follows the argument made by Taniguchi Yasuyo, "Kandai no kōgō ken" and "Kandai no Taigō rinchō," that the empress was ritually the most significant female figure in the empire, and this was converted into political power. Other senior palace women such as dowager empresses and grand dowager empresses should be understood as retaining authority from their previous position as empress.

35 Bray, *Technology and Gender*, 191–92; and Wu Fanglang, "Handai sizhiye yanjiu," 17–24.

36 This argument is based on the analysis found in Walthall, "Introducing Palace Women," in emphasizing the work performed by women recruited into the Rear Palace. For important studies of the various roles performed by palace women in later dynasties in China, see Chung, *Palace Women of the Northern Song*; Hsieh, "Empress' Grove" and "From Charwoman to Empress Dowager"; Soulliere, "Palace Women in the Ming Dynasty" and "Women in the Imperial Household."

37 This system was in constant evolution, with changes in the precise standing of each rank and their subsequent entitlements at various times throughout the Han dynasty; see Sun Wenbo, "Ershi deng jue queli."

38 This prescription is recorded in *Shiji*, 9:400; and *Hanshu* 18:678. In practice, however, there were a small number of kings within the borders of the Han empire who were not members of the Liu family, particularly in the early part of the dynasty.

39 Xu Fu's fortune-telling activities are described in a number of Han dynasty texts; see, for example, *Shiji*, 49:1970.

40 The official histories of the Han dynasty record a number of women who held the title of *furen*. In some cases, women who both held rank and were concubines of the emperor were designated by a double title: *furen* and their rank within the Rear Palace. This shows that a clear distinction was maintained between these groups, though one woman might be involved in both roles.

41 The title of *bazi*, or "consort of the eighth rank," was previously used in the Qin palace; on the appointment of King Xiaowen of Qin (r. 250 BCE), his mother, Tang Bazi, become Dowager Queen Tang; similarly the mother of King Zhaoxiang of Qin (r. 306–251 BCE), Mi Bazi (d. 265 BCE), was appointed Dowager Queen Xuan after her son came to the throne. See *Shiji*, 5:218 and 72:2323, respectively. Throughout Chinese history palace women were given ranks suggestive of an attractive appearance. It is only in the Tang dynasty that women working in the Rear Palace were temporarily given more formal, non-gender- or appearance-specific ranking nomenclature. See Jo-shui Chen, "Empress Wu and Proto-Feminist Sentiments."

42 *Shiji*, 49:1983–84, says: "In the time of Emperor Wu, he favored Consort Yin Jieyu. Consort Xing had the title *xing'e*, but everyone called her '*xinghe*.' A *xinghe*'s rank is comparable to that of an official with a salary of a full two thousand bushels of grain, a *ronghua*'s rank is comparable to that of an official with a salary of two thousand bushels of grain, while a *jieyu* is ranked like a *liehou*. It was quite common to see a *jieyu* be promoted to the position of empress." The origin of this name was apparently derived from Qin dialect; see *Shuowen jiezi zhu*, 624 ["Nübu"].

43 Women of *zhaoyi* and *jieyu* rank would thus have had salaries of ten thousand bushels of grain a year. It is known that salaries of government officials in the Han dynasty were calculated in bushels (*dan*) of grain, but were actually paid partly in coin; see Huang Huixian and Chen Feng, *Zhongguo fenglu zhidu shi*, 36–50.

44 *Hanshu*, 97A:3935. For an alternative translation of this passage, see McMahon, *Women Shall Not Rule*, 63. Titles in this book are all translated according to Hucker, *A Dictionary of Official Titles in Imperial China*.

45 *Hanshu*, 97B:4000.

46 *Hou Hanshu*, 10A:400.

47 *Hanguan jiuyi*, 44.

48 Li Yufang, "Han Chang'ancheng Weiyang gong de kaogu"; and Yang Hongxiu, *Gongdian kaogu tonglun*, 232.

49 *Hanguan jiuyi*, 44.

50 Zhu Ziyan, "Qin-Han hougong zhidu shulun." The political importance of women is also stressed in Nylan, "Golden Spindles and Axes"; and Gu Lihua, *Handai funü shenghuo qingtai*, 266.

51 This quotation is derived from the account of the investiture of Empress Song in 171 CE, attributed to the Han dynasty government official Cai Zhi; see *Hou Hanshu, zhi* 5:3121n3.

52 *Hou Hanshu*, 10A:421. The concept that the ritual position of empress should be considered equal to that of emperor is mentioned a number of times in Eastern Han dynasty texts; see, for example, *Hou Hanshu*, 56:1832; and *Dongguan Hanji jiaozhu*, 5:166.

53 Eisenberg, *Kingship in Early Medieval China*, 33.

54 As noted by Wang Zijin and Zhang Jing, *Zhongguo funü tongshi* (190), although this important role is not mentioned in prescriptive texts, there are sufficient records in historical texts to indicate this was an area of government in which these women were considered to have special rights.

55 The invention of palace poetry is usually ascribed to the Tang dynasty poet Wang Jian (ca. 751–ca. 830), who wrote a cycle of one hundred poems based on information gathered from a palace eunuch friend. See Chi Naipeng, *Wang Jian yanjiu conggao*, 89–90; and He Zhong, "Tangdai shiren Wang Jian."

56 The question of authenticity of experience, whereby even an emperor writing about his own harem was criticized for introducing a male perspective on a feminine space, is considered in Egan, "Huizong's Palace Poems."

57 In recent years, a number of important collections of these unorthodox histories have been produced; see *Zhongguo yeshi jicheng* Bianji Weiyuanhui and Sichuan Daxue Tushuguan, *Zhongguo yeshi jicheng*; and *Zhongguo yeshi jicheng xubian* Bianweihui and Sichuan Daxue Tushuguan, *Zhongguo yeshi jicheng xubian*. Although very popular with readers, such pseudo-historical writings have been the subject of little academic research. For pioneering studies, see Liao Ruiming, *Mingdai yeshi de fazhan yu tese*; Lei Ge, "Shi shi qiu zhu ye"; and Xia Zuen, "Qingdai yeshi de shixue diwei chutan." For English-language readers, virtually the only serious consideration of such texts can be found in McMahon, *Women Shall Not Rule* and *Celestial Women*.

58 For a history of book banning in China, which included prohibitions on numerous unorthodox histories, see An Pingqiu and Zhang Peiheng, *Zhongguo jinshu daguan*.

59 Anon., *Hangong chunse*, 1377–1423. This compilation has an introduction claiming the various short stories included therein date to the Eastern Jin dynasty, and were based upon Han tomb texts, but in fact the whole thing was written in the late Qing; see Xue Hongji, "Wan Qing 'Huanghou xilie xiaoshuo' shulüe."

60 Anon., *Han zashi mixin*. This novella is generally attributed to the Ming dynasty scholar Yang Shen (1488–1559), and was apparently intended to explain the early history of footbinding; see Ko, *Cinderella's Sisters*, 118–25.

61 *Songshu*, 14:337–39.

62 Anon., *Daye shiyi ji*. Victor Cunrui Xiong, *Historical Dictionary of Medieval China*, 129, dates this text to the Northern Song dynasty. For the official biography of Empress Xiao, which stresses her beauty, charm, and sweet nature, see *Suishu*, 36:1111–13. The most obvious conjunction between the fictional and the historical character is the expertise both show in divination techniques.

63 Anon., *Milou ji*, 2. This text, and other similar unorthodox histories about Emperor Yang, is now generally dated to the late Tang; see Li Jianguo, "*Daye shiyi ji* deng wu pian chuanqi."

64 For the importance of this text in the history of bondage literature in China, see Van Gulik, *Sexual Life in Ancient China*, 119–21. *Record of the Labyrinth* makes repeated reference to the way that the women were trapped within the maze building of the title, and then further imprisoned within cages for sexual purposes.

65 Qidong yeren, *Sui Yangdi yanshi*. Other Silk Pillow writings that tackle the subject of women resisting objectification include *The Tale of Green Pearl* (Lüzhu zhuan), attributed to the historian and scholar Yue Shi (930–1007), which describes its eponymous main character in the context of other palace women who committed suicide rather than be treated as trophies or conquests; see Yue Shi, *Lüzhu zhuan*, 1803–8.

66 Chu Renhuo, *Sui-Tang yanyi*, 28:654–78. The importance of the earlier text as a source for subsequent novels is discussed in Cai Qing, "*Sui-Tang yanyi* de chengshu guocheng xiaokao"; and Zeng Ya, "Lun Ming-Qing xiaoshuo zhong de Sui Yangdi." For *Romance of the Sui and Tang Dynasties* as a kind of anthology of earlier writings on Emperor Yang, see Hegel, *The Novel in Seventeenth-Century China*, 189–208, and "Aesthetics of the Seventeenth Century Suchou Elite."

67 For a complete translation and detailed study of this text, see Stone, *The Fountainhead of Chinese Erotica*.

68 Yue Shi, *Yang Taizhen waizhuan*. The first of these texts was sufficiently innocuous to remain legal, but the second, *The Seductive History of the Jade Consort*, was banned during the Qing dynasty, which seems to have resulted in the book disappearing completely. See Pan Jianguo, *Zhongguo gudai xiaoshuo shumu yanjiu*, 176–77, for a list of the "lascivious" (*yin*) books banned in 1837.

69 The dating and authenticity of *The Tale of the Plum-Blossom Consort* has been much contested; see, for example, Cheng Jie, "Guanyu Mei Fei yu *Mei Fei zhuan*"; Zhang Peiheng, "*Daye shiyi ji, Mei Fei zhuan* deng wupian chuanqi"; and Zhang Chengjian, "'Changhen ge' yu *Mei Fei zhuan*." *The Tale of the Plum-Blossom Consort* was transmitted into Korea and had an important influence on early fiction writing on the peninsula; see Yoo Hee Jun and Min Dong Kuan, "Munhak munhwa." For a complete translation of this novella, see Zhengjun Zhang, "Anonymous, 'The Tale of the Plum-Blossom Consort.'"

70 Anon., *Li Shishi waizhuan*, 1588.

71 Anon., *Da-Song Xuanhe yishi*, 50–66. For a translation of this text, see Hennessey, *Proclaiming Harmony.*

72 *Forgotten Events of the Xuanhe Reign Era of the Song Dynasty* has been much studied because of its relationship with *The Water Margin*; see, for example, Yu Xiaohong, "*Da-Song Xuanhe yishi* zhong de *Shuihu* renwu gushi"; Wei Huijuan, "*Da-Song Xuanhe yishi* he *Shuihu zhuan*"; and Zhang Xiuying and Huang Haiyan, "*Da-Song Xuanhe yishi* he *Shuihu zhuan* zhong de Yang Zhi."

73 Xu Tong, *Jinfeng waizhuan*, 231–40.

74 Wu Renchen, *Shiguo chunqiu*, 94:1360–62. The relationship between the erotic novel and the work of history is discussed in McMahon, *Women Shall Not Rule*, 251–55.

75 Tao Zongyi, *Yuanshi yeting ji*, 1849–61.

76 For an important group of writings recounting Empress Bumbutai's involvement in an incestuous relationship with her brother-in-law and their sexual orgies in Buddhist temples, see Zheng Chenggong and Zheng Jing, *Yanping erwang yiji.* Such texts are indicative of the political uses of Silk Pillow writings within the Southern Ming (1644–83) regime, to discredit the nascent Qing dynasty.

77 Lié Sou [Georges Soulié de Morant], *T'seu Hsi*; and Segalen, *René Leys.*

78 Backhouse, *Décadence Mandchoue.* Although this "memoir" was written in 1943, it was not published until 2011, thanks to Hugh Trevor-Roper's *Hermit of Peking*, which demonstrated that Backhouse's writings were largely the work of his fevered imagination. This group of foreign-language writings is considered in McMahon, *Celestial Women*, 201–31.

79 Ebrey, *Women and the Family in Chinese History*, 189.

CHAPTER TWO: *THE SCANDALOUS TALE OF ZHAO FEIYAN*

1 The importance of this novella as the very earliest surviving example of Chinese erotic fiction is stressed in Mao Dun, "Zhongguo wenxuenei de xingyu miaoxie," 22–23.

2 Li Jianguo, "'Chuanqi zhi shou,'" 40; Wu Liquan, *Zhongguo yanqing xiaoshuo shi*, 18; and On Shionoya, *Zhongguo wenxue gailun*, 340.

3 See, for example, Pak Kyehwa and Min Kwantong, "Chungguk munŏn sosŏrŭi kungnaeyuipkwa suyongyangsang"; and Min Kwantong, "Chungguk aejŏngnyu sosŏrŭi kungnaeyuipkwa p'anbonyŏn'gu."

4 Empress Xu and Ban Jieyu appear in the official history of the dynasty; see *Hanshu*, 97B:3973–83 and 3983–88, respectively. Empress Ma's great-aunts are mentioned in *Hou Hanshu*, 10A:408.

5 One of the few scholars writing about this text to have commented on the performative aspect is Xing Peishun, "*Zhao Feiyan waizhuan* tanlun," 61.

6 As with *The Scandalous Tale*, a number of expressions commonly used in the Chinese language are derived from this preface. Furthermore, the portrayal of the companionate relationship between Ling Xuan and his concubine would prove very influential in later literature; for a groundbreaking study of the use of this preface in the writings of the great Song poet Su Shi (1037–1101), see Wang Jiantang, "Su

Shi yu *Zhao Feiyan waizhuan*." Other references to this text in the writings of Su Shi are considered in Zhiyi Yang, *Dialectics of Spontaneity*, 35–36.

7 Li Jianguo, *Songdai zhiguai chuanqi xulu*, 161, is unusual for considering the preface attributed to Ling Xuan to be a forgery, but accepting the authenticity of those attributed to Huan Tan and Xun Xu, thus allowing him to accept the authenticity of *The Scandalous Tale* as a genuine Han dynasty text.

8 For an interesting analysis of this genre, with its emphasis on reckless spending by the female characters to compensate for circumscribed lives and concerns about male infidelity, see Scanlon, "What's an Acquisitive Girl to Do?" Meanwhile, Brown, "Sex 'n' Shopping," notes the significance of brand names and other such details in this kind of consumerist fiction: this being the very information found in *The Scandalous Tale* that we today lack the skills to interpret.

9 All references in this book to *The Scandalous Tale of Zhao Feiyan*, unless otherwise specified, refer to the text found in *The Complete Collection of Books from Various Collectanea* (Congshu jicheng) edition.

10 The title of *xielü sheren*—which literally means "retainer in charge of music," here translated as "orchestral master"—is not recorded in any other text. The office of *xielü duwei*, or "director of imperial music," which carried with it a salary of two thousand bushels of grain, was apparently originally created by Emperor Wu for the brother of one of his favorites: Li Yannian (d. 87 BCE); see *Shiji*, 49:1980; and *Hanshu*, 97A:3952. In *Hou Hanshu*, *zhi* 1:3000, the appointment of this official to check the orchestras performing for the emperor is considered part of the "rectification of music" (*zheng yue*) that took place in the reign of Emperor Wu. The author of *The Scandalous Tale* seems to be suggesting that the empress's grandfather held a similar kind of position, but at the lower level of a kingly household.

11 The only female member of the royal family of Jiangdu to have been recorded in Han dynasty texts is the daughter of Liu Jian, the second king: Liu Xijun (d. 101 BCE), who married the king of Wusun; see *Hanshu*, 96B:3903.

12 Zhao Man is an invented figure. The title here translated as "commandant" (*zhongwei*) referred to a senior military official responsible for defense in the service of a kingly house. In his partial translation of *The Scandalous Tale*, Lin Yutang, *The Wisdom of China and India*, 449, gives the commandant's personal name as Manman, probably as a result of misreading the unpunctuated text.

13 The term *xing*, here translated as "favored," is used throughout *The Scandalous Tale* in a sexual sense, though elsewhere it is applied to the relationship between men and women. It is quite possible that the reader is intended here to understand the relationship between Zhao Man and Feng Wanjin as a homosexual one. The motif of a homoerotic relationship leading to further sexual license between the man's lover and his wife or concubine would become a staple of later Chinese erotic fiction; see McMahon, "The Polyandrous Empress," 40.

14 To quote Vitiello, *The Libertine's Friend*, 2, on the perceived dangers of having male lovers in the household: "[Such] favorites might have the pernicious ambition of penetrating the women's quarters, and the women inhabiting them, under the nose of their legitimate men."

15 The personal name here attributed to Zhao Feiyan, Yizhu, literally means "appropriate to rule" and hence serves to presage her future greatness. Neither the personal name of the future empress nor that of her younger sister seems to have been recorded prior to *The Scandalous Tale*; however, many later texts refer specifically to Zhao "Hede."

16 The terms in which Zhao Feiyan's birth is described suggest that the author was attempting to link these events with the scandalous family background of an earlier entertainer turned empress: Wei Zifu. The biography of her half brother Wei Qing (d. 106 BCE) in *History of the Han Dynasty* states: "His father, Zheng Ji, . . . had an illicit sexual relationship with a maidservant in his master's household named Wei, and she gave birth to Qing. Qing had an older half brother, Wei Changjun, and half sister, Wei Zifu; Zifu went from the household of the Princess of Pingyang to be favored by Emperor Wu; therefore Qing adopted the surname Wei even though he had no claim upon it." See *Hanshu*, 55:2471. The similarities between this account and *The Scandalous Tale* are striking, and are unlikely to be coincidental.

17 Although this particular title is not mentioned elsewhere, Pengzu was commonly associated with texts detailing sexual arts. *Pengzu's Classic* (Pengzu jing) is mentioned in *The Master of Embracing Simplicity* (Baopuzi), and *Pengzu on Self-Cultivation* (Pengzu yangxing) appears in the catalogue of the imperial library in the Sui dynasty, preserved in the official history; see *Baopuzi neipian jiaoshi*, 333 ["Xialan"]; and *Suishu*, 34:1043, respectively.

18 The theme of a young girl obtaining an esoteric text that allows her to develop sexual techniques that give her strange powers is extremely ancient in China; the earliest known example is the story of Nü Wan (also occasionally given as Nü Ji), who is said to have learned her skills from a text titled *The Plain Girl's Classic* (Sunü jing), recorded in *Biographies of Exemplary Transcendents* (Liexian zhuan); see *Liexian zhuan jiaojian*, B:156.

19 As noted in Stone, *The Fountainhead of Chinese Erotica*, 91, the protagonists of Chinese erotic fiction were often portrayed as orphans, because this would imply a lack of proper guidance and moral control in their lives. In real life, Zhao Feiyan had not only her younger sister but also her father and two brothers living at the time she was introduced to court.

20 According to *Hanshu*, 97B:3989, Zhao Lin was the name of Empress Zhao's father. He was made Marquis of Chengyang in 16 BCE, with a view to facilitating his daughter's elevation to the position of empress. The introduction of this otherwise undeveloped and unnecessary character in *The Scandalous Tale* seems to be prompted by the need to include a father figure named Zhao Lin, presumably because some readers were aware of the existence of this historical individual.

21 Here, the Qing dynasty Wu family manuscript recension of the text in the collection of the National Library of China may make better sense: "Lin was delighted and loved her very much" (Lin yue ai zhi).

22 The author or authors of *The Scandalous Tale* appear to have imagined the Feathered Forest (Yulin) to be some kind of hunting park. This is not a mistake that could

have been made by a Han dynasty person, particularly not an official of the kind described in the preface. The Feathered Forest was in fact a division of the imperial guard, established by Emperor Wu in 104 BCE, staffed entirely by carefully selected men of good family; see *Hanshu*, 19A:727 and 28B:1644. Yang Hongnian, "Huben Yulin," 130–46, gives a detailed account of what is known of the workings of this elite unit.

23 The locus classicus of the term here translated as "to be exposed to the elements" (*luli*) seems to be *Sanguo zhi*, 55:1290.

24 The Chengguang Palace is mentioned in a number of Han dynasty historical texts; see, for example, *Lienü zhuan buzhu*, 382; and *Hanshu*, 99C:4162. There is also a reference to Chengguang in "Rhapsody on the Western Capital" (Xijing fu) by the Eastern Han dynasty poet Zhang Heng (78–139); this is glossed in the commentary by Xue Zong (d. 243 CE) as meaning the Chengguang Tower; see *Wenxuan*, 21. The title of *siyi*, which seems to mean something like "directress of tapestries," is not recorded in any ancient text.

25 This reference to Lady Cao is impossible to understand, since it is not at all clear which "Lady Cao" Emperor Cheng means to refer to.

26 In other early imperial-era descriptions of femme fatales, there are similar accounts of their abilities to control the internal workings of their bodies; see, for example, *Lienü zhuan buzhu*, 306 ["Niebi"]. This account of Empress Zhao seems to draw on something of the same idea. In the Ming dynasty, a later reworking of *The Scandalous Tale* titled *The Remarkable History of the Zhaoyang Palace* (Zhaoyang qushi) associates her ability to "control her breathing and allow her *qi* to circulate freely" with this kind of muscle control; see Guhang Yanyansheng, *Zhaoyang qushi*, 150.

27 The Mandarin Ducks Hall (Yuanyang Dian) is known to have been one building within the Weiyang Palace complex; see *Wenxuan*, 5 ["Xidu fu"]. According to *Sanfu huangtu jiaoshi*, 163, this building was one of eight constructed in the Rear Palace by Emperor Wu of Han. Thanks to a reference to mandarin ducks in *Book of Songs*, they became a popular symbol of marital harmony; see *Mao Shi zhengyi*, 864–67 ["Yuanyang"].

28 According to *Xijing zaji jiaozhu*, 82, Zhuo Wenjun, the wife of the famous poet Sima Xiangru (ca. 179–117 BCE), had "eyebrows as lovely as looking at distant hills" (*meise ru wang yuan shan*); this is thought to be the origin of this expression.

29 According to *Xijing zaji jiaozhu*, 39, this hall was part of the complex known as the Lateral Courts, where palace women below the rank of *jieyu* resided.

30 The Hall of Spreading Perfume (Pixiang Dian) is known to have been the name of one part of the Rear Palace complex at the Weiyang Palace; see, for example, *Sanfu huangtu jiaoshi*, 163; and *Wenxuan*, 5 ["Xidu fu"].

31 Here "Fire" represents the Han dynasty. It is often stated that the link between the element and the dynasty was an Eastern Han dynasty development, and therefore this proves that *The Scandalous Tale* cannot be a Western Han dynasty text; see, for example, Li Jianguo, "'Chuanqi zhi shou,'" 34; and Xing Peishun, "*Zhao Feiyan waizhuan* tanlun," 59. However, as noted by Yang Quan, *Xin wude lilun yu*

Liang-Han zhengzhi, 139–45, this is not actually correct—the link between the element "Fire" and the authority of the Han dynasty was first proposed by the erudite Liu Xiang in the reign of Emperor Cheng.

32 The name of the palace here given as Empress Zhao Feiyan's residence—Extending Shoots House (Yuantiao Guan)—is derived from a quotation from *Book of Songs* that concerns the Sichuan pepper plant, a symbol of fertility; see *Mao Shi zhengyi*, 386 ["Jiaoliao"].

33 Until the invention of aniline dyes in the mid-nineteenth century, purple was a notoriously costly color to produce, derived as it was from murex shells. For the use of this kind of dye in Tang dynasty China, see Schafer, *The Golden Peaches of Samarkand*, 211. The reference to the color is probably given here to emphasize the associated expense.

34 The translation here follows the Wu family manuscript recension of the text. The term *chijin*, which literally means "red metal," was often used in ancient Chinese texts to refer to copper; see, for example, *Shiji*, 30:1426; and *Hanshu*, 24B:1163. These texts make it quite clear that copper was considered inferior to both gold and silver. Hence, *chijin* has here been translated in another meaning, "gold," since the emphasis in every account of imperial spending in this text is on luxurious extravagance.

35 The Realm of White Clouds (Baiyun Xiang) as the term denoting the abode of immortals is originally derived from the line "[The sage] rides on white clouds to reach the realm of the gods" in *Book of Master Zhuang* (Zhuangzi); see *Zhuangzi jishi*, 421 ["Tiandi"].

36 In the late Eastern Han dynasty, broad sleeves were worn by elite women as a sign of their wealth and status; see, for example, *Yutai xinyong jianzhu*, 27 ["Hanshi tongyao ge"]. Whether this fashion can be projected back two hundred years to the court of Emperor Cheng is unclear.

37 "Five Skandhas" is a term derived from Buddhist thought, referring to the five senses—clinging to these forms of perception causes suffering. The use of this clearly Buddhist term indicates that this section of the text cannot date to the Western Han dynasty. *Tongxiang*, which literally means "penetrating fragrance," is a perfumery term of unknown meaning, which probably refers to some kind of scented wood.

38 This type of incense seems to have been an invention of the author. However, the idea that the gods were to be summoned by scent is extremely ancient in China, figuring in many descriptions of sacrifice; see, for example, *Liji zhengyi*, 952 ["Jiao tesheng"]. The idea that scent could be used as a means to communicate with deities resulted in the development of sacrifices of scent; see Zhang Xiuhua, "Cong jinwen cailiao kan yin chai liao."

39 This scent is not mentioned in any other early or medieval text.

40 The idea that elite women were recognizable by the scents they used was often mentioned in medieval Chinese literature, and occasionally projected back to an earlier period, such as the Han dynasty. The representation of the empress and the *zhaoyi*'s personal scents links them with other romantic figures such

as Consort Li, the beloved of Emperor Wu of Han. According to *Records Gleaned from Lost Works*, a compendium of historical stories and myths "lost" from other texts compiled by Wang Jia (d. 390 CE), Emperor Wu's mourning for his favorite concubine was rendered much more painful by a powerful olfactory memory: "[The emperor] was asleep and dreamed that Consort Li gave him some *hengwu* aromatic. His Majesty woke up in alarm and the scent still perfumed his clothes and bedding, and for more than a month it did not disappear." *Shiyi ji yizhu*, 5:140.

41 The term here translated as "musk" is *xiongluqi*, which literally means "male musk deer's navel." The origins of this extremely odd term are most likely derived from Sanskrit, where "deer's navel" (*mṛganābhi*) is a standard synonym for "musk"; see McHugh, *Sandalwood and Carrion*, 174.

42 Here the reading given in the Wu family manuscript recension of the text is perhaps preferable: "In the end she never became pregnant" (Zhong buneng shen).

43 The earliest reference to the state of Zhenla in Chinese literature is found in the *Suishu*, 82:1835–37. This kingdom is said to have originally been a subordinate state to Funan, based in the Mekong delta region, but to have eventually achieved independence and then conquered Funan in approximately 550 CE. As noted by Chen Lijun, "*Shiyi ji* xinci xinyi kaoshi," 47, the term "night-shining pearl" (*yemingzhu*) is not attested to in Chinese literature prior to the medieval period—in fact the first known reference is in *Records Gleaned from Lost Works* by Wang Jia.

44 However the list is counted up (either by the number of different types of things mentioned or by the total number of objects), there are not twenty-six items. It is likely the text is in some way corrupt at this point.

45 The term here translated as "clove" is *hanxiang*, which literally means "aromatic that is held in the mouth." This name for cloves (*Syzygium aromaticum*) is derived from a story attributed to *Ceremonial Regulations for Han Dynasty Officials*, which describes how Emperor Huan gave his officials cloves when they suffered from bad breath. See *Taiping yulan*, 981:6b. This quotation was incorporated into the text of *Ceremonial Regulations for Han Dynasty Officials* when it was recompiled from quotations by the Qing dynasty scholar Sun Xingyan (1753–1818); see *Hanguan yi*, 135–36.

46 In the original text it says that one item on the gift list was "One sandalwood statue [ornamented with] *tongxiang*-scented tiger-skin." It is very difficult to imagine what this might look like, and by analogy with the previous item, it is most likely that the *tongxiang*-scented tiger-skin item was a rug, and the sandalwood statue is therefore an entirely different object. It may be that the reason there is not the correct number of items in the list of objects presented to Empress Zhao is because textual loss has occurred at this point.

47 Sandalwood images were specifically associated with Buddhism, since according to legend, one of the early patrons of the Buddha had a sandalwood statue made to cheer him up when the Buddha was temporarily absent—such stories would have an enormous influence on Chinese material culture from the medieval period onward; see Kieschnick, *The Impact of Buddhism on Chinese Material*

Culture, 53. It is not possible that such an object could exist in the Western Han dynasty, before the arrival of Buddhism in China.

48 Ambergris is an intensely scented substance derived from the intestinal tracts of whales. Extremely soft, it melts at approximately 62 degrees Celsius. The task of carving it would be extremely delicate, but not impossible; the New York Metropolitan Museum of Art has an extraordinary sixteenth-century Italian pendant made of carved ambergris ornamented with gold; see McConnell, *Metropolitan Jewelry*, 40. Schafer, *The Golden Peaches of Samarkand*, 174, suggests that this substance was not imported into China until the late Tang dynasty.

49 Prior to the Sui-Tang period, all Chinese mirrors were either round or square. Mirrors of the type described here, in the shape of a flower, do not appear to have been produced before the Tang. Interestingly, reference works show that such Tang floral mirrors usually had even numbers of "petals": four, six, or eight lobes being the most common; see, for example, Shanghai Bowuguan, *Lianxing shenye, yingzhi lianggong*, 213–87; and Hua Guangpu, *Zhongguo lidai tongjing mulu*, 202–62. Asymmetric mirrors do not seem to have been popular at all.

50 As noted by Yang Gang, "Xian-Qin zhi Qin-Han de xunxiang xisu wenhua," 176, although there are a number of early references in literature that may refer to incense burners designed to perfume bedding, excavated examples of this type of object date only to the Tang dynasty.

51 In the Han dynasty, Yizhou Commandery covered a large area of what is today Shaanxi, Sichuan, Yunnan, and Guizhou Provinces. According to *Hanshu*, 28A:1601, it had a population of 81,946 households, consisting of a total of 580,463 individuals. The idea that the entire tax revenues of such a vast area for three years could be spent on ornaments for the palace of a court favorite is intended to stress Emperor Cheng's extravagance and besotted love.

52 According to *Shiji*, 28:1402, this pool was constructed at the Jianzhang Palace, with islands named after the abode of the immortals in its midst, ornamented with sculptures of turtles and fish. *Sanfu huangtu jiaoshi*, 261, quoting a lost text named *A Record of Passes in the Capital Region* (Guanfu ji), thought to be a mistake for *A Record of the Lands inside the Passes* (Guanzhong ji), also mentions sculptures of whales and fish, stating that the Taiyi Pool was designed to represent the North Sea. The accuracy of this description can be seen by the excavation of a 4.9-meter-long stone sculpture of just such a fish; see Hei Guang, "Xi'an Han Taiyichi chutu yijian juxing shiyu."

53 Yingzhou is the name of one of the islands on which immortals dwell; see, for example, *Liezi jishi*, 151 ["Tangwen"]; and *Shiji*, 6:247. In the Tang dynasty, when Emperor Taizong (r. 626–649) had images of famous scholars produced to hang in his Hall of Worthies, this was referred to as "Ascending to the Immortals' Realm" (*deng Yingzhou*); see *Jiu Tangshu*, 72:2583; and *Xin Tangshu*, 102:3977. This usage of the term would have rendered it familiar to the Tang dynasty educated elite.

54 The kingdom of Nanyue was destroyed by the forces of Emperor Wu of Han in 111 BCE; see *Shiji*, 113:2975–76. However, this term does seem to have continued to serve as a useful general designation for the far south at least into the Tang dynasty.

55 This tune is recorded in a number of accounts of early music for the *qin*; see, for example, the list given in *Chuxue ji*, 16:386.

56 As it stands, the text at this point does not make sense without some reference to an attempt by the empress to throw herself from the tower, thus tearing her skirts. It is possible that this omission, which is common to all extant versions of *The Scandalous Tale*, and all known quotations of this section, is indicative of textual loss.

57 There is a variant reported in some Song dynasty collectanea for these two lines, where they are replaced by the line "The Emperor ordered his entourage to grab hold of her skirts" (Di ling zuoyou chi qi qun); see, for example, Zhu Shengfei, *Ganzhu ji*, 1:16b; and Zhu Mu, *Gujin shiwen leiju*, 21:6b.

58 Wang Xuxiao, "Handai richang fushi yanjiu," 8, uncritically taking this text as evidence of Han dynasty high fashion, suggests that when Feng Wufang saved the empress from falling, her skirt was ripped short, and this was the origin of this style of short pleated skirts.

59 The name of this residence seems to be an invention of the author, since no such place is recorded in any description of the palaces of the Western Han capital.

60 The name of this chamber is not recorded elsewhere. However, the practice of bathing in perfumed waters is extremely ancient in China; see *Chuci buzhu*, 57 ["Yunzhong jun"]; see also *Da Dai Liji huijiao jizhu*, 257 ["Xia xiaozheng"]. For a study of this practice, see Yang Zhishui, "Lantang yu xiangshui."

61 This reference associates this gate with the Jade-Disc Gate (Bimen) constructed by Emperor Wu of Han at the Jianzhang Palace with a view to enticing immortals to visit him. This structure is mentioned in *Shiji*, 12:482; and *Hanshu*, 28:1402. For a study of this gate and its influence on Han dynasty representations of the Gate of Heaven (Tianmen), see Tseng, *Picturing Heaven in Early China*, 206–11.

62 The name of this people seems to be an invention of the author of *The Scandalous Tale*. It does not appear to be recorded elsewhere.

63 According to *Records of Searching for Immortals* (Soushen ji), attributed to the Jin dynasty scholar Gan Bao (286–336): "On the fifteenth day of the tenth lunar month, everyone went to the Lingnü Temple. . . . They played the flute and strummed the zither, singing the song 'Supremely Numinous.' Then they marched shoulder to shoulder with one another, stamping the ground to mark time, while singing 'The Arrival of the Red Phoenix.'" See *Soushen ji jiaozhu*, 2:16. A very similar account is also given in *Xijing zaji jiaozhu*, 138. The crucial distinction seems to be in the dating: *The Scandalous Tale* and *Miscellaneous Records of the Western Capital* both give the date of this festival as the fifth day of the tenth lunar month; *Records of Searching for Immortals* gives it as the fifteenth day.

64 The title *guifei*, or "honored consort," was first coined by Liu Jun, Emperor Xiaowu of the Liu-Song dynasty (r. 453–464); see *Songshu*, 41:1269. As with the Han dynasty title of *zhaoyi*, it refers to the most senior of the emperor's consorts, after the empress herself. The appearance of this title in a text that otherwise preserves Han dynasty usage is clear evidence of later rewriting or interpolation.

65 "*Shenxu* paste" (*shenxujiao* 脋岫膠) is described here as an aphrodisiac substance of some kind. This is undoubtedly the source of inspiration for the *shenxu jiao*

慎卹膠 mentioned in the late Tang dynasty collection of short stories and anecdotes titled *Stories Surviving from the Kaiyuan and Tianbao Reign Eras, 713–741 and 742–756* (Kaiyuan Tianbao yishi) by Wang Renyu (880–956): "An Lushan [ca. 703–757] once presented one hundred pills of 'Assisting Romance' floral aromatic to His Majesty. They were about the size of a grain of rice and red in color. Every time he went to bed, he would consume one of these aromatic pills, and once the 'Assisting Romance' [pill] started to work, his strength would then be inexhaustible. His Majesty thought this was amazing and said: 'This is just like the *shenxu* paste of the Han dynasty!'" See Wang Renyu, *Kaiyuan Tianbao yishi*, 21. For a study of early aphrodisiac use in China, see Harper, "Ancient and Medieval Chinese Recipes."

66 A number of scholars, including Li Jianguo, "'Chuanqi zhi shou,'" 40, and Wu Liquan, *Zhongguo yanqing xiaoshuo shi*, 18, have cited this description as the source for the account of the death of Ximen Qing given in *The Plum in the Golden Vase* in which he is poisoned by an overdose of aphrodisiac.

67 The Lateral Courts were the abode of palace women who held a rank lower than that of *jieyu*; see *Hanguan jiuyi*, 44. These women would have been constantly involved in the smallest details of the emperor's life, hence the formulation in *Sanfu huangtu jiaoshi*, 162: "The Lateral Courts palace [women] are by the emperor's side, like his elbows and knees." The director of this institution would therefore have privileged access to information about the private life of the imperial household.

68 For example, "The Tale of Miss Ren" (Renshi zhuan) by Shen Jiji (ca. 750–ca. 797), a story about a fox-spirit, features a conclusion stating that the author was informed of these events by one of the protagonists. Meanwhile, "The Record of the Sundered Soul" (Lihun ji), a tale of supernatural happenings and suspended animation by Chen Xuanyou (fl. 779 CE), has the author claim to have been told all about it by a relative of the family concerned; see Yuan Lükun and Xue Hongji, *Tang-Song chuanqi zongji*, 175 and 162, respectively. For a study of the role of this kind of narrative technique in creating the impression of authenticity and reliability, see Li Qiu, "Cong 'shishixing xugou' de xushi celüe kan Tang chuanqi xushi zhuti."

69 Hong Mai, *Rongzhai wubi*, 7:1b–2a ["Shengshuai buke chang"].

70 Huan Tan's official biography is given in *Hou Hanshu*, 28A:955–61; he is known to have been a close associate of Yang Xiong and other leading intellectuals of the period.

71 *Shangshu zhengyi*, 331–40.

72 See, for example, *Shiji*, 33:1516; and *Zhushu jinian*, B:1a.

73 Xun Xu was a close friend and adviser to Emperor Wu of Jin (r. 265–290) for much of his reign, and his official biography is given in *Jinshu*, 39:1152–57.

74 This major scholarly project and Xun Xu's role in it are discussed in detail in Shaughnessy, *Rewriting Early Chinese Texts*, 131–84; and Goodman, *Xun Xu and the Politics of Precision*, 279–349.

75 Ling Xuan's postface also appears in Yan Kejun, *Quan Hanwen*, 578.

76 Lushui is not a place mentioned in any Han dynasty text. However, as described in *Commentary on the Classic of Waterways* (Shuijing zhu), the Zhuozhang River

was known as the Lushui or Lu River when passing through Lu County (Lu Xian) in what is now Shanxi Province; see Chen Qiaoyi, *Shuijing zhu jiaozheng*, 10:256.

77 Yang Xiong was by far the most important scholar of his day, and he is honored with a two-chapter biography in *History of the Han Dynasty*. The character recorded in his official biography is quite different from that portrayed here; see *Hanshu*, 87A:2513–87B:2588.

78 As noted by Wang Shouliang, "*Zhao Feiyan waizhuan* jianlun," 59, in the Western Han dynasty, the period to which this preface purports to date, the text was not yet known as *Records of the Grand Historian* (Shiji). It is not recorded under this title until the Eastern Han dynasty.

79 By representing Fan Tongde throwing a shadow in the lamplight, this account echoes the episode in which the shade of Consort Li appeared to Emperor Wu of Han after her death; see *Hanshu*, 97:3952. The emperor's passion is thus depicted as the pursuit of shadows. As noted by Tian, *Beacon Fire and Shooting Star*, 242–47, in Age of Disunion literature there is much discussion of women and their shadows, derived from Buddhist discourse on reality and illusion.

80 Thanks to this reference, from the Song dynasty onward for a woman to "hold her chignon in her hand" (*yi shou yong ji*) became a recognized gesture to express anguish. There are a number of references to this term in the works of Su Shi; see, for example, Yang Jialuo, *Su Dongpo quanji*, 179 ["He Wang Gong liushou bing ciyun"].

81 Although both the Zhao sisters held the title of *jieyu* at one point in their careers, it is likely that this reference is to Ban Jieyu. There are a number of writings attributed to her that bewail her unhappy fate; see Knechtges, "The Poetry of an Imperial Concubine."

82 This title is one of the many designations by which *The Scandalous Tale* was traditionally known.

83 Although the genealogy of the various members of the Ban family and the details of their careers are extremely well recorded in *History of the Han Dynasty*, this supposed cousin is not documented there. The preface, of course, serves as a useful excuse to justify why the Ban family did not incorporate this material in their own work; see Zhu Rundong, *Badai zhuanxu wenxue shulun*, 51.

84 In editions of *The Scandalous Tale* that include this text, Huan Tan's statement is normally untitled.

85 The name Bian Li does not appear to be recorded elsewhere.

86 The family name Xiahou here is probably intended to suggest Xiahou Sheng (dates unknown), one of the most important Confucian scholars of the late Western Han dynasty. His official biography appears in *Hanshu*, 75:3155–59.

87 The Red Eyebrows uprising took place from approximately 17 CE to 27 CE; although their earliest activities are recorded on the Shandong Peninsula, they would at different times hold both Chang'an and Luoyang. It is not impossible that some violence occurred in the region of Maoling, the site of the tomb of Emperor Wu of the Han dynasty, though nothing of this kind is recorded in any surviving historical text.

88 Liu Gong is a genuine historical figure, a member of the Han imperial family who was caught up in the Red Eyebrows uprising as a child; his younger brother Liu Penzi (b. 10 CE) was chosen by the rebels as their candidate to become the next Han emperor. Eventually Liu Gong became a staunch supporter of Emperor Gengshi (r. 23–25 CE), considering him to be the rightful leader of the restoration of the Han dynasty. Some biographical information about Liu Gong, an intelligent and energetic man who found himself living through very difficult times, is given in *Hou Hanshu*, 11:477–86.

89 Jia Ziyi seems to be an invention of the author of this statement; this individual is not otherwise recorded.

90 The reference here to Ling Xuan as a player and teacher of the *qin* is very obscure; this is an aspect of his biography not mentioned elsewhere, though it serves to explain the acquaintanceship between the two men.

91 As with Huan Tan's comments on the text, this piece is usually untitled.

CHAPTER THREE: ZHAO FEIYAN'S BIOGRAPHY IN HISTORICAL SOURCES

1 In no case are the textual parallels particularly close, though they are sufficiently similar to be recognizable as referring to the same events. Given these differences, it is entirely possible that *The Scandalous Tale* drew on other sources of this period that have not survived, and indeed on popular traditions—this has been well documented elsewhere. See Zhao Xiupei, "Song chuanqi 'diangu lihe' de chuanqi shoufa."

2 *Hanshu*, 97B:3988–99. This account also forms the basis of the biography given in *Further Biographies of Exemplary Women* (Xu Lienü zhuan); see *Lienü zhuan buzhu*, 363–65 ["Han Zhao Feiyan"]. Traditionally, *Further Biographies of Exemplary Women* has been ascribed to the authorship of Ban Zhao (45–ca. 116), making it another example of a work produced by this family, which was resolutely opposed to Empress Zhao; see, for example, Zeng Gong, *Zeng Gong ji*, 179. However, although *Further Biographies of Exemplary Women* is indeed most likely to be an Eastern Han dynasty text, the association with the Ban family is not at all secure. For the importance of the Ban family in constructing early biographies of Zhao Feiyan, see Yang Qing, "Zhao Feiyan gushi ji qi xiaoshuo bianzou," 112.

3 *Hanshu*, 97B:3984.

4 This point is emphasized in *Hanshu*, 97B:3973: "Emperor Yuan mourned the fact that his much-injured mother, the respected and lamented empress, had been established for but a short time when she was murdered by the Huo family, so he selected [Xu] Jia's daughter to become the crown prince's wife."

5 The most detailed record of distinguished antecedents of the Ban family appears to be that given in *Hanshu*, 100A:4197–98. Some of the same information is repeated in the official biography of Ban Biao (3–54 CE) in *Hou Hanshu*, 40A:1323.

6 See *Hanshu*, 97B:3974; and *Hanshu*, 97B:3984, respectively.

7 As noted by Owen, "One Sight," Ban Gu was extremely hostile to powerful women from entertainment backgrounds. In this study of the biography of Emperor Wu of Han's beloved Consort Li, he demonstrates the way in which *History of the Han Dynasty* is deliberately constructed to present her slightest actions in a negative light.

8 This translation of the term *gongren* as "palace slave" follows the commentary by Yan Shigu, quoted in *Hanshu*, 97B:3988n1. Although the term *gongren* could also refer to a freeborn woman servant working in the Rear Palace, Yan Shigu bases his interpretation of Zhao Feiyan's original family background on the account given in *Old Ceremonial Regulations of the Han Dynasty* (Han jiuyi): "Palace slaves [*gongren*] are selected from female government slaves above the age of eight *sui*, and they serve [women in the Rear Palace] from the empress down, until they are married off at the age of thirty-five." See *Hanguan jiuyi*, 46.

9 As noted in Kinney, *Exemplary Women of Early China*, xxiii, the presence of Zhao Feiyan's younger sister in Emperor Cheng's harem represents an informal attempt to return to the preunification model of sororal polygyny, whereby an alliance was guaranteed by multiple marriages between the same man and sisters or cousins. In the event of one marriage failing to produce children, there was every hope that another would succeed.

10 *Hanshu*, 97B:3988.

11 Kinney, "Dyed Silk," 25. The case of Zhao Feiyan is specifically cited here as an instance of this kind of equation between life force as a child and a remarkable destiny as an adult.

12 This point is made in Bossler, "Gender and Entertainment at the Song Court," 274. It appears to have been true in the Han dynasty as well, since both Empress Wei Zifu and Empress Zhao Feiyan originally served in the households of imperial family members and not in the Rear Palace itself, which apparently gave them the opportunity to meet the emperor in an unsupervised way.

13 For a detailed study of how the Wang family brought down Empress Xu, see Shaoyun Yang, "The Politics of Omenology in Chengdi's Reign."

14 *Hanshu*, 97B:3989. The official biography of Emperor Cheng specifies that the appointment of the then Zhao Jieyu's father as a marquis occurred in the fourth lunar month of 16 BCE; his appointment of Zhao Feiyan as empress took place in the sixth lunar month of the same year; see *Hanshu*, 10:319.

15 *Hanshu*, 93:3730–33.

16 *Hanshu*, 98:4013.

17 *Hanshu*, 77:3252. Other complaints on the same subject are reported in *Hanshu*, 60:2667–74, 81:3341–42, and 85:3443–53. *Shiji*, 49:1981, records similar concerns expressed at an earlier period, when Emperor Wu found himself unable to promote a beloved consort because of her humble background: "When Consort Li died, Yin Jieyu and other women of her ilk were even more favored. However, they were all of artiste background and not the daughters of kings, marquises, or gentlemen in possession of estates, so they were not suitable matches for the ruler."

18 This translation follows the commentary by Yan Shigu in identifying "Wei" as Li Ping, a maid in Ban Jieyu's staff that she presented to the emperor as a sexual partner in the hope that she might bear children. She became known by the surname Wei, because Emperor Cheng thought her career mirrored that of an earlier artiste turned empress: Wei Zifu. It is likely that Wei Zifu was herself the subject of great criticism in her own day, but given that all subsequent Western Han emperors from Emperor Xuan onward were descended from her, it is probable that official documents were heavily pruned to remove such material. Zhao Feiyan and Li Ping, with no children and hence with no one with a vested interest in defending them, were not so lucky.

19 *Hanshu*, 36:1957–58.

20 Schwarzenbach, "Imagined Queens between Heaven and Hell." A number of empresses in subsequent Chinese dynasties also came from entertainer-courtesan backgrounds, but maintained better posthumous reputations than Zhao Feiyan did. For example, the careers of a couple of Song dynasty empresses with such origins are considered in Bossler, "Gender and Entertainment at the Song Court"; and Lee, *Empresses, Art, and Agency*, 163–69. However, in both cases, these women played a crucial role in ensuring the smooth transition of the throne to the next emperor, and hence the dynasty had a vested interest in downplaying their scandalous origins.

21 For Procopius's scandalous portrayal of Empress Theodora's early career as a prostitute, actress, and striptease performer, see Dewing, *Procopius*, 105–13 [ix.8–28]. Her belief in magic and dealings with other persons claiming to be able to contact evil spirits is described in *Procopius*, 263 [xxii.25–28].

22 According to *Sanfu huangtu jiaoshi*, 163, the Zhaoyang Hall was one of the eight main buildings established within the Rear Palace, in the Weiyang Palace complex, during the reign of Emperor Wu of Han. As noted by Chen Zhi, *Hanshu xinzheng*, 441, a mirror has been excavated in Xi'an with an inscription indicating that it pertained to this residence.

23 Close studding is a construction technique in which a timber framework, usually with many vertical rails, is set into the wall and left visible for decorative purposes. From the description here, that is what is intended.

24 *Hanshu*, 97B:3989. A virtually identical description of the Zhaoyang Hall is also found in *Sanfu huangtu jiaoshi*, 165, though this account has a slightly different opening: "The Zhaoyang Residence had rooms [made fragrant with] orchids and walls of Sichuan pepper [crushed into the plaster], the central courtyard was [painted] vermillion. . . ."

25 Nylan, introduction to *Chang'an 26 BCE*, 5.

26 The importance of such women appearing in public wearing distinctive costume and regalia is considered in Carney, *Fairy Tale Queens*, 117–45. The giving of precious gifts has also been extensively studied, with some cultures engaging in extremely codified practices; see, for example, Auble, "Bejeweled Majesty"; and Tillander-Godenheilm, *Jewels from Imperial St. Petersburg.*

27 In the Han dynasty, time was measured by water clocks, divided into twelve "double hours," or one hundred *ke*, or "quarters" (approximating 14.4 modern minutes). Emperor Cheng thus died within roughly two and a half hours of his initial collapse, leading modern scholars to suggest that his death was probably the result of a stroke; see, for example, Zheng Fu, "Han Chengdi zhi si yu 'yinghou shouxin,'" 125.

28 *Hanshu*, 97B:3990.

29 *Hanshu*, 97B:3998–99. According to *Sanfu huangtu jiaoshi*, 136, the North Palace was located within the walls of Chang'an, north of the Weiyang Palace and close to the Cinnamon Palace (Guigong). At the same time that Empress Zhao was sent to live at the North Palace (the usual residence assigned to deposed empresses when there was no immediate intention to execute them), the widow of Emperor Ai was ordered to live in the Cinnamon Palace; see *Hanshu*, 97B:4005.

30 When Emperor Zhao of Han (r. 86–74 BCE) came to the throne without any senior women in the Rear Palace, his sister, Princess Eyi (d. 80 BCE), joined him in "mutually nurturing the palace" (*gongyang shengzhong*); see *Hanshu*, 7:217. From the reference given here to Empress Zhao's failings, this seems to have been understood as a key aspect of the role of the Mother of All-under-Heaven in the Han dynasty.

31 *Hanshu*, 97B:3998–99.

32 *Hanshu*, 97B:3991.

33 Meng Xiangcai, "Pushuo mili de Zhao Feiyan zimei mousha huangzi an," argues on the basis that this report was compiled under the auspices of Dowager Empress Wang Zhengjun that very little reliance should be placed on any conclusion that it reached. For the Wang family to maintain power, it was crucial that the Zhao family should fall and that their names should be blackened by accusations of heinous crimes.

34 *Xijing zaji jiaozhu*, 279. It has long been noted that some sections of the transmitted *Miscellaneous Records of the Western Capital* are either identical or very closely related to *History of the Han Dynasty*, making the claim that the former was intended to complement the latter difficult to substantiate; see, for example, Yong Rong et al., *Siku quanshu zongmu*, 140:1182.

35 *Miscellaneous Records of the Western Capital* is described as anonymous in the catalogue of the Sui imperial library—the first known bibliographic reference to this work; see *Suishu*, 33:966. What may be the earliest reference to the attribution to Ge Hong appears in the work of Zhang Jianzhi (625–706); however, the original text does not survive: Zhang Jianzhi's comment is recorded in a Song dynasty text; see Chao Zaizhi, *Xu tan zhu*, 16–17 ["Dongming ji ba"]. There are later indubitably Tang dynasty references to Ge Hong's authorship of *Miscellaneous Records of the Western Capital*; see Liu Zhiji, *Shitong*, 193.

36 The earliest reference to the theory that this book was the work of Wu Jun seems to have been the scholar and author Duan Chengshi (ca. 803–863) in the late Tang dynasty: he attributes this idea to the Liang dynasty diplomat and poet Yu Xin

(513–581); see Duan Chengshi, *Youyang zazu*, 76. The attribution to Wu Jun seems to have been a strong local tradition in the Yangzi delta region; see Chao Gongwu, *Junzhai dushu zhi*, 6:242. Alternatively, the attribution to Xiao Ben is based upon the fact that he is said to have authored a text titled *Miscellaneous Records of the Western Capital* in sixteen *juan*; see *Nanshi*, 44:1106. The theory that this compilation should be attributed to Xiao Ben is discussed in some detail in Nienhauser, "Authorship of the *Hsi-ching tsa-chi*."

37 Knechtges, "*Xijing zaji*." For different perspectives on the vexed issue of the authorship and dating of this book, see Lao Gan, "Lun *Xijing zaji* zhi zuoshe ji chengshu shidai"; Cheng Zhangcan, "*Xijing zaji* de zuozhe"; Ding Hongwu, "Cong xushi shijiao kan *Xijing zaji* yuanshi wenben"; and Wang Shouliang, "*Xijing zaji* zuozhe wenti shukao."

38 In their commentary on this passage, Cheng Lin and Cheng Zhangcan, *Xijing zaji quanyi*, 28–29, suggest that the meaning of the term *jiuzi* is not clear. It is likely that *jiuzi* here refers to the nine stars of the constellation Wei, or "Tail," a meaning that is well attested in Han dynasty literature; see, for example, *Shiji*, 27:1298.

39 The term *dian* normally refers to a mat made from woven bamboo; see, for example, *Shuowen jiezi zhu*, 341 ["Zhubu"]. Here, however, this item is specifically said to have been made from ivory, so it would seem to refer to some kind of low stool, which would then be covered with a bearskin rug. By according such an item to the *zhaoyi*, *Miscellaneous Records of the Western Capital* links her with a previous imperial consort with a background in the performing arts: Consort Li. According to *Xijing zaji jiaozhu*, 248, Emperor Wu of Han had a special *dian* made for her from ivory.

40 Chinese artisans began making glass in the late Spring and Autumn period (771–475 BCE); the recipe used for their potash silicate-barium silicate-lead silicate glass is unique in the premodern period, and the technology used (casting in ceramic molds) points to an independent invention; see Gan Fuxi, "Zhongguo gudai boli de qiyuan yu fazhan." Given that much early Chinese glass was cast, they had the technological capacity to make plaques and sheets of this material approximately one thousand years earlier than anywhere else in the world. Some plaques of Han dynasty glass do survive; see, for example, Guangzhoushi Wenwu Guanli Weiyuanhui, Zhongguo Shehui Kexueyuan Kaogu Yanjiusuo, and Guangdongsheng Bowuguan, *Xi-Han Nanyue wang mu*, 133–34. Early Chinese window glass is not known, but it would have been quite possible to produce.

41 The artisan Ding Huan is mentioned elsewhere in *Xijing zaji jiaozhu*, 59, for his amazing inventive skills, including the manufacture of a ball-shaped pomander in which the internal arrangement of interlocking rings keeps the inner bowl forever upright. A Tang dynasty example of this design of pomander was excavated from Famensi; see Shaanxisheng Kaogu Yanjiuyuan and Famensi Bowuguan, *Famensi kaogu fajue baogao*, 126.

42 As noted by Cheng Lin and Cheng Zhangcan, *Xijing zaji quanyi*, 28–29, the text appears to be corrupt at this point. Li Jianguo, "'Chuanqi zhi shou,'" 35, suggests

the name mentioned here, Fan Yannian, is in some way the source for the surname of the Fan family as it appears in *The Scandalous Tale*.

43 *Xijing zaji jiaozhu*, 41. For an alternative translation of this passage, featuring a different interpretation of the meaning of some of the terms concerning the appointments of this hall, see Barbieri-Low, *Artisans in Early Imperial China*, 180–81.

44 The original text reads *ziluo*, or "purple silk gauze," but this translation follows the commentary by Cheng Lin and Cheng Zhangcan, *Xijing zaji quanyi*, 41, in reading *luo* (silk gauze) as a mistake for *lun* (clock), suggesting that the veil matched the hat in the previous item.

45 This variety of silk brocade is not recorded in any Western Han dynasty text. However, according to *Hou Hanshu*, *zhi* 30:3664, in the Eastern Han dynasty, wearing this kind of fabric was restricted to government officials below the ranks of duke (*gong*), marquis (*hou*), and the nine chief ministers (*jiuqing*).

46 This reference to *saptaratna*, or "seven jewels" (*qibao*) designs, shows that the account of gifts given by the *zhaoyi* must postdate the arrival of Buddhism in China. Different sutras, however, give various combinations of precious metals and stones within the *saptaratna* set.

47 A *buyao*, or *en tremblant* hairpin, featured a gold element, from which hung strings of pearls or jade beads that swung with every move of the wearer; see Gao Meijin, "Chunqiu Zhanguo ji Qin-Han funü shoushi chutan," 71; Zhang Yu'an, "Han Wei Nanbeichao buyao yanjiu"; and Sun Ji, "Buyao, buyaoguan yu yaoye shipian." These hairpins were the height of fashion for many centuries, though the design was significantly modified over time.

48 The original text of *Miscellaneous Records of the Western Capital* gives "Hehuan earspools" (*Hehuan yuandang*); however, as noted by Yan Kejun, *Quan Hanwen*, 109, there is a textual variant that gives the place-name Hepu, which makes much better sense. In the Han dynasty, Hepu was a major terminus for much international trade in luxury goods; see Han Huchu, *Hepu Handai wenwu tan*; and Wu Chuanjun and Lü Yusheng, *Haishang sichou zhi lu yanjiu*.

49 Mica (a generic term designating a variety of mineral silicate) forms large crystalline sheets. Rickwood, "The Largest Crystals," 901, reports a single sheet of mica more than 150 × 250 cm discovered in Ontario, Canada, though individual crystals of this size are extremely rare. It would be quite possible to make a mica screen, and such a unique item would demonstrate the prestige of the emperor's favorite.

50 The term *jiuhua* refers to a multilobed shape, and also to the chrysanthemum flower. The existence of *jiuhua* fans, made of woven bamboo, in elite culture in the late Eastern Han dynasty and early Age of Disunion is attested to in a number of works of literature; see, for example, Zhao Youwen, *Cao Zhi ji jiaozhu*, 38.

51 The *wuming* fan was traditionally said to have been designed by the sage-king Shun, and used by members of the ruling elite in the Han dynasty; see Cui Bao, *Gujin zhu*, A:8a; and Xu Jian, *Chuxue ji*, 25:604.

52 Mountain-shaped incense burners were introduced into China in the reign of Emperor Wu of Han. Some scholars have traced the evolution of this design from Achaemenid and Assyrian examples; see, for example, Rawson, "The Chinese Hill

Censer." Other connections with indigenous Chinese traditions are considered in Lin Xiaojuan, "Boshanlu kao"; Zhang Xiang, "Shuangmian guanzhao"; and Dong Xueying, "Shaanxi diqu Han huaxiangshi zhong de boshanlu tuxiang chutan."

53 The meaning of this term is not known. Barbieri-Low, *Artisans in Early Imperial China*, 182, suggests some kind of revolving fan.

54 Identifying *qingmu* aromatic is not simple. From the late imperial era onward, this term was applied to *Aristolochia debilis*, and some scholars have understood it as a reference to this plant; see Barbieri-Low, *Artisans in Early Imperial China*, 182. However, modern research has clarified that *Aristolochia debilis* is highly toxic and a carcinogen, hardly the kind of thing that one would give as a gift, or desire to receive. Laufer, *Sino-Iranica*, 464, suggests that *qingmu* aromatic was a portmanteau term comprising a variety of different scented woods.

55 Jiuzhen Commandery was created in 111 BCE, following the conquest of the kingdom of Nanyue by Emperor Wu of Han; see *Hanshu*, 28B:1630. Jiuzhen would correspond roughly to the area of modern-day Thanh Hóa Province in Vietnam. This area was famous in antiquity for the many aromatics produced and traded there, which may have included musk.

56 *Xijing zaji jiaozhu*, 62.

57 Barbieri-Low, *Artisans in Early Imperial China*, 181, suggests not merely that the list genuinely dates to the Western Han dynasty (specifically to the year 16 BCE), but that it was actually derived from the imperial archives, as a genuine record of the presents given to Empress Zhao Feiyan by her younger sister.

58 In the case of gharuwood, Jung, "The Cultural Biography of Agarwood," 108, suggests that this aromatic was not imported into China until the widespread adoption of Buddhism, which probably precludes a genuinely Han dynasty date. There appears, for example, to be no archaeologically recovered examples of this aromatic from an undisputed early imperial context.

59 Li Fang et al., *Wenyuan yinghua*, 346:281.

60 Wan Jingjun, *Cui Hao shizhu*, 25.

61 The description of Zhao Zhaoyi's appearance here as "fine boned and with a delicate skin" (*ruoti fengji*) is a direct quotation from "Rhapsody on a Beautiful Woman" (Meiren fu) attributed to Sima Xiangru; see Yan Kejun, *Quan Hanwen*, 219.

62 *Xijing zaji jiaozhu*, 66.

63 Moral training through the contemplation of pictures of female exemplars is first mentioned in the reign of Emperor Wu of Han; see *Hanshu*, 100A:4200–201. This important form of instruction is mentioned with particular approval in *Hou Hanshu*, 10B:438, where the outstandingly virtuous and well-educated Empress Liang Na (116–150), the wife of Emperor Shun of Han (r. 125–144), constantly viewed this kind of image. For a study of this practice in the context of the images of exemplary women found in Eastern Han dynasty art, see Hung Wu, *The Wu Liang Shrine*, 170–80.

64 The biography of Ban Jieyu in *History of the Han Dynasty* contains two references to her self-cultivation practices, through the viewing of pictures of moral exemplars. The first is found in the account of one of her conversations with Emperor

Cheng; see *Hanshu*, 97B:3983. The second is included within a rhapsody she composed; see *Hanshu*, 97B:3985.

65 *Xijing zaji jiaozhu*, 166. Although *The Scandalous Tale* makes little overt use of this anecdote, the same tune is said to have been performed by Zhao Feiyan for the delectation of the emperor.

66 Xu Jian, *Chuxue ji*, 16:386, identifies these two song titles as famous early pieces of *qin* music. They appear on the same list as that recording the two titles that Empress Zhao was said to perform.

67 *Xijing zaji jiaozhu*, 85. The same passage is also translated in McMahon, *Women Shall Not Rule*, 81. As the author notes, fictional accounts have traditionally characterized Empress Zhao as a quintessential "wanton woman" (*yinfu*), engaging in sexual acts with multiple male partners in spite of being supposedly cloistered within the imperial harem.

68 This theory is discussed in Zhang Xiaofeng, "Zhengshuo Zhao Feiyan," 76.

69 For the biography of this violent and uncontrolled woman, see *Jinshu*, 31:963–66.

70 Chao Gongwu, *Junzhai dushu zhi*, 2B:167. For the original reference, see *Suishu*, 33:982.

71 The significance of the difference in *juan* numbers for indicating that these may in fact be completely different texts is stressed in He Qinggu, "*Sanfu huangtu* de chengshu ji qi banben," 28.

72 Cheng Dachang, *Yonglu*, 1:7a–8a.

73 For example, one item in *Sanfu huangtu jiaoshi*, 37, states: "The Guo Palace was constructed by Dowager Empress Xuan, and it stands on the border of what is today Guo County [Guo Xian] in Qi Prefecture [Qi Zhou]." The name of Qi Prefecture is not a Han dynasty term; it was introduced in 619 CE, and in 756 CE it was changed again, to Fengxiang Commandery. Guo County itself was not established until 691 CE, in the reign of Wu Zetian. This example and others are discussed as evidence of the formation of the text in its present form in He Qinggu, "*Sanfu huangtu* de chengshu ji qi banben," 29.

74 For the former, see Miao Changyan, "Sanfu huangtu xu," quoted in *Sanfu huangtu jiaoshi*, 5. See also Chen Zhensun, *Zhizhai shulu jieti*, 8:235.

75 The Sharpshooters were an elite regiment of archers founded by Emperor Wu of the Han dynasty in 104 BCE; see *Hanshu*, 19A:731.

76 See *Sanfu huangtu jiaoshi*, 264–65; and *Shiyi ji yizhu*, 6:168, respectively.

77 For studies of the text and its influence on later Chinese literature, see Wu Liwen, "*Shiyi ji* dui houshi wenxue de yingxiang juli"; Wang Xingfen, "Zashi zazhuan wei ti, dili bowu wei yong"; and Zhang Chunhong, "*Shiyi ji* chuangzuo de shenqihua zhuiqiu."

78 The text of Xiao Qi's preface is given in Mei Dingzuo, *Liangwen ji*, 14:34a–35b ["Wang Zinian *Shiyi ji* xu"]. Thus, in the catalogue of the Sui imperial library, this text is recorded as "Wang Zinian's [Wang Jia] *Record of Gleanings from Lost Works*" (Wang Zinian *Shiyi ji*) recompiled by Xiao Qi, in ten *juan*; see *Suishu*, 33:961. Xiao Qi's intervention in the text is considered in Zhang Kan, "Shitan Xiao Qi dui *Shiyi ji* de zhengli he piping."

79 Hu Yinglin, *Shaoshi shanfang bicong*, 318.

80 Campany, *Strange Writings*, 64–67, 306–18.

81 A palace of this name was constructed by Murong Xi, Emperor Zhaowen of Later Yan (r. 401–407). This complex is mentioned in *Jinshu*, 124:3105. However, there is no evidence that a palace of the same name was constructed by Emperor Cheng of Han.

82 *Shiyi ji yizhu*, 6:166–67.

83 *Shiyi ji yizhu*, 6:167.

84 Yi is a comparatively unusual posthumous title; however, it appears in the detailed list of the meanings of such titles given in *Surviving Zhou Documents* (Yi Zhoushu) and is explained as follows: "One who is happy to correct oneself and change one's old ways is called 'Willing to Reform'" (Hao geng gai jiu yue Yi); see *Yi Zhoushu huijiao jizhu*, 749 ["Shifa jie"].

85 The full details of this massive excavation have yet to be published; however, for early results, see Li Zebin and Chen Gang, "Jiangsu Xuyixian Dayunshan Xi-Han Jiangdu wangling yihao mu"; Li Zebin, Qi Jun, Tian Changyou, Bai Ji, and Chen Gang, "Jiangsu Xuyi Dayunshan Jiangdu wangling erhao mu fajue jianbao"; and Li Zebin, "Jiangsu Xuyi Dayunshan Jiangdu wangling M9, M10 fajue jianbao."

86 Jay Xu, *Tomb Treasures*, 146–47; for a discussion of related finds, see Chen Hai, "G dian yu Xi-Han nüyong xingwanju kao"; and Li Ling, *Wanbian*, 405–25.

87 *Shiji*, 59:2096. This assessment of the personality of the first king of Jiangdu is simply repeated in *Hanshu*, 53:2414.

88 *Shiji*, 59:2096; see also Goldin, *The Culture of Sex in Ancient China*, 85. The same author argues elsewhere that accusations of sexual immorality often appear in charges launched against senior male members of the imperial house during the Han dynasty, since this represented an effective means of getting rid of them, while besmirching their reputations; see Goldin, "Copulating with One's Stepmother—or Birth Mother?" In the account in *Records of the Grand Historian* of the life of the second king of Jiangdu, however, Sima Qian states that his sexual misconduct was not a direct factor in his downfall.

89 These events took place in 121 BCE. It is not at all clear from the account in *Records of the Grand Historian* what the king of Jiangdu was up to with his shamans and invocators (*wuzhu*), and *History of the Han Dynasty* does not mention this at all. However, given that in 91 BCE Emperor Wu would have literally thousands of people killed in a witch hunt against those accused of cursing him with *gu* poison, the second king of Jiangdu's activities were undoubtedly extremely dangerous.

90 *Hanshu*, 53:2414.

91 This change in emphasis may reflect changes in social attitudes; studies of early Han dynasty law show that sexual misconduct by a widow in the wake of her spouse's demise was likely to offend the family of the deceased, but was not punishable as adultery, since the bond between the couple was broken on death; see Nylan, "Notes on a Case of Illicit Sex from Zhangjiashan."

92 The name of this unfortunate woman, Lady Zhuo, may well be a source for the surname for Lady Zhuo in *The Scandalous Tale*. According to *Hanshu*, 53:2421, after

the death of King Yi and her rape by his son, the historical Lady Zhuo ended up in the household of Liu Pengzu, king of Zhao (r. 152–92 BCE).

93 *Hanshu*, 53:2414.

94 *Hanshu*, 53:2415–16.

95 In Han dynasty law, grain pounding was the penalty imposed upon women for serious crimes such as conspiracy to commit murder or assault inflicting grievous bodily harm; see Zhangjiashan Ersiqihao Hanmu Zhujian Zhengli Xiaozu, *Zhangjiashan Hanmu zhujian*, 11–12. Shaving of the head was the penalty for a woman who offended but did not physically injure a senior member of the family: this statute may be relevant for the way the king of Jiangdu punished his household. Surviving slave collars of the period would have been extremely unpleasant to wear: weighing approximately one kilogram, they might even include a spike to impale the unfortunate person concerned if they bent forward; see Qin Zhonghang, "Han Yangling fujin qiantu mu de fajue."

96 *Hanshu*, 53:2416.

CHAPTER FOUR: INTERPRETING *THE SCANDALOUS TALE*

1 The importance of this text in the history of Chinese literature is recognized in one of the standard assessments of *The Scandalous Tale*, that it is the "finest of all *chuanqi*" (*chuanqi zhi shou*). This designation was first given in Hu Yinglin, *Shaoshi shanfang bicong*, 283, and has frequently been repeated since.

2 See, for example, Kazuyuki Fukazawa, "Sinsue shijin ga *Chō Hien* o nozoku," for a useful overview of some of the large body of poetry produced from the Song dynasty onward, inspired by this novella.

3 Lin Yuhong, "*Zhao Feiyan waizhuan* chengshu."

4 The textual history of this *congshu* is comparatively complicated, since the original 100-*juan* form was later re-edited and revised to form a 120-*juan* edition, and there seems to have been some textual loss. For an account of the history of the compilation and recompilation of *Stories from the Suburbs*, see Chang Bide, *Shuofu kao*.

5 This recension of the text was published in a collection titled *Fiction from the Gu Family Library* (Gushi wenfang xiaoshuo) in 1522; subsequently, this was reprinted in Taiwan in modern times. Today, the *Gushi wenfang xiaoshuo* recension is readily available through the Database of Chinese Classic Ancient Books (Zhongguo Jiben Guji Ku).

6 For example, *The Complete Collection of Books from Various Collectanea* recension of the text is based upon the version found in *Fiction from the Gu Family Library*, collated with *The Collectanea of Literature from the Han and Wei Dynasties* (Han-Wei congshu) and *Secret Books from Longwei* (Longwei mishu) editions.

7 *The Collectanea of Literature from the Han and Wei dynasties* has been repeatedly reprinted. The text of *The Scandalous History* is found in Cheng Rong, *Han Wei congshu*, 1640–43, a photolithographic reproduction of the 1592 edition. In addition, *The Scandalous Tale* is reproduced in Ma Junliang, *Longwei mishu*, 7:1a–8b.

8 See, for example, Wu Zengqi, *Jiu xiaoshuo*; and Wubai mingjia, *Wuchao xiaoshuo daguan*, 31–36.

9 This manuscript, now in the National Library of China, has been reprinted in *Xu Siku quanshu*, 595–99.

10 See Ling Xuan, *Zhao Feiyan waizhuan* (Congshu jicheng ed.), 4; and Ling Xuan, *Feiyan waizhuan* (Xu Siku quanshu ed.), 595, respectively.

11 See, for example, *Wenxuan*, 5 ["Xidu fu"].

12 See Ling Xuan, *Zhao Feiyan waizhuan* (Congshu jicheng ed.), 2; and Ling Xuan, *Feiyan waizhuan* (Xu Siku quanshu ed.), 595 respectively.

13 Zeng Zao, *Leishuo*, 1:12a–17a.

14 This has not prevented many scholars from suggesting that *The Scandalous Tale* dates to an earlier period; quite how this is possible—particularly for those aware of modern methods of textual criticism—is not clear. For example, Wu Zhida, *Zhongguo wenyan xiaoshuo shi*, 58, dates the text to the Age of Disunion. Xue Hongji, *Chuanqi xiaoshuo shi*, 34, dates *The Scandalous Tale* to the Jin dynasty. Meanwhile, Li Jianguo, *Songdai zhiguai chuanqi xulu*, 161, argues for a date in the Eastern Han dynasty, claiming that this is supported by textual analysis.

15 *Suishu*, 82:1835–37.

16 As has been noted by a number of scholars, the appearance of this name in *The Scandalous Tale* precludes a Han dynasty date for the text. See, for example, Lin Feiyun, "Guanyu 'jin suojian Hanren xiaoshuo' xiezuo niandai de yanjiu," 54.

17 See *Hanshu*, 97B:3990; and Ling Xuan, *Zhao Feiyan waizhuan*, 15, respectively.

18 Xing Peishun, "*Zhao Feiyan waizhuan* tanlun," 59.

19 Some scholars have dated the composition of *The Scandalous Tale* to the Northern Song period; see, for example, Zhou Zhongfu, *Zhengtang dushu ji*, 1243–44; and Chang Bide, *Shuofu kao*, 227. This would imply that the author of the text had carefully culled all suitable quotations of material concerning the character of Zhao Feiyan from these late Tang dynasty poems, not to mention arranging for the insertion of spurious quotations into earlier compendia. This is fundamentally impossible; hence this theory should be dismissed.

20 Liu Xuekai and Yu Shucheng, *Li Shangyin shige jijie*, 1932 ["Ketan"].

21 Wang Jiantang and Song Haiying, "*Feiyan waizhuan* de wenshi yu liubo," 36; and Hou Zhongyi, *Han Wei Liuchao xiaoshuo jianshi*, 19.

22 Chen Jilong, *Han Wo shi zhu*, 358. The golden "cakes" mentioned here were round discs specially made in the early imperial era to be given as rewards. Interestingly, Han Wo was the nephew by marriage of Li Shangyin; it seems likely that the two men must have had access to a family copy of *The Scandalous Tale*. This impression is strengthened by the fact that Han Wo's poem "Rhapsody on a Red Banana" (Hong bajiao fu) is the first known text after *The Scandalous Tale* to name Zhao Hede; see Chen Yuanlong et al., *Yuding lidai fu hui*, 15:22a–23b.

23 Cao Yin, Peng Dingqiu, et al., *Quan Tangshi*, 7628.

24 Wang Jiantang and Song Haiying, "*Feiyan waizhuan* de wenshi yu liubo," 36, notes the existence of what appears to be a further quotation of this kind, though it is apparently derived from a lost section of the text. Duan Chengshi mentions

in an essay titled "Jewels to Encircle the Chignon" (Jihuan pin) that "Zhao Hede wore the chignon [called] 'Enjoying Sorrow'" (Zhao Hede you Xinchouji); see Tao Zongyi, *Shuofu*, 77:3602. It is likely that this is indeed derived from *The Scandalous Tale*, because this is the earliest known text to record Zhao Hede's name. If that is the case, then this is another reference to the text that appears in mid-ninth-century literature.

25 See, for example, Feng Zhi, *Yunxian zaji*, 9:72 ["Yan Chifeng"] and 10:76 ["Wenrou xiang"].

26 He Zhu, *Qinghu yilao shiji*, 4:16a.

27 Ma Chun, *Taozhu xinlu*, 50.

28 Yao Mian, *Xuepo ji*, 21:1b.

29 Ge Weijun and Wang Xiaohong, *Shanzhong baiyun ci*, 142.

30 In some later accounts of the circumstances in which *The Scandalous Tale* was written, it is said that Fan Tongde was Empress Zhao's personal secretary (*nüshi*); see, for example, Zhang Ying, Wang Shizhen, Wang Tan, et al., *Yuding yuanjian leihan*, 247:23b.

31 See, for example, Chao Gongwu, *Junzhai dushu zhi*, 2B:173.

32 Chen Zhensun, *Zhizhai shulu jieti*, 7:188.

33 Yang Jialuo, *Su Dongpo quanji*, 504 ["Zhaoyun shi"]. For a study of Su Shi's many references to *The Scandalous Tale* and its preface in his writings, see Wang Jiantang, "Su Shi yu *Zhao Feiyan waizhuan*." The relationship between Su Shi and Wang Zhaoyun is considered in Bossler, *Courtesans, Concubines, and the Cult of Female Fidelity*, 93–99.

34 As noted by Nylan, introduction to *Chang'an 26 BCE*, 5, Emperor Cheng was frequently compared to his detriment with Emperor Wu, because the former tended to eschew the expensive military campaigns that the latter so much enjoyed. Although at the time there were many who were deeply concerned about the viability of Emperor Wu's foreign conquests, in later dynasties his expansionist aims came to be much admired.

35 The reference here to the Xiongnu Khan concerns the events of the reign of Emperor Xuan when Huhanye (d. 31 BCE) made a series of visits to the Han imperial capital, in 51 and 49 BCE; see *Hanshu*, 8:270–71, 273. It seems likely that the poet was particularly interested in the events of 51 BCE, when Emperor Xuan commemorated the success of his diplomatic efforts by installing in the main hall of the Weiyang Palace portraits of the eleven officials who had brought it about.

36 The Master of Hongjia refers to Emperor Cheng; the Hongjia reign era ran from 20 BCE to 17 BCE.

37 In this poem, Zhang Nie comments on one of the odd features of *The Scandalous Tale*. In the early part of the narrative, the strange sexual skills learned by the eponymous heroine form an important part of the narrative. However, in the later sections, there is no mention of this aspect at all—the poor integration of themes from one part of the text to another is possibly the result of multiple authorship.

38 Zhang Nie, *Ziwei ji*, 10:10b–11a.

39 Much information concerning Emperor Wu's difficult private life is preserved in the official histories of the dynasty. *Shiji*, 49:1978–80, discusses his terrible relationship with his first empress. Similar information also appears in *Hanshu*, 97A:3948–49, with particular stress on the problems the emperor had with producing any children early in his reign. Meanwhile, the main stages in the witchcraft accusations are recounted in *Hanshu*, 6:208–10 and 97A:3950.

40 This text is included in a number of collections, including *Stories from the Suburbs* and *The Complete Collection of Books from Various Collectanea*.

41 A particular problem is that *The Alternative Tale of Zhao Feiyan* was frequently printed under the title *Surviving Records of Empress Zhao*; see Li Jianguo, "Qin Chun *Zhao Feiyan biezhuan* kaolun," 1.

42 For a study of this text, see Xue Hongji, "*Zhao Feiyan biezhuan*," 744–45; and Li Jianguo, *Songdai zhiguai chuanqi xulu*, 160–63. Liu Jianguo dates *The Alternative Tale of Zhao Feiyan* to approximately the period 1078–85. A complete translation of this text is available in English; see Zhengjun Zhang, "Qin Chun, 'Supplementary Biography of Empress Zhao.'"

43 Qin Chun, *Zhao Feiyan biezhuan*, 145.

44 Xu Liming, "Shuangfeng bing zhi chuan er mei," 31, suggests that this text can be read as a description of the oppression of women within harem life. Such a reading can be made, but ignores the strong moral perspective of the original author, who clearly wished to portray the Zhao women as evil.

45 Yue Shi, *Yang Taizhen waizhuan*, 665. The text titled *The Private History of Emperor Cheng of the Han Dynasty* may well be an invention of the author of this text; it is certainly known only from this context. This particular story is also found in another Song dynasty text; see Zhu Shengfei, *Ganzhu ji*, 1:18a.

46 Yue Shi, *Yang Taizhen waizhuan*, 665.

47 Huangdu Fengyue Zhuren, *Lüchuang xinhua*.

48 Yang Qing, "Zhao Feiyan gushi ji qi xiaoshuo bianzou," 115.

49 Wang Shizhen, *Yanyi bian*. As discussed in McCausland, "Exemplary Complicity," 96–113, Wang Shizhen possessed a manuscript version of *The Scandalous Tale* in the calligraphy of the famous Ming dynasty literati artist Wen Zhengming (1470–1559); he also commissioned the painter Qiu Ying (1494?–1552) to produce illustrations for the text. This manuscript was offered for sale by the Chuo Auction House in Tokyo in 2016; the catalogue dates this exceptional work of art to 1540.

50 This text today exists in both two- and four-*juan* versions. The interrelationship between the different reworkings of the earlier novella is considered in Li Mengsheng, *Jinhui xiaoshuo yetan*, 93–100.

51 Guhang Yanyansheng, *Zhaoyang qushi*, 149–50.

52 Yanyansheng, *Zhaoyang yanshi*, 3–58.

53 Lin Yutang, *The Wisdom of China and India*, 955–63. The section of this compilation dealing exclusively with China was subsequently published independently, and the translation of *The Scandalous Tale* appears in Lin Yutang, *The Wisdom of China*, 449–58.

54 Lin Yutang, *The Wisdom of China*, 448.

55 Bauer and Franke, *Die goldene Truhe*, 49–51.

56 Bauer and Franke, *The Golden Casket*, 53–66. *The Scandalous Tale* is here called "The Emperor and the Two Sisters," a direct translation of the way the title was rendered in German.

57 See, for example, Song, *The Fragile Scholar*, 31.

58 Xiong Ming, "*Zhao Feiyan waizhuan* kaolun," 60–61, notes the strong relationship here between the preface and the main text, whereby the author's preface establishes the narrative as an articulation of female experience, and then the text itself is dominated by its female characters. Although Zhao Feiyan and Zhao Hede are the most important women, the other individuals, such as Fan Yi, the erudite Lady Zhuo, the pharmacist Shangguan Wu, and so on each have a role to play.

59 This tradition of a strongly female perspective also applies to palace literature produced elsewhere in East Asia. For example, *Diary of Kyech'uk Year, 1613* (Kyech'uk ilgi), a Korean text concerning the persecution and murder of many of Queen Inmok's (1584–1632) closest relatives by her stepson, presents all events from the perspective of a palace woman in Her Majesty's service; see Kang Hanyŏng, *Kyech'uk ilgi*. For a study of this particular text, see Haboush, "The Vanished Women of Korea." It is the readers' perception of the author as eyewitness to the events described that give the text its power, and allows the claim that this record is "authentic" even when it is contradicted by other sources.

60 This point is made in Wu Xueling, "Nüshiren: Nüxing huayu de zifazhe" and "Nanshiren: Nüxing huayu de shenhuazhe"; and Guo Zhusong, "Yinyong gongnü shenghuo, kanbu shiji quezai."

61 The unusual characterization of the text, with the prominence given to female characters, is stressed in Xiong Ming, *Han-Wei Liuchao zazhuan yanjiu*, 213.

62 Ling Xuan, *Zhao Feiyan waizhuan*, 13–14.

63 This point is emphasized in On Shionoya, *Zhongguo wenxue gailun*, 338. The same point is also stressed by Xiong Ming, "*Zhao Feiyan waizhuan* kaolun," 61–62, who nevertheless somewhat overstates the case with respect to the centrality within the narrative of Zhao Hede's conflicts with her older sister.

64 Ling Xuan, *Zhao Feiyan waizhuan*, 9.

65 Wei Yuchuan, "*Feiyan waizhuan* kaolun," stresses in her study of this text that the two sisters are always portrayed as bending to the emperor's demands the moment they are expressed; it is impossible for them to decide for themselves what they wish to do. This leaves them with little choice but to lie or deceive others, since they cannot openly acknowledge even the smallest difference of opinion. This is seen by the author as an example of the way in which *The Scandalous Tale* highlights the corruption of life at court.

66 See, for example, Xing Peishun, "*Zhao Feiyan waizhuan* tanlun," 59.

67 See Xie Siwei, *Bai Juyi shi ji jiaozhu*, 943–56; and Chen Hong, *Changhen zhuan*, 105–20, respectively. The textual history of *Changhen zhuan* is considered in Li Jianguo, *Tang Wudai zhiguai chuanqi xulu*, 350–61.

68 The problem of how to handle the issue of Yang Guifei's first marriage continued to bother the producers of the official history of the dynasty: the compilers of *Old*

History of the Tang Dynasty (Jiu Tangshu) (completed in 945) try to avoid any reference to these events. The compilers of *New History of the Tang Dynasty* (completed 1060), working a century later, seem more comfortable with acknowledging that the marriage took place; see *Xin Tangshu*, 76:3943.

69 For studies of the developing portrayal of Yang Guifei in different Song dynasty texts, see, for example, Chao Hsiu-Pay, "Cong huojie dao huoshou"; Li Chunyan, "Lun Tang Minghuang gushi"; and Wang Li, "Yu yunyou qie chang."

70 Yue Shi, *Yang Taizhen waizhuan*, 663.

71 The official biographies of the emperor are given in *Jiu Tangshu*, 19A:649–88; and *Xin Tangshu*, 9:255–63. In addition, Guo Shufei has her own separate biography in *Xin Tangshu*, 77:3511.

72 Su E, *Duyang zabian*. The story also appears in Li Fang et al., *Taiping guangji*, 237:1822–23 ["Tongchang gongzhu"]. For a discussion of the textual history of *The Duyang Miscellany*, and "The Scandalous Tale of the Tongchang Princess" in independent circulation, see Li Jianguo, *Tang Wudai zhiguai chuanqi xulu*, 118–40.

73 *Jiu Tangshu*, 177:4605–7. The text of Liu Zhan's memorial also appears in Dong Gao et al., *Quan Tangwen*, 747:3431. For a study of these events, see Cheng Jin, "Tongchang gongzhu yian xiaokao."

74 *Xin Tangshu*, 77:3511.

CHAPTER FIVE: GENDERING EMPRESS ZHAO

1 Yuan Zai's career and that of his wife are described in *Jiu Tangshu*, 118:3409–14; and *Xin Tangshu*, 145:4711–14. Both accounts make it clear that she was executed at the same time as her husband, but the circumstances are not recorded.

2 The earliest account of Wang Yunxiu's last words appears to come from Fan Lu, *Yunxi youyi*, 12:71. While the Zhaoyang Palace refers to Zhao Feiyan and her sister, the Changxin Palace refers to Ban Jieyu. After the collapse of her marriage to Emperor Cheng, even though she successfully defended herself against charges of engaging in witchcraft, Ban Jieyu served Dowager Empress Wang Zhengjun, who was resident in this palace; see *Hanshu*, 897B:3965.

3 *Shuowen jiezi zhu*, 1082 ["Nübu"], defines *du* as meaning "when a wife is jealous of her husband."

4 There has been little study of the history of negative emotions in early imperial China; for a series of pioneering work on the subject in the Ming and Qing dynasties, see Santangelo, *Materials for an Anatomy of Personality* and *Sentimental Education in Chinese History*; and Santangelo and Guida, *Love, Hatred, and Other Passions*.

5 Numerous examples of this usage can be found in pre-imperial and early imperial texts; see *Shangjun shu zhuizhi*, 84 ["Xiuquan"]; *Xunzi jishi*, 217–18 ["Wangba"]; and *Shuoyuan jiaozheng*, 432 ["Zayan"].

6 In *Shuowen jiezi zhu*, 1082 ["Nübu"], *mao* is glossed as meaning "when a husband is jealous of his wife."

7 For a listing of the seven reasons for divorce, see, for example, *Da Dai Liji huijiao jizhu*, 1376 ["Benming"]. According to *Lienü zhuan buzhu*, 65 ["Xianming"], jealousy was the most important of the *qichu*. For an overview of early imperial divorce law, see Chen Guyuan, *Zhongguo hunyin shi*, 233–56. For detailed studies of this topic, see, for example, Pang Xiangyu, "Jianlun Zhongguo gudai qichu sanbuqu de falü zhidu"; Wang Geya, "Zhongguo gudai de lihun moshi"; and Cui Lanqin, "Zhongguo gudai fashang de heli."

8 For a demonstration of the point that emotional outbursts of whatever kind were often "performed" and appear in certain predictable, even stereotypical, situations with a view to forcing a resolution, see White, "The Politics of Anger," 139.

9 The locus classicus of this term is thought to be *Shiji*, 8:381, where it is applied to Xiang Yu (232–202 BCE). Subsequently, this term appears in many discussions of unsuccessful rulers.

10 See *Hanshu*, 44:2135, 27A:1330, 44:2154, 97A:3946, 55:2472, 53:2434, and 97B:3985, respectively.

11 According to *Hanshu*, 76:3205, the accusation was unjustified, and since it appeared malicious, it proved instrumental in bringing about Zhao Guanghan's downfall.

12 See *Shiji*, 118:3075, 9:403–4, 118:3095, 49:1976, 111:2922, 59:2102, and 20:1065, respectively.

13 *Hou Hanshu*, *zhi* 18:3363, 10B:435, 10B:453–54, and 32:1132. The marriage between the Princess of Liyi and Yin Feng represented a major alliance between the families of Emperor Guangwu and his second wife, Empress Yin Lihua (5–64 CE). Hence, the murder of the princess by her husband posed a serious political problem—Yin Feng was executed for the crime, and his parents both committed suicide, which allowed Emperor Ming of Han (r. 58–75 CE) to treat the rest of his mother's family with leniency.

14 *Hou Hanshu*, 10B:448.

15 Just in case any reader of *History of the Han Dynasty* did not get the point, this characterization of the pair is repeated in different chapters; see *Hanshu*, 27A:1337 and 97B:3985.

16 According to *Hanshu*, 27A:1330–31, first the icehouse at the Weiyang Palace and then the Weaving House caught fire. Liu Xiang associated these events with the appointment a few days later of Empress Zhang, who (though of very eminent birth) would fail to support the interests of the Liu family against her grandmother, Dowager Empress Lü. His condemnation of her is couched in almost exactly the same words as those he subsequently applies to Empress Zhao Feiyan.

17 Other Han dynasty texts are silent on the origins of Emperor Xuan's grandmother. Elsewhere in *History of the Han Dynasty*, her name is given as Shi Liangdi. According to the commentary by Fu Qian (ca. 125–195), *liangdi* was an official title; see *Hanshu*, 8:235n3. According to Wei Zhao (201–273), it was the title accorded to a type of woman official in the household of the heir to the throne; see *Hanshu*, 63:2742n5.

18 *Hanshu*, 27A:1336–37.

19 According to *Hanshu*, 97B:3999, when Emperor Cheng went out incognito with Zhang Fang, Marquis of Fuping, he would proclaim himself a member of the same family. Supposedly, Zhang Fang was present on the occasion that Emperor Cheng first met and became infatuated with Zhao Feiyan.

20 The door is understood as a reference to the imperial palace, which Zhao Feiyan should have been too lowborn to ever enter.

21 *Hanshu*, 97B:3999. The same song is also quoted in 27B:1395.

22 *Weishu*, 21A:563. For a detailed study of the implications of this story, see Zhang Yunhua, "Lun Beichao funü de duhan fengqi."

23 This interpretation of the role of jealousy is derived from the discussion found in Epstein, "Turning the Authorial Table," 179.

24 See, for example, Wang Wanying, "Wei Jin Nanbeichao shiqi shangliu shehui guiting de duhan zhi feng."

25 *Bei Qishu*, 38:385. In Ban Zhao's original text, women's virtue is defined as "being quiet and gentle, modest and correct, behaving appropriately and acting according to the law," and women's work as "concentrating on your weaving, not indulging in jokes and gossip, and showing moderation in your consumption of food and alcohol, serving your guests [first]." See *Hou Hanshu*, 84:2789. This text is translated in full in Idema and Grant, *The Red Brush*, 36–42.

26 For example, Ouyang Xun, *Yiwen leiju*, 35:614, quotes an account from *Records of the Wei Dynasty* (Weizhi) of the murder of five of the late Eastern Han dynasty warlord Yuan Shao's (d. 202 CE) favorite concubines by his wife, Lady Liu. Meanwhile, *Sanguo zhi*, 6:210n2, quotes the description given in *Spring and Autumn Annals of the Nine Regions* (Jiuzhou chunqiu) of the garroting of warlord Yuan Shu's (d. 199 CE) wife, Lady Feng, by his other jealous consorts and their subsequent faking of the scene of the crime as a suicide. *Sanguo zhi*, 50:1199, also records the murder of Empress Pan, the second wife of Sun Quan, Emperor Da of Wu (r. 229–252), in revenge for her jealous attacks on other palace women. Again, since this was a crime committed against a senior woman within the Rear Palace, attempts were initially made to disguise the murder as death by natural causes, but eventually the truth was revealed and a number of palace women were punished.

27 *Jinshu*, 5:136.

28 *Mao Shi zhengyi*, 43 ["Zhongsi"].

29 *Weishu*, 13:337.

30 *Songshu*, 41:1290. This book seems to have survived until the Tang dynasty, since it is mentioned in the catalogues of the imperial library in *Suishu*, 33: 978; and *Xin Tangshu*, 58:1486. However, it seems that by the Song dynasty, bibliophiles were no longer able to locate copies of this text; see Chao Gongwu, *Junzhai dushu zhi*, 3B:1a. Hence it survives today only in quotations.

31 When his minister and regular chess partner, Rong Yanyuan, came to the palace with an injured face after a quarrel with his jealous wife, Emperor Ming ordered her execution. Another minister, Liu Xiu, was given concubines, while his wife was caned and ordered to perform menial labor as punishment for her jealousy; see *Nan Qishu*, 34:612. Whether this was quite what either man wanted is not clear.

32 Both of these songs were considered especially important for the edification of elite women; see Huang Linmeng, "Guanju"; and Zhou Chunjian, "Zhounan 'Zhongsi' shi jiaoyi fawei."

33 Ouyang Xun, *Yiwen leiju*, 35:614–15.

34 The earliest version of this story is found in *New Tales of the World* (Shishuo xinyu); see Zhu Chuyu, *Shishuo xinyu huixiao jizhu*, 35:765. It was subsequently included in *Jinshu*, 40:1170, thus giving this tale official validation.

35 Alternative accounts of Guo Huai's behavior are given in contemporary sources; see, for example, Fu Chang's (d. 330) *Encomium on the Lords of Jin* (Jin zhugong zan), and the commentary by Liu Xiaobiao (462–521), quoted in *Shishuo xinyu huixiao jizhu*, 35:765. Furthermore, the impression given by Guo Huai's epitaph, excavated in 1930, is also quite different. For a translation and study of this epitaph and contrasting sources of Guo Huai's biography; see Davis, *Entombed Epigraphy and Commemorative Culture*, 262–73.

36 Han Wan, *Yushitai ji*, 788. To emphasize that Ren Gui's wife was merely defending her own interests in the face of almost overwhelming social pressure, the version of this story preserved in Zhang Ao, *Chaoye qianzai*, 3:3b–4a, has her explain her situation to Emperor Taizong: "[Ren] Gui and I got married very young. We both came from extremely humble backgrounds, and thanks to our support for one another, he has achieved glory and obtained an official position. Gui now already has many favored concubines and my life really is not worth living." A very similar tale was also recorded of the wife of Fang Xuanling; see Liu Su, *Sui-Tang jiahua*, B:13.

37 *Zhao Feiyan waizhuan*, 13.

38 Xu Zhaopei's murderous jealousy, alcoholism, affairs with other men, and habit of making up only one half of her face to make fun of her husband for being blind in one eye are recorded in detail in *Nanshi*, 12:341–42. The present text of *Master of the Golden Tower* makes only veiled references to Xu Zhaopei's difficult behavior, but there are reasons to believe that the book was originally more explicit; see *Jinlouzi shuzheng jiaozhu*, 292n29 ["Houfei"]. The official history of the Liang dynasty merely says that the future Emperor Yuan was justified in ordering his wife to commit suicide; see *Liangshu*, 7:163–64. Emperor Wen's lament is recorded in *Suishu*, 56:1109.

39 Other positive fictional representations of jealousy also mention the idea that this adds spice to a marriage; see Epstein, "Turning the Authorial Table," 179. Constant submissiveness on the part of wives might be advocated by ritual and moral texts, but was not necessarily always portrayed as desirable in other literary genres.

40 This rhapsody is translated in full in Idema and Grant, *The Red Brush*, 80–82. For studies of Ban Jieyu's writings, see, for example, Knechtges, "The Poetry of an Imperial Concubine"; and Li Tong, "Ban Jieyu he ta de fu."

41 *Hanshu*, 97B:3987.

42 The songs in question are "Green Robes" (Lüyi) and "White Flowers" (Baihua); see *Mao Shi zhengyi*, 117–21 and 925–33, respectively.

43 See, for example, the poems "In Praise of Ban Jieyu" (Ban Jieyu zan) by Zuo Fen (ca. 255–300); "Harmonizing with the Rhymes of [Ban] Jieyu's Plaint" (He jieyu

yuan) by Liu Lingxian (fl. 525); and "Changxin gong" by Tian E, an obscure female Tang dynasty poet; quoted in Ouyang Xun, *Yiwen leiju*, 18:337; Wu Zhaoyi et al., *Yutai xinyong jianzhu*, 359; and Wang Yandi, *Zhongguo gudai nüzuojia ji*, 247, respectively. Of these women poets, Zuo Fen, a consort of Emperor Wu of the Jin dynasty and member of a very distinguished literati family, is by far the best known.

44 Zhang Yuniang, *Lanxue ji*, 16:654. For an analysis of Zhang Yuniang's writings in the context of literary activities by Song dynasty women, see Egan, *The Burden of Female Talent*, 37–42.

45 The official biography of Empress Xiao Guanyin is given in *Liaoshi*, 71:1205.

46 See, for example, Chen Shanshan, "Pinglun Liaodai shitan de yizuo gaofeng"; and Xiu Xinyu, "Lun Liaodai dihou."

47 The terms "rain and clouds" (*yuyun*) or "clouds and rain" (*yunyu*) conventionally refer to sexual activity. This expression is derived from the preface to "Rhapsody on the Gaotang Shrine" (Gaotang fu) attributed to Song Yu (fl. 298–263 BCE); see *Wenxuan*, 250.

48 Wang Ding, *Fenjiao lu*, 3.

49 Other writings attributed to Empress Xiao Guanyin, also derived from *An Account of Burned Pepper*, are translated in Idema and Grant, *The Red Brush*, 301–4. For an overview of her poetic oeuvre in the context of the information given in *An Account of Burned Pepper* (here treated as a reputable historical source), see Zhang and Schlepp, "Xiao Guanyin."

50 The publication history of *An Account of Burned Pepper* is considered in Zhongguo Guji Shanben Shumu Bianji Weiyuanhui, *Zhongguo guji shanben shumu*, 243, which suggests that it only entered circulation in the late Ming. See also You Li, "*Fenjiao lu* ji qi shiliao jiazhi kaoshi."

51 Yan Wanzhang, "Liao Daozong Xuanyi huanghou fu wei Xiao Xiaohui kao."

52 Zhao Weiyi is a genuine historical figure, and he was executed for the crime of an adulterous affair with the empress; see *Liaoshi*, 71:1205.

53 In real life, Zhang Xiaojie was instrumental in ensuring that Empress Xiao Guanyin and her son, the crown prince, would both be killed in order to facilitate the installation of another empress from a faction favorable to Yelü Yixin. He was therefore accorded second place within the biographies of evil ministers in the official history of the dynasty, right behind his co-conspirator; see *Liaoshi*, 110:1486–87.

54 Wang Ding, *Fenjiao lu*, 5.

55 Wang Ding, *Fenjiao lu*, 6.

56 See, for example, Mann, *Precious Records*, 208–18; and Gao Chunhua, "Man-Han jiazu ronghe."

57 Yun Zhu, *Hongxiangguan shicao*, no *juan*:13a.

58 Ji Lanyun, *Chuwan'ge ji*, 9:12a. Thanks to her marriage to Qu Songman (1792–1815), Ji Lanyun was a member of the intellectual community centered upon the Qu family of Changshu, which encouraged the literary endeavors of both male and female members of the clan. For a study of the literary works produced within

the extended clan over the course of the Qing dynasty, see Mei Xinlin and Lou Xinxing, "Lun Qingdai Changshu Qushi jiazu nüxing de wenxue huodong yu chuanbo."

59 Li Shuyi, *Shuyinglou mingshu baiyong*, no *juan*.23b.

60 Li Shuyi, *Shuyinglou mingshu baiyong*, no *juan*.24a.

61 Wang Renpei, *Peishanshan shi shicun*, 1:7b.

APPENDIX TWO: CHINESE TEXT OF *THE SCANDALOUS TALE OF ZHAO FEIYAN*

1 Ling Xuan, *Zhao Feiyan waizhuan* (Gushi wenfang xiaoshuo ed.).

2 Ling Xuan, *Zhao Feiyan waizhuan* (Han Wei congshu ed.); and Ling Xuan, *Zhao Feiyan waizhuan* (Longwei mishu ed.).

3 Ling Xuan, *Zhao Feiyan waizhuan* (Shuofu ed.); Ling Xuan, *Zhao Feiyan waizhuan* (Jiu xiaoshuo: Han Wei Liuchao ed.); Ling Xuan, *Zhao Feiyan waizhuan* (Wuchao xiaoshuo daguan ed.); Ling Xuan, *Zhao Feiyan waizhuan* (Biji xiaoshuo daguan: Sanbian ed.); and Ling Xuan, *Feiyan waizhuan* (Xu Siku quanshu ed.), respectively.

BIBLIOGRAPHY

ANCIENT TEXTS AND DYNASTIC HISTORIES

Baihu tong shuzheng 白虎通疏證. Annot. Chen Li 陳立. Beijing: Zhonghua Shuju, 1994.

Baopuzi neipian jiaoshi 抱樸子内篇校釋. Annot. Wang Ming 王明. Beijing: Zhonghua Shuju, 1986.

Bei Qishu 北齊書. Comp. Li Baiyao 李百藥 et al. Beijing: Zhonghua Shuju, 1972.

Chuci buzhu 楚辭補注. Annot. Hong Xingzu 洪興祖. Beijing: Zhonghua Shuju, 1983.

Chunqiu fanlu yizheng 春秋繁露義證. Annot. Su Yu 蘇輿. Beijing: Zhonghua Shuju, 1992.

Chunqiu Gongyang zhuan zhushu 春秋公羊傳注疏. Annot. He Xiu 何休 and Xu Yan 徐彥. Beijing: Beijing Daxue Chubanshe, 1999.

Chunqiu Guliang jingzhuan buzhu 春秋穀梁經傳補注. Annot. Zhong Wenzheng 鍾文烝. Beijing: Zhonghua Shuju, 1996.

Chunqiu Zuozhuan zhu 春秋左傳注. Annot. Yang Bojun 楊伯峻. Beijing: Zhonghua Shuju, 1993.

Da Dai Liji huijiao jizhu 大戴禮記彙校集注. Annot. Huang Huaixin 黃懷信. Xi'an: San-Qin Chubanshe, 2004.

Dongguan Hanji jiaozhu 東觀漢記校注. Annot. Wu Shuping 吳樹平. Beijing: Zhonghua Shuju, 2008.

Fengsu tongyi jiaozhu 風俗通義校注. Annot. Wang Liqi 王利器. Taipei: Dingyuan Wenhua, 2004.

Guanzi jiaozhu 管子校注. Annot. Li Fengxiang 黎鳳翔. Beijing: Zhonghua Shuju, 2004.

Han Feizi jishi 韓非子集釋. Annot. Chen Qiyou 陳奇猷. Shanghai: Shanghai Guji Chubanshe, 2000.

Hanguan jiuyi 漢官舊儀. Comp. Wei Hong 衛宏. In *Hanguan liuzhong* 漢官六種, comp. Sun Xingyan 孫星衍. Beijing: Zhonghua Shuju, 1990.

Hanguan yi 漢官儀. Comp. Ying Shao 應劭. In *Hanguan liuzhong*, comp. Sun Xingyan. Beijing: Zhonghua Shuju, 1990.

Hanshu 漢書. Comp. Ban Gu 班固 et al. Beijing: Zhonghua Shuju, 1962.

Hanyi 漢儀. Comp. Ding Fu 丁孚. In *Hanguan liuzhong*, comp. Sun Xingyan. Beijing: Zhonghua Shuju, 1990.

Hou Hanshu 後漢書. Comp. Fan Ye 范曄 et al. Beijing: Zhonghua Shuju, 1965.

Jinlouzi shuzheng jiaozhu 金樓子疏證校注. Annot. Chen Zhiping 陳志平 and Xiong Qingyuan 熊清元. Shanghai: Shanghai Guji Chubanshe, 2014.

Jinshu 晉書. Comp. Fang Xuanling 房玄齡 et al. Beijing: Zhonghua Shuju, 1974.

Jiu Tangshu 舊唐書. Comp. Liu Xu 劉昫 et al. Beijing: Zhonghua Shuju, 1975.

Liangshu 梁書. Comp. Yao Silian 姚思廉 et al. Beijing: Zhonghua Shuju, 1974.

Liaoshi 遼史. Comp. Tuotuo 脫脫 et al. Beijing: Zhonghua Shuju, 1974.

Lienü zhuan buzhu 列女傳補注. Annot. Wang Zhaoyuan 王照圓. Shanghai: Donghua Shifan Daxue Chubanshe, 2012.

Liexian zhuan jiaojian 列仙傳校箋. Annot. Wang Shumin 王叔岷. Beijing: Zhonghua Shuju, 2007.

Liezi jishi 列子集釋. Annot. Yang Bojun. Beijing: Zhonghua Shuju, 1979.

Liji zhengyi 禮記正義. Annot. Kong Yingda 孔穎達. Beijing: Beijing Daxue Chubanshe, 1999.

Lüshi chunqiu xin jiaoshi 呂氏春秋新校釋. Annot. Chen Qiyou. Shanghai: Shanghai Guji Chubanshe, 2002.

Mao Shi zhengyi 毛詩正義. Annot. Kong Yingda. Beijing: Beijing Daxue Chubanshe, 1999.

Mozi xiangu 墨子閒詁. Annot. Sun Yirang 孫詒讓. Beijing: Zhonghua Shuju, 2001.

Nan Qishu 南齊書. Comp. Xiao Zixian 蕭子顯 et al. Beijing: Zhonghua Shuju, 1974.

Nanshi 南史. Comp. Li Yanshou 李延壽 et al. Beijing: Zhonghua Shuju, 1975.

Sanfu huangtu jiaoshi 三輔黃圖校釋. Annot. He Qinggu 何清谷. Beijing: Zhonghua Shuju, 2005.

Sanguo zhi 三國志. Comp. Chen Shou 陳壽 et al. Beijing: Zhonghua Shuju, 1959.

Shangjun shu zhuizhi 商君書錐指. Annot. Jiang Lihong 蔣禮鴻. Beijing: Zhonghua Shuju, 1986.

Shangshu zhengyi 尚書正義. Annot. Kong Yingda. Beijing: Beijing Daxue Chubanshe, 1999.

Shiji 史記. Comp. Sima Qian 司馬遷 et al. Beijing: Zhonghua Shuju, 1959.

Shishuo xinyu huixiao jizhu 世說新語彙校集注. Annot. Zhu Chuyu 朱鑄禹. Shanghai: Shanghai Guji Chubanshe, 2008.

Shiyi ji yizhu 拾遺記譯注. Annot. Meng Qingxiang 孟慶祥. Harbin: Heilongjiang Renmin Chubanshe, 1989.

Shuowen jiezi zhu 說文解字注. Annot. Duan Yucai 段玉裁. Taipei: Yiwen Yinshugan, 1964.

Shuoyuan jiaozheng 說苑校證. Annot. Xiang Zonglu 向宗魯. Beijing: Zhonghua Shuju, 1987.

Songshu 宋書. Comp. Shen Yue 沈約 et al. Beijing: Zhonghua Shuju, 1974.

Soushen ji jiaozhu 搜神記校注. Annot. Wang Shaoying 汪紹楹. Beijing: Zhonghua Shuju, 1985.

Suishu 隋書. Comp. Wei Zheng 魏徵 et al. Beijing: Zhonghua Shuju, 1973.

Weishu 魏書. Comp. Wei Shou 魏收 et al. Beijing: Zhonghua Shuju, 1974.

Wenxuan 文選. Annot. Li Shan 李善 et al. Taipei: Zhengzhong Shuju, 1971.

Xijing zaji jiaozhu 西京雜記校注. Annot. Xiang Xinyang 向新陽 and Liu Keren 劉克任. Shanghai: Shanghai Guji Chubanshe, 1991.

Xin Tangshu 新唐書. Comp. Ouyang Xiu 歐陽修 et al. Beijing: Zhonghua Shuju, 1975.

Xunzi jishi 荀子集釋. Annot. Li Disheng 李滌生. Beijing: Zhonghua Shuju, 1988.

Yi Zhoushu huijiao jizhu 逸周書彙校集注. Annot. Huang Huaixin, Zhang Maorong 張懋鎔, and Tian Xudong 田旭東. Shanghai: Shanghai Guji Chubanshe, 1995.

Zhuangzi jishi 莊子集釋. Annot. Guo Qingfan 郭慶藩. Beijing: Zhonghua Shuju, 2008.

Zhushu jinian 竹書紀年. Annot. Hong Yixuan 洪頤煊. Sibu beiyao ed.

WORKS CITED

Allan, Sarah. "Not the *Lun yu*: The Chu Script Bamboo Slip Manuscript, *Zigao*, and the Nature of Early Confucianism." *Bulletin of the School of Oriental and African Studies* 72.1 (2009): 115–51.

An Pingqiu 安平秋 and Zhang Peiheng 章培恒. *Zhongguo jinshu daguan* 中國禁書大觀. Shanghai: Shanghai Wenhua Chubanshe, 1990.

Anon. *Da-Song Xuanhe yishi* 大宋宣和遺事. Wanyou wenku ed.

———. *Daye shiyi ji* 大業拾遺記. In *Tangdai biji xiaoshuo* 唐代筆記小說, ed. Zhou Guangpei 周光培, 2:27–29. Shijiazhuang: Hebei Jiaoyu Chubanshe, 1994.

———. *Han zashi mixin* 漢雜事秘辛. Beijing: Zhonghua Shuju, 1991.

———. *Hangong chunse* 漢宮春色. In *Biji xiaoshuo daguan: Wubian* 筆記小說大觀: 五編, comp. Lidai xueren 歷代學人. Taipei: Xinxing Chubanshe, 1983.

———. *Li Shishi waizhuan* 李師師外傳. In *Biji xiaoshuo daguan: Wubian* 筆記小說大觀: 五編, comp. Lidai xueren 歷代學人. Taipei: Xinxing Chubanshe, 1983.

———. *Milou ji* 迷樓記. Congshu jicheng ed.

Auble, Cassandra. "Bejeweled Majesty: Queen Elizabeth I, Precious Stones, and Statecraft." In *The Emblematic Queen: Extra-literary Representations of Early Modern Queenship*, ed. Debra Barrett-Graves, 35–52. New York: Palgrave Macmillan, 2013.

Backhouse, Sir Edmond. *Décadence Mandchoue: The China Memoirs of Sir Edmund Trelawny Backhouse.* Ed. Derek Sandhaus. Shanghai: Earnshaw Books, 2011.

Barbieri-Low, Anthony J. *Artisans in Early Imperial China.* Seattle: University of Washington Press, 2007.

Bauer, Wolfgang, and Herbert Franke, comps. *Die goldene Truhe: Chinesische Novellen aus zwei Jahrtausenden.* Munich: Carl Hanser Verlag, 1959.

———. *The Golden Casket: Chinese Novellas of Two Millennia.* Trans. Christopher Levenson. Harmondsworth, U.K.: Penguin, 1967.

Beijing Daxue Guwenxian Yanjiusuo 北京大學古文獻研究所, ed. *Quan Songshi* 全宋詩. Beijing: Beijing Daxue Chubanshe, 1991.

Bodde, Derk. *Festivals in Classical China: New Year and Other Annual Observances during the Han Dynasty, 206 B.C.–A.D. 220.* Princeton, N.J.: Princeton University Press, 1975.

Booth, Marilyn, ed. *Harem Histories: Envisioning Places and Living Spaces.* Durham, N.C.: Duke University Press, 2010.

Bossler, Beverly. *Courtesans, Concubines, and the Cult of Female Fidelity: Gender and Social Change in China, 1000–1400.* Cambridge, Mass.: Harvard University Asia Center, 2013.

———. "Gender and Entertainment at the Song Court." In *Servants of the Dynasty: Palace Women in World History*, ed. Anne Walthall, 261–79. Berkeley: University of California Press, 2008.

Bray, Francesca. *Technology and Gender: Fabrics of Power in Late Imperial China.* Berkeley: University of California Press, 1997.

Brown, Stephen. "Sex 'n' Shopping: A 'Novel' Approach to Consumer Research." *Journal of Marketing Management* 11.8 (1995): 769–83.

Cai, Liang. *Witchcraft and the Rise of the First Confucian Empire.* Albany: State University of New York Press, 2014.

Cai Qing 蔡卿. "*Sui-Tang yanyi* de chengshu guocheng xiaokao" 隋唐演義的成書過程小考. *Beijing huaxue daxue xuebao* (Shehui kexueban) 北京化學大學學報(社會科學版), 2005.2, 69–74.

Campany, Robert. *Strange Writings: Anomaly Accounts in Early Medieval China.* Albany: State University of New York Press, 1996.

Cao Yin 曹寅, Peng Dingqiu 彭定求, et al., comps. *Quan Tangshi* 全唐詩. Beijing: Zhonghua Shuju, 1960.

Carney, Jo Eldridge. *Fairy Tale Queens: Representations of Early Modern Queenship.* New York: Palgrave Macmillan, 2012.

Carrier, Hubert. *Les mazarinades.* Vol. 1, *La conquête de l'opinion.* Geneva: Droz, 1989.

———. *Les mazarinades.* Vol. 2, *Les hommes du vivre.* Geneva: Droz, 1991.

Chang, K. C. *Art, Myth, and Ritual: The Path to Political Authority in Ancient China.* Cambridge, Mass.: Harvard University Press, 1983.

Chang Bide 昌彼得. *Shuofu kao* 說郛考. Taipei: Wenshizhe Chubanshe, 1979.

Chao Gongwu 晁公武. *Junzhai dushu zhi* 郡齋讀書志. Shanghai: Shanghai Guji Chubanshe, 1990.

Chao Hsiu-Pay 趙修霈. "Cong huojie dao huoshou: Yue Shi *Yang Taizhen waizhuan* de shuxie shoufa" 從禍階到禍首: 樂史楊太真外傳的書寫手法. *Chengda zhongwen xuebao* 成大中文學報 34 (2011): 131–57.

Chao Zaizhi 晁載之. *Xu tan zhu* 續談助. Congshu jicheng ed.

Chen, Jo-shui. "Empress Wu and Proto-Feminist Sentiments in T'ang China." In *Imperial Rulership and Cultural Change in Traditional China*, ed. Frederick P. Brandauer and Chün-chieh Huang, 77–116. Seattle: University of Washington Press, 1994.

Chen Caixun 陳才訓 and Lü Jingfen 呂敬芬. "Shuo Jiaofang" 說椒房. *Tangshan shifan xueyuan xuebao* 唐山師範學院學報 23.6 (2001): 17–18.

Chen Guyuan 陳顧遠. *Zhongguo hunyin shi* 中國婚姻史. Taipei: Taiwan Shangwu Yinshugan, 1992.

Chen Hai 陳海. "G dian yu Xi-Han nüyong xingwanju kao" 點與西漢女用性玩具考. *Kaogu yu wenwu* 考古與文物, 2004.3, 62–67.

Chen Hong 陳鴻. *Changhen zhuan* 長恨傳. In *Tangren xiaoshuo jiaoshi* 唐人小說校釋, ed. Wang Meng'ou 王夢鷗. Beijing: Zhonghua Shuju, 1983.

Chen Jilong 陳繼龍. *Han Wo shi zhu* 韓偓詩注. Shanghai: Xuelin Chubanshe, 2000.

Chen Lijun 陳麗君. "*Shiyi ji* xinci xinyi kaoshi" 拾異記新詞新義考釋. *Ningbo daxue xuebao* (Renwen kexueban) 寧波大學學報 (人文科學版) 19.2 (2006): 47–51.

Chen Qiaoyi 陳橋驛. *Shuijing zhu jiaozheng* 水經注校證. Beijing: Zhonghua Shuju, 2007.

Chen Shanshan 陳珊珊. "Pinglun Liaodai shitan de yizuo gaofeng: Cong *Fenjiao lu* kan Xiao Guanyin de wenxue chengjiu" 評論遼代詩壇的一座高峰: 從焚椒錄看蕭觀音的文學成就. *Changchun gongye daxue xuebao* (Shehui kexueban) 長春工業大學學報 (社會科學報), 2014.1, 96–98.

Chen Yuanlong 陳元龍 et al., comps. *Yuding lidai fu hui: Buyi* 御定歷代賦彙: 補遺. Siku quanshu ed.

Chen Zhensun 陳振孫. *Zhizhai shulu jieti* 直齋書錄解題. Taipei: Taiwan Shangwu Yinshugan, 1968.

Chen Zhi 陳直. *Hanshu xinzheng* 漢書新證. Beijing: Zhonghua Shuju, 2008.

Cheng Dachang 程大昌. *Yonglu* 雍錄. Siku quanshu ed.

Cheng Jie 程傑. "Guanyu Mei Fei yu *Mei Fei zhuan*" 關於梅妃與梅妃傳. *Nanjing shifan daxue wenxueyuan xuebao* 南京師範大學文學院學報, 2006.3, 125–29.

Cheng Jin 程錦. "Tongchang gongzhu yian xiaokao" 同昌公主醫案小考. *Wenshi zazhi* 文史雜志, 2017.2, 50–56.

Cheng Lin 成林 and Cheng Zhangcan 程章燦. *Xijing zaji quanyi* 西京雜記全譯. Guiyang: Guizhou Renmin Chubanshe, 1993.

Cheng Zhangcan. "*Xijing zaji* de zuozhe" 西京雜記的作者. *Zhongguo wenhua* 中國文化 2 (1994): 93–96.

Chi Naipeng 遲乃鵬. *Wang Jian yanjiu conggao* 王建研究叢稿. Chengdu: Ba-Shu Shushe, 1997.

Ching, Julia. "Son of Heaven: Sacral Kingship in Ancient China." *T'oung Pao* 83 (1997): 2–41.

Chu Renhuo 褚人穫. *Sui-Tang yanyi* 隋唐演義. Shanghai: Shanghai Guji Chubanshe, 1994.

Chung, Priscilla Ching. *Palace Women of the Northern Song, 960–1126*. Leiden: Brill, 1981.

Cui Bao 崔豹. *Gujin zhu* 古今注. Siku quanshu ed.

Cui Lanqin 崔蘭琴. "Zhongguo gudai fashang de heli" 中國古代法上的和離. *Faxue yanjiu* 法學研究, 2010.5, 170–82.

Cutter, Robert Joe, and William Gordon Cromwell. *Empresses and Consorts: Selections from Chen Shou's "Records of the Three States" with Pei Songzhi's Commentary*. Honolulu: University of Hawai'i Press, 1999.

Darnton, Robert. *The Corpus of Clandestine Literature in France, 1769–1789*. New York: W. W. Norton, 1995.

———. *The Forbidden Best-Sellers of Pre-revolutionary France*. New York: W. W. Norton, 1995.

Davis, Timothy M. *Entombed Epigraphy and Commemorative Culture in Early Medieval China: A History of Early Muzhiming*. Leiden: Brill, 2015.

Deng Peiling 鄧佩玲. *Tianming, guishen yu zhudao: Dong Zhou jinwen guci tanlun* 天命, 鬼神與祝禱: 東周金文嘏辭探論. Taipei: Yiwen Yinshugan, 2011.

Dewing, H. B., ed. and trans. *Procopius: The Anecdota or Secret History*. Cambridge, Mass.: Harvard University Press, 1969.

Ding Hongwu 丁宏武. "Cong xushi shijiao kan *Xijing zaji* yuanshi wenben de zuozhe ji xiezuo shidai" 從敘事視角看西京雜記原始文本的作者及寫作時代. *Tushuguan zazhi* 圖書館雜志 29.4 (2010): 68–76.

Dong Gao 董誥 et al., comps. *Quan Tangwen* 全唐文. Shanghai: Shanghai Guji Chubanshe, 1990.

Dong Xueying 董雪迎. "Shaanxi diqu Han huaxiangshi zhong de boshanlu tuxiang chutan" 陕西地區漢畫像石中的博山爐圖像初探. *Wenwu shijie* 文物世界, 2014.3, 15–18.

Duan Chengshi 段成式. *Youyang zazu* 酉陽雜俎. Jinan: Qi-Lu Shushe, 2008.

Durrant, Stephen. "Ssu-ma Ch'ien's Portrayal of the First Ch'in Emperor." In *Imperial Rulership and Cultural Change in Traditional China*, ed. Frederick P. Brandauer and Chün-chieh Huang, 28–50. Seattle: University of Washington Press, 1994.

Ebrey, Patricia Buckley. *Women and the Family in Chinese History.* New York: Routledge, 2003.

Egan, Ronald. *The Burden of Female Talent: The Poet Li Qingzhao and Her History in China.* Cambridge, Mass.: Harvard University Asia Center, 2013.

———. "Huizong's Palace Poems." In *Emperor Huizong and Late Northern Song China: The Politics of Culture and the Culture of Politics*, ed. Patricia Buckley Ebrey and Maggie Bickford, 361–94. Cambridge, Mass.: Harvard University Press, 2006.

Eisenberg, Andrew. *Kingship in Early Medieval China.* Leiden: Brill, 2008.

Epstein, Maram. "Turning the Authorial Table: Women Writing Wanton Women, Shame, and Jealousy in Two Qing *Tanci*." In *Wanton Women in Late-Imperial Chinese Literature: Models, Genres, Subversions and Traditions*, ed. Mark Stevenson and Wu Cuncun, 157–83. Leiden: Brill, 2017.

Fan Lu 范攄. *Yunxi youyi* 雲溪友議. Beijing: Zhonghua Shuju, 1985.

Feng Zhi 馮贄. *Yunxian zaji* 雲仙雜記. Congshu jicheng ed.

Gan Fuxi 干福熹. "Zhongguo gudai boli de qiyuan yu fazhan" 中國古代玻璃的起源和發展. *Ziran zazhi* 自然雜志 28.4 (2006): 187–93.

Gao Chunhua 高春花. "Man-Han jiazu ronghe yu chucai yangde zhi dao: Lun Qingdai nü shiren Yun Zhu de caiming huode yu chucai celüe" 滿漢家族融合與處才養得之道: 論清代女詩人惲珠的才名獲得與處才策略. *Heilongjiang minzu congkan* 黑龍江民族叢刊, 2014.5, 130–34.

Gao Meijin 高梅進. "Chunqiu Zhanguo ji Qin-Han funü shoushi chutan" 春秋戰國及秦漢婦女首飾初探." *Guanzi xuekan* 管子學刊, 2015.3, 70–73.

Ge Weijun 葛渭君 and Wang Xiaohong 王曉紅. *Shanzhong baiyun ci* 山中白雲詞. Shenyang: Liaoning Jiaoyu Chubanshe, 2001.

Goldin, Paul Rakita. "Copulating with One's Stepmother—or Birth Mother?" In *Behaving Badly in Early and Medieval China*, ed. N. Harry Rothschild and Leslie V. Wallace, 56–69. Honolulu: University of Hawai'i Press, 2017.

———. *The Culture of Sex in Ancient China.* Honolulu: University of Hawai'i Press, 2002.

Goodman, Howard L. *Xun Xu and the Politics of Precision in Third-Century AD China.* Leiden: Brill, 2010.

Gu Lihua 顧麗華. *Handai funü shenghuo qingtai* 漢代婦女生活情態. Beijing: Shehui Kexue Chubanshe, 2011.

Guangzhoushi Wenwu Guanli Weiyuanhui 廣州市文物管理委員會, Zhongguo Shehui Kexueyuan Kaogu Yanjiusuo 中國社會科學院考古研究所, and Guangdongsheng Bowuguan 廣東省博物館. *Xi-Han Nanyue wang mu* 西漢南越王墓. Beijing: Wenwu Chubanshe, 1991.

Guhang Yanyansheng 古杭艷艷生. *Zhaoyang qushi* 昭陽趣史. In *Siwuxie huibao* 思無邪匯寶, ed. Chen Qinghao 陳慶浩 and Wang Qiugui 王秋桂, vol. 3. Taipei: Taiwan Daying Baike, 1994.

Guo Zhusong 郭祝崧. "Yinyong gongnü shenghuo, kanbu shiji quezai: Tan Huarui furen gongci de shiliao jiazhi" 吟詠宮女生活堪補史籍缺載: 談花蕊夫人宮詞的史料價值. *Chengdu daxue xuebao* 成都大學學報, 2001.2, 36–40.

Gupta, Subhadra Sen. *Mahal: Power and Pageantry in the Mughal Harem*. New Delhi: Hachette, 2019.

Haboush, JaHyun Kim. "The Vanished Women of Korea: The Anonymity of Texts and the Historicity of Subjects." In *Servants of the Dynasty: Palace Women in World History*, ed. Anne Walthall, 280–98. Berkeley: University of California Press, 2008.

Han Huchu 韓湖初. *Hepu Handai wenwu tan* 合浦漢代文物談. Guilin: Guangxi Shifan Daxue Chubanshe, 2011.

Han Wan 韓琬. *Yushitai ji* 御史臺記. In *Jiu xiaoshuo* 舊小說, comp. Wu Zengqi 吳曾祺. Shanghai: Shangwu Yinshugan, 1957.

Harper, Donald. "Ancient and Medieval Chinese Recipes for Aphrodisiacs and Philters." *Asian Medicine* 1.1 (2005): 91–100.

He Qinggu 何清谷. "*Sanfu huangtu* de chengshu ji qi banben" 三輔黃圖的成書及其版本. *Wenbo* 文博, 1990.2, 28–32.

He Zhong 賀忠. "Tangdai shiren Wang Jian yu huanguan Wang Shoucheng guanxi kaolun: Yi Wang Jian 'Zeng Shumi shi' wei zhongxin" 唐代詩人王建與宦官王守澄關係考論: 以王建 '贈樞密詩' 爲中心. *Shenyang gongcheng xueyuan xuebao* (Shehui kexue ban) 沈陽工程學院學報 (社會科學版) 5.4 (2009): 531–35.

He Zhu 賀鑄. *Qinghu yilao shiji* 慶湖遺老詩集. Siku quanshu ed.

Hegel, Robert. *The Novel in Seventeenth-Century China*. New York: Columbia University Press, 1981.

———. "*Sui T'ang Yen-i* and the Aesthetics of the Seventeenth Century Suchou Elite." In *Chinese Narrative: Critical and Theoretical Essays*, ed. Andrew Plaks, 124–59. Princeton, N.J.: Princeton University Press, 1977.

Hei Guang 黑光. "Xi'an Han Taiyichi chutu yijian juxing shiyu" 西安漢太液池出土一件巨形石魚. *Wenwu* 文物, 1975.6, 91–92.

Hennessey, William O. *Proclaiming Harmony*. Ann Arbor: Center for Chinese Studies, University of Michigan, 1981.

Hong Mai 洪邁. *Rongzhai wubi* 容齋五筆. Sibu congkan ed.

Hou Zhongyi 侯忠義. *Han Wei Liuchao xiaoshuo jianshi* 漢魏六朝小說簡史. Taiyuan: Shanxi Renmin Chubanshe, 2005.

Hsieh, Bao Hua. "Empress' Grove: Ritual and Life in the Ming Palace." *Jindai Zhongguo funüshi yanjiu* 近代中國婦女史研究 11 (2003): 99–187.

———. "From Charwoman to Empress Dowager: Serving-Women in the Ming Palace." *Ming Studies* 1 (1999): 26–80.

Hu Yinglin 胡應麟. *Shaoshi shanfang bicong* 少室山房筆叢. Shanghai: Shanghai Shudian, 2001.

Hua Guangpu 華光普. *Zhongguo lidai tongjing mulu* 中國歷代銅鏡目錄. Beijing: Zhongguo Huanjing Kexue Chubanshe, 1998.

Huang Huixian 黃惠賢 and Chen Feng 陳鋒. *Zhongguo fenglu zhidu shi* 中國俸祿制度史. Wuhan: Wuhan Daxue Chubanshe, 2005.

Huang Linmeng 黃林蒙. "Guanju. *Mao Shi xu* 'Houfei zhi de shuo' zhi bianxi" 關雎. 毛詩序 '后妃之德說' 之辨析. *Ningbo guangbo dianshi daxue xuebao* 寧波廣播電視大學學報, 2014.1, 20–23.

Huangdu Fengyue Zhuren 皇都風月主人. *Lüchuang xinhua* 綠窗新話. Shanghai: Shanghai Guji Chubanshe, 1991.

Hucker, Charles. *A Dictionary of Official Titles in Imperial China*. Stanford, Calif.: Stanford University Press, 1985.

Idema, Wilt, and Beata Grant. *The Red Brush: Writing Women of Imperial China*. Cambridge, Mass.: Harvard University Asia Center, 2004.

Ji Lanyun 季蘭韻. *Chuwan'ge ji* 楚畹閣集. Qing woodblock print, 1847.

Jouhaud, Christian. *Mazarinades: La fronde des mots*. Paris: Aubier, 1985.

Jung, Dinah. "The Cultural Biography of Agarwood: Perfumery in Eastern Asia and the Asian Neighbourhood." *Journal of the Royal Asiatic Society* 23.1 (2013): 103–25.

Kang Hanyŏng 姜漢永, annot. *Kyech'uk ilgi* 癸丑日記. Seoul: Minhyŏp Ch'ulp'ansa, 1962.

Kaplan, M. Lindsay. *The Culture of Slander in Early Modern England*. Cambridge: Cambridge University Press, 1997.

Kazuyuki Fukazawa 深澤一幸. "Sinsue shijin ga *Chō Hien* o nozoku" 清末詩人が趙飛燕を窺く. *Zinbun gakuhō* 人文學報, 2008, 33–66.

Kieschnick, John. *The Impact of Buddhism on Chinese Material Culture*. Princeton, N.J.: Princeton University Press, 2003.

Kinney, Anne Behnke. "Dyed Silk: Han Notions of the Moral Development of Children." In *Chinese Views of Childhood*, ed. Anne Behnke Kinney, 17–56. Honolulu: University of Hawai'i Press, 1995.

———, trans. and ed. *Exemplary Women of Early China: The "Lienü zhuan" of Liu Xiang*. New York: Columbia University Press, 2014.

Knechtges, David R. "The Poetry of an Imperial Concubine: The Favorite Beauty Ban." *Oriens Extremus* 36.2 (1993): 127–44.

———. "*Xijing zaji* 西京雜記 (Diverse Notes on the Western Capital)." In *Ancient and Early Medieval Chinese Literature: A Reference Guide*, ed. David R. Knechtges and Taiping Chang, 3:1648–55. Leiden: Brill, 2014.

Ko, Dorothy. *Cinderella's Sisters: A Revisionist History of Footbinding*. Berkeley: University of California Press, 2005.

Lam, Lap. "A Reconsideration of Liu Yong and His 'Vulgar' Lyrics." *Journal of Song-Yuan Studies* 33 (2003): 1–47.

Lao Gan 勞榦. "Lun *Xijing zaji* zhi zuoshe ji chengshu shidai" 論西京雜記之作者及成書年代. *Zhongyang yanjiuyuan lishi yuyan yanjiusuo jikan* 中央研究院歷史語言研究所季刊 33 (1962): 19–34.

Laufer, Berthold. *Sino-Iranica: Chinese Contributions to the History of Civilization in Ancient Iran*. Chicago: Field Museum of Natural History, 1919.

Laynesmith, J. L. *The Last Medieval Queens: English Queenship 1445–1503*. Oxford: Oxford University Press, 2004.

Lee, Hui-shu. *Empresses, Art, and Agency in Song Dynasty China*. Seattle: University of Washington Press, 2010.

Lei Ge 雷戈. "Shi shi qiu zhu ye: Zhongguo gudai yeshi guannian yanjiu" 史失求諸野: 中國古代野史觀念研究. *Tianjin shehui kexue* 天津社會科學, 2011.1, 139–44.

Li Binghai 李炳海. *Handai wenxue de qingli shijie* 漢代文學的清理世界. Changchun: Dongbei Shifan Daxue Chubanshe, 2000.

Li Chunyan 李春燕. "Lun Tang Minghuang gushi chuanqishu xie de miwenhua, yanqinghua taishi" 論唐明皇故事傳奇書寫的秘聞化, 艷情化態勢. *Yindu xuekan* 殷都學刊, 2018.1, 75–79.

Li Fang 李昉 et al., comps. *Taiping guangji* 太平廣記. Beijing: Zhonghua Shuju, 1986.

———. *Taiping yulan* 太平御覽. Shanghai: Shanghai Shudian, 1985.

———. *Wenyuan yinghua* 文苑英華. Taipei: Taiwan Shangwu Yinshugan, 1983.

Li Jianguo 李建國. "'Chuanqi zhi shou': *Zhao Feiyan waizhuan*" 傳奇之首: 趙飛燕外傳. *Gudian wenxue zhishi* 古典文學知識, 2004.1, 33–40.

———. "*Daye shiyi ji* deng wu pian chuanqi xiezuo shidai de zai taolun" 大業拾遺記等五篇傳奇寫作時代的再討論. *Wenxue yichan* 文學遺產, 2009.1, 21–28.

———. "Qin Chun *Zhao Feiyan biezhuan* kaolun: Jian yi *Lishan ji, Wenquan ji*" 秦醇趙飛燕別傳考論: 兼議驪山記, 溫泉記. *Guyuan shizhuan xuebao* (Shehui kexue ban) 固原師專學報 (社會科學版), 2001.1, 1–9.

———. *Songdai zhiguai chuanqi xulu* 宋代志怪傳奇敘錄. Tianjin: Nankai Daxue Chubanshe, 1997.

———. *Tang Wudai zhiguai chuanqi xulu* 唐五代志怪傳奇敘錄. Beijing: Zhonghua Shuju, 2017.

Li Ling 李零. *Wanbian* 萬變. Beijing: Sanlian Shudian, 2017.

Li Mengsheng 李夢生. *Jinhui xiaoshuo yetan* 禁毀小說夜譚. Shanghai: Shanghai Shudian, 2008.

Li Qiu 李秋. "Cong 'shishixing xugou' de xushi celüe kan Tang chuanqi xushi zhuti" 從'事實性虛構'的敘事策略看唐傳奇敘事主體. *Beihua daxue xuebao* (Shehui kexueban) 北華大學學報 (社會科學版) 17.1 (2016): 131–35.

Li Shuyi 李淑儀. *Shuyinglou mingshu baiyong* 疏影樓名姝百詠. Qing woodblock print, 1833.

Li Tong 李彤. "Ban Jieyu he ta de fu" 班婕妤和她的賦. *Shenyang daxue xuebao* 瀋陽大學學報 18.6 (2006): 64–68.

Li Yufang 李毓芳. "Han Chang'ancheng Weiyang gong de kaogu fajue yu yanjiu" 漢長安城未央宮的考古發掘與研究. *Wenbo* 文博, 1995.3, 82–93.

Li Zebin 李則斌. "Jiangsu Xuyi Dayunshan Jiangdu wangling M9, M10 fajue jianbao" 江蘇盱眙大雲山江都王陵 M9, M10 發掘簡報. *Dongnan wenhua* 東南文化, 2013.1, 51–64.

Li Zebin 李則斌 and Chen Gang 陳剛. "Jiangsu Xuyixian Dayunshan Xi-Han Jiangdu wangling yihao mu" 江蘇盱眙縣大雲山西漢江都王陵一號墓. *Kaogu* 考古, 2015.10, 3–68.

Li Zebin 李則斌, Qi Jun 齊軍, Tian Changyou 田長有, Bai Ji 白繼, and Chen Gang. "Jiangsu Xuyi Dayunshan Jiangdu wangling erhao mu fajue jianbao" 江蘇盱眙大雲山江都王陵二號墓發掘簡報. *Wenwu* 文物, 2013.2, 25–66.

Liao Ruiming 廖瑞銘. *Mingdai yeshi de fazhan yu tese* 明代野史的發展與特色. Taipei: Hua Mulan Wenhua Chubanshe, 2009.

Lié Sou [Georges Soulié de Morant]. *T'seu Hsi: Impératrice des Boxers*. Paris: Éditions d'Art et de Littérature, 1911.

Lin Feiyun 林飛雲. "Guanyu 'jin suojian Hanren xiaoshuo' xiezuo niandai de yanjiu" 關於'今所見漢人小說'寫作年代的研究. *Wuzhou xueyuan xuebao* 梧州學院學報, 2007.10, 47–55.

Lin Xiaojuan 林小娟. "Boshanlu kao" 博山爐考. *Sichuan wenwu* 四川文物, 2008.3, 65–67.

Lin Yuhong 林于弘. "*Zhao Feiyan waizhuan* chengshu ji banben chuancheng bijiao yanjiu" 趙飛燕外傳成書及版本傳承比較研究. *Guoli zhongyang tushuguan Taiwan fenguan guankan* 國立中央圖書館臺灣分館館刊 9.3 (2003): 86–91.

Lin Yutang, ed. *The Wisdom of China*. London: Michael Joseph, 1944.

———. *The Wisdom of China and India*. New York: Random House, 1942.

Ling Xuan 伶玄. *Feiyan waizhuan* 飛燕外傳. Xu Siku quanshu ed.

———. *Zhao Feiyan waizhuan* 趙飛燕外傳. Congshu jicheng ed.

———. *Zhao Feiyan waizhuan*. In *Biji xiaoshuo daguan: Sanbian* 筆記小說大觀:三編, comp. Lidai xueren 歷代學人. Taipei: Xinxing Shuju, 1974.

———. *Zhao Feiyan waizhuan*. In *Gushi wenfang xiaoshuo* 顧氏文房小說. National Central Library, Taipei, microfilm no. 15238 [1522].

———. *Zhao Feiyan waizhuan*. In *Han Wei congshu* 漢魏叢書, comp. Cheng Rong 程榮. Taipei: Xinxing Shuju, 1978.

———. *Zhao Feiyan waizhuan*. In *Jiu xiaoshuo: Han Wei Liuchao* 舊小說: 漢魏六朝, comp. Wu Zengqi 吳曾祺. Shanghai: Shangwu Yinshugan, 1914.

———. *Zhao Feiyan waizhuan*. In *Longwei mishu* 龍威秘書, comp. Ma Junliang 馬俊良. Shimen: Mashi Dayoushanfang Kan, 1794.

———. *Zhao Feiyan waizhuan*. In *Shuofu* 說郛, comp. Tao Zongyi 陶宗儀. Shanghai: Shanghai Guji Chubanshe, 1988.

———. *Zhao Feiyan waizhuan*. In *Wuchao xiaoshuo daguan* 五朝小說大觀, comp. Wubai mingjia 五百名家. Taipei: Xinxing Shuju, 1960.

Liu Qingzhu 劉慶柱. "Han Chang'ancheng de kaogu faxian ji xiangguan wenti yanjiu: Jinian Han Chang'ancheng kaogu gongzuo sishi nian" 漢長安城的考古發現及相關問題研究: 紀念漢長安城考古工作四十年. *Kaogu* 考古, 1996.10, 1–14.

Liu Su 劉餗. *Sui-Tang jiahua* 隋唐嘉話. Congshu jicheng ed.

Liu Xuekai 劉學鍇 and Yu Shucheng 余恕誠. *Li Shangyin shige jijie* 李商隱詩歌集解. Beijing: Zhonghua Shuju, 2004.

Liu Zehua 劉澤華, Wang Maohe 汪茂和, and Wang Lanzhong 王蘭仲. *Zhuanzhi quanli yu Zhongguo shehui* 專制權力與中國社會. Tianjin: Tianjin Guji Chubanshe, 2005.

Liu Zhiji 劉知幾. *Shitong* 史通. Shanghai: Shanghai Shiji Chubanshe, 2008.

Loewe, Michael. *Crisis and Conflict in Han China, 104 BC to AD 9*. London: George Allen and Unwin, 1974.

———. *The Government of the Qin and Han Empires, 221 BCE–220 CE*. Indianapolis: Hackett Publishing, 2006.

———. *The Men Who Governed Han China*. Leiden: Brill, 2004.

Love, Harold. *English Clandestine Satire, 1660–1702*. Oxford: Oxford University Press, 2002.

Luo Xinhui 羅新慧. "Zhoudai tianming guannian de fazhan yu shanbian" 周代天命觀念的發展與嬗變. *Lishi yanjiu* 歷史研究, 2012.5, 4–18.

Ma Chun 馬純. *Taozhu xinlu* 陶朱新錄. Beijing: Zhonghua Shuju, 1985.

Ma Ruichen 馬瑞辰. *Mao Shi zhuanjian tongshi* 毛詩傳箋通釋. Beijing: Zhonghua Shuju, 1989.

Mann, Susan. *Precious Records: Women in China's Long Eighteenth Century*. Stanford, Calif.: Stanford University Press, 1987.

Mao Dun 矛盾. "Zhongguo wenxuenei de xingyu miaoxie" 中國文學內的性欲描寫. In *Zhongguo gudai xiaoshuo de xing miaoxie* 中國古代小說的性描寫, ed. Zhang

Guoxing 張國星 and Fu Zengxiang 傅憎享, 18–30. Tianjin: Baihua wenyi Chubanshe, 1993.

McCausland, Shane. "Exemplary Complicity: The Pictorial Lives of Han Court Beauties in Two Narrative Handscrolls of Mid-Ming Suzhou." In *On Telling Images of China: Essays in Narrative Painting and Visual Culture*, ed. Shane McCausland and Yin Hwang, 89–117. Hong Kong: Hong Kong University Press, 2014.

McConnell, Sophie. *Metropolitan Jewelry*. New York: Metropolitan Museum of Art, 1991.

McHugh, James. *Sandalwood and Carrion: Smell in Indian Religion and Culture*. Oxford: Oxford University Press, 2012.

McMahon, Keith. *Celestial Women: Imperial Wives and Concubines in China from Song to Qing*. Lanham, Md.: Rowman and Littlefield, 2016.

———. "The Polyandrous Empress: Imperial Women and Their Male Favorites." In *Wanton Women in Late-Imperial Chinese Literature: Models, Genres, Subversions and Traditions*, ed. Mark Stevenson and Wu Cuncun, 29–53. Leiden: Brill, 2017.

———. *Women Shall Not Rule: Imperial Wives and Concubines in China from Han to Liao*. Lanham, Md.: Rowman and Littlefield, 2013.

Mei Dingzuo 梅鼎祚. *Liangwen ji* 梁文紀. Siku quanshu ed.

Mei Xinlin 梅新林 and Lou Xinxing 婁欣星. "Lun Qingdai Changshu Qushi jiazu nüxing de wenxue huodong yu chuanbo" 論清代常熟屈氏家族女性的文學活動與傳播. *Suzhou daxue xuebao* (Zhexue shehui kexueban) 蘇州大學學報 (哲學社會科學版), 2016.2, 160–67.

Meng Xiangcai 孟祥才. "Pushuo mili de Zhao Feiyan zimei mousha huangzi an" 撲朔迷離的趙飛燕姊妹謀殺皇子案. *Liaocheng shiyuan xuebao* 聊城師院學報, 2000.6, 1–5, 11.

Min Kwantong 閔寬東. "Chungguk aejŏngnyu sosŏrŭi kungnaeyuipkwa p'anbonyŏn'gu" 中國愛情類小說의國內流入과板本研究. *Chungguk sosŏl nonch'ong* 중국소설논총 25 (2007): 185–212.

Nienhauser, William. "Once Again, the Authorship of the *Hsi-ching tsa-chi* (Miscellanies of the Western Capital)." *Journal of the American Oriental Society* 98.3 (1978): 219–36.

Nylan, Michael. "Golden Spindles and Axes: Elite Women in the Achaemenid and Han Empires." In *Early China / Ancient Greece: Thinking through Comparisons*, ed. Steven Shankman and Stephen Durrant, 251–81. Albany: State University of New York Press, 2002.

———. Introduction to *Chang'an 26 BCE: An Augustan Age in China*, ed. Michael Nylan and Griet Vankeerberghen, 3–52. Seattle: University of Washington Press, 2015.

———. "Notes on a Case of Illicit Sex from Zhangjiashan: A Translation and Commentary." *Early China* 30 (2005–6): 25–45.

On Shionoya 鹽谷溫. *Zhongguo wenxue gailun* 中國文學概論. Trans. Sun Lianggong 孫俍工. Taipei: Kaiming Shudian, 1976.

Ouyang Xun 歐陽詢. *Yiwen leiju* 藝文類聚. Shanghai: Shanghai Guji Chubanshe, 1999.

Owen, Stephen. "One Sight: The *Han shu* Biography of Lady Li." In *Rhetoric and the Discourses of Power in Court Culture: China, Europe, and Japan*, ed. David R. Knechtges and Eugene Vance, 239–56. Seattle: University of Washington Press, 2005.

———. "Reproduction in the *Shijing* (Classic of Poetry)." *Harvard Journal of Asiatic Studies* 61.2 (2001): 287–315.

Pak Kyehwa 朴桂花 and Min Kwantong. "Chungguk munŏn sosŏrŭi kungnaeyuip-kwa suyongyangsang: Songdae ijŏn munŏn sosŏrŭl chungshimŭro" 中國文言小┌의 국내유입과 수용양상: 宋代以前文言小┌을 중심으로. *Chungguk ŏmunhak nonjip* 中國語文學論集 82 (2013): 329–45.

Pan Jianguo 潘建國. *Zhongguo gudai xiaoshuo shumu yanjiu* 中國古代小說書目研究. Shanghai: Shanghai Guji Chubanshe, 2005.

Pang Xiangyu 龐翔宇. "Jianlun Zhongguo gudai qichu sanbuqu de falü zhidu" 簡論中國古代七出三不去的法律制度. *Fazhi yu shehui* 法制與社會 33 (2015): 13–15.

Peirce, Leslie. *The Imperial Harem: Women and Sovereignty in the Ottoman Empire*. Oxford: Oxford University Press, 2010.

Pines, Yuri. "Subversion Unearthed: Criticism of Hereditary Succession in the Newly Discovered Manuscripts." *Oriens Extremus* 45 (2005–6): 159–78.

Qidong yeren齊東野人. *Sui Yangdi yanshi* 隋煬帝艷史. Shanghai: Shanghai Guji Chubanshe, 1994.

Qin Chun 秦醇. *Zhao Feiyan biezhuan* 趙飛燕別傳. In *Gudai duanpian xiaoshuo mingzuo pingzhu* 古代短篇小說名作評注, ed. He Manzi 何滿子 and Li Shiren 李時人, 139–47. Shanghai: Shanghai Guji Chubanshe, 2000.

Qin Zhonghang 秦中行. "Han Yangling fujin qiantu mu de fajue" 漢陽陵附近鉗徒墓的發掘. *Wenwu* 文物, 1972.7, 51–53.

Rabb, Melinda. *Satire and Secrecy in English Literature from 1650–1750*. London: Palgrave Macmillan, 2007.

Rawson, Jessica. "The Chinese Hill Censer, *boshan lu*: A Note on Origins, Influence and Meanings." *Arts Asiatiques* 61 (2006): 75–86.

Rickwood, Peter. "The Largest Crystals." *American Mineralogist* 66 (1981): 885–907.

Santangelo, Paulo. *Materials for an Anatomy of Personality in Late Imperial China*. Leiden: Brill, 2010.

———. *Sentimental Education in Chinese History: An Interdisciplinary Textual Research on Ming and Qing Sources*. Leiden: Brill, 2003.

Santangelo, Paulo, and Donatella Guida, eds. *Love, Hatred, and Other Passions: Questions and Themes on Emotions in Chinese Civilization*. Leiden: Brill, 2006.

Scanlon, Jennifer. "What's an Acquisitive Girl to Do? Chick Lit and the Great Recession." *Women's Studies* 42 (2013): 904–22.

Schafer, Edward. *The Golden Peaches of Samarkand: A Study of T'ang Exotics*. Berkeley: University of California Press, 1963.

Schwartz, Benjamin. "The Primacy of Political Order in East Asian Societies: Some Preliminary Generalizations." In *Foundations and Limits of State Power in China*, ed. S. R. Schram, 1–10. London: School of Oriental and African Studies, 1987.

Schwarzenbach, Alexis. "Imagined Queens between Heaven and Hell." In *The Body of the Queen: Gender and Rule in the Courtly World, 1500–2000*, ed. Regina Schulte, 306–26. New York: Berghahn Books, 2006.

Segalen, Victor. *René Leys*. Paris: Éditions G. Cres, 1922.

Seigle, Cecilia Segawa, and Linda H. Chance. *Ōoku: The Secret World of the Shogun's Women*. Amherst, N.Y.: Cambria Press, 2014.

Shaanxisheng Kaogu Yanjiuyuan 陝西省考古研究院 and Famensi Bowuguan 法門寺博物館, eds. *Famensi kaogu fajue baogao* 法門寺考古發掘報告. Beijing: Wenwu Chubanshe, 2007.

Shanghai Bowuguan 上海博物館, ed. *Lianxing shenye, yingzhi lianggong: Shanghai bowuguan zang tongjing jingpin* 練形神冶, 瑩質良工: 上海博物館藏銅鏡精品. Shanghai: Shanghai Shuhua Chubanshe, 2005.

Shaughnessy, Edward L. *Rewriting Early Chinese Texts*. Albany: State University of New York Press, 2006.

Shirakawa Shizuka 白川靜. *Kinbun tsūshaku* 金文通釋. Kobe: Hakatsuru Bijutsukanshi, 1962–.

Song, Geng. *The Fragile Scholar: Power and Masculinity in Chinese Culture*. Hong Kong: Hong Kong University Press, 2004.

Soulliere, Ellen. "Palace Women in the Ming Dynasty." Ph.D. diss., Princeton University, 1987.

———. "Women in the Imperial Household at the Close of China's Ming Dynasty: 1573–1644." *Asia Pacific Perspectives* 12.1 (2013–14): 33–60.

Stone, Charles R. *The Fountainhead of Chinese Erotica: The Lord of Perfect Satisfaction (Ruyijun zhuan)*. Honolulu: University of Hawai'i Press, 2003.

Su E 蘇鄂. *Duyang zabian* 杜陽雜編. Beijing: Zhonghua Shuju, 1985.

Sun Ji 孫機. "Buyao, buyaoguan yu yaoye shipian" 步搖步搖冠與搖葉飾片. *Wenwu* 文物, 1991.11, 55–64.

Sun Wenbo 孫聞博. "Ershi deng jue queli yu Qin-Han juezhi fenceng de fazhan" 二十等爵確立與秦漢爵制分層的發展. *Zhongguo renmin daxue xuebao* 中國人民大學學報, 2016.1, 131–37.

Taniguchi Yasuyo 谷口やすよ. "Kandai no kōgō ken" 漢代の皇后權. *Shigaku zasshi* 史學雜志 87.11 (1978): 1578–96.

———. "Kandai no Taigō rinchō" 漢代の太后臨朝. *Rekishi hyōron* 歷史評論 159 (1980): 86–98.

Tao Zongyi 陶宗儀, comp. *Shuofu* 說郛. Shanghai: Shanghai Guji Chubanshe, 1988.

———. *Yuanshi yeting ji* 元氏掖庭記. In *Biji xiaoshuo daguan: Wubian* 筆記小說大觀: 五編, comp. Lidai xueren 歷代學人. Taipei: Xinxing Chubanshe, 1983.

Tian, Xiaofei. *Beacon Fire and Shooting Star: The Literary Culture of the Liang (502–557)*. Cambridge, Mass.: Harvard University Asia Center, 2007.

Tillander-Godenheilm, Ulla. *Jewels from Imperial St. Petersburg*. St. Petersburg: Liki Rossii, 2012.

Trevor-Roper, Hugh. *Hermit of Peking: The Hidden Life of Sir Edmund Backhouse*. London: Macmillan, 1976.

Tseng, Lillian Lan-ying. *Picturing Heaven in Early China*. Cambridge, Mass.: Harvard University Press, 2011.

Van Gulik, Robert. *Sexual Life in Ancient China: A Preliminary Survey of Chinese Sex and Society from ca. 1500 B.C. till 1644 A.D.* Leiden: Brill 2003.

Vitiello, Giovanni. *The Libertine's Friend: Homosexuality and Masculinity in Late Imperial China*. Chicago: University of Chicago Press, 2011.

Walthall, Anne. "Introducing Palace Women." In *Servants of the Dynasty: Palace Women in World History*, ed. Anne Walthall, 1–21. Berkeley: University of California Press, 2008.

Wan Changhua 萬昌華 and Zhao Xingbin 趙興彬. *Qin-Han yilai jizeng xingzheng yanjiu* 秦漢以來基層行政研究. Jinan: Qi-Lu Shushe, 2008.

Wan Jingjun 萬競君. *Cui Hao shizhu* 崔顥詩注. Shanghai: Shanghai Guji Chubanshe, 1985.

Wang Ding 王鼎. *Fenjiao lu* 焚椒錄. Congshu jicheng ed.

Wang Geya 王歌雅. "Zhongguo gudai de lihun moshi yu lihun daode kaolüe" 中國古代的離婚模式與離婚道德考略. *Heilongjiang shehui kexue* 黑龍江社會科學, 2004.3, 84–88.

Wang Jiantang 王建堂. "Su Shi yu *Zhao Feiyan waizhuan*" 蘇軾與趙飛燕外傳. *Leshan shifan xueyuan xuebao* 樂山師範學院學報, 2007.1, 18–20.

Wang Jiantang 王建堂 and Song Haiying 宋海鷹. "*Feiyan waizhuan* de wenshi yu liubo" 飛燕外傳的問世與流播. *Jindongnan shifan zhuanke xueyuan xuebao* 晉東南師範專科學院學報 19.4 (2002): 35–40.

Wang Li 王立. "Yu yunyou qie chang: Yang *Guifei* xingxiang zai Tang-Song chuanqi zhong de liubian" 余韵悠且長: 楊貴妃形象在唐宋傳奇中的流變. *Chifeng xueyuan xuebao* 赤峰學院學報 37.3 (2016): 181–82.

Wang Renpei 王紉佩. *Peishanshan shi shicun* 佩珊珊室詩存. Qing woodblock print, 1893.

Wang Renyu 王仁裕. *Kaiyuan Tianbao yishi* 開元天寶遺事. Beijing: Zhonghua Shuju, 2006.

Wang Shizhen 王世貞. *Yanyi bian* 艷異編. Shanghai: Shanghai Guji Chubanshe, 1994.

Wang Shouliang 王守亮. "*Xijing zaji* zuozhe wenti shukao" 西京雜記作者問題述考. *Linyi daxue xuebao* 臨沂大學學報 34.2 (2012): 56–58.

———. "*Zhao Feiyan waizhuan* jianlun" 趙飛燕外傳簡論. *Shandong nüzi xueyuan xuebao*山東女子學院學報, 2011.10, 58–60.

Wang Wanying 王萬盈. "Wei Jin Nanbeichao shiqi shangliu shehui guiting de duhan zhi feng" 魏晉南北朝時期上流社會閨庭的妒悍之風. *Xibei shida xuebao* (Shehui kexue ban) 西北師大學報 (社會科學版) 37.5 (2000): 77–82.

Wang Xingfen 王興芬. "Zashi zazhuan wei ti, dili bowu wei yong: Lun *Shiyi ji* de wenti tezheng" 雜史雜傳爲體, 地理博物爲用: 論拾遺記的文體特徵. *Xibei shida xuebao* (Shehui kexue ban) 46.3 (2009): 35–40.

Wang Xuxiao 王旭曉. "Handai richang fushi yanjiu" 漢代日常服飾研究. *Fushi daokan* 服飾導刊 6.2 (2013): 6–12.

Wang Yandi 王延娣, ed. *Zhongguo gudai nüzuojia ji* 中國古代女作家集. Jinan: Shandong Daxue Chubanshe, 1999.

Wang Yinglin 王應麟. *Yuhai* 玉海. Siku quanshu ed.

Wang Zijin 王子今 and Zhang Jing 張經. *Zhongguo funü tongshi: Xian-Qin juan* 中國婦女通史: 先秦卷. Hangzhou: Hangzhou Chubanshe, 2010.

Wei Huijuan 魏慧娟. "*Da-Song Xuanhe yishi* he *Shuihu zhuan* zhong Song Jiang xingxiang duibi fenxi" 大宋宣和遺事和水滸傳中宋江形象對比分析. *Puyang zhiye jishu xueyuan xuebao* 濮陽職業技術學院學報, 2011.4, 75–76.

Wei Yuchuan 魏玉川. "*Feiyan waizhuan* kaolun" 飛燕外傳考論. *Tangdu xuekan* 唐都學刊 21.6 (2005): 38–40.

White, Stephen D. "The Politics of Anger." In *Anger's Past: The Social Uses of an Emotion in the Middle Ages*, ed. Barbara H. Rosenwein, 127–52. Ithaca, N.Y.: Cornell University Press, 1998.

Woodacre, Elena, and Carey Fleiner, eds. *Royal Mothers and Their Ruling Children: Wielding Political Authority from Antiquity to the Early Modern Era*. New York: Palgrave Macmillan, 2015.

Wu, Hung. *The Wu Liang Shrine: The Ideology of Early Chinese Pictorial Art*. Stanford, Calif.: Stanford University Press, 1989.

Wu Chuanjun 吳傳鈞 and Lü Yusheng 呂余生, eds. *Haishang sichou zhi lu yanjiu* 海上絲綢之路研究. Beijing: Kexue Chubanshe, 2006.

Wu Congxiang 吳從祥. "Liang Han nüguan kao" 兩漢女官考. *Shandong nüzi xueyuan xuebao* 山東女子學院學報 122.4 (2015): 37–41.

Wu Fanglang 吳方浪. "Handai sizhiye yanjiu" 漢代絲織業研究. Master's thesis, Jiangxi Shifan Daxue, 2013.

Wu Liquan 吳禮權. *Zhongguo yanqing xiaoshuo shi* 中國言情小說史. Taipei: Taiwan Shangwu Yinshugan, 1995.

Wu Liwen 吳俐雯. "*Shiyi ji* dui houshi wenxue de yingxiang juli" 拾遺記對後世文學的影響舉例. *Dalu zazhi* 大陸雜志 85.2 (1992): 4–48.

Wu Renchen 吳任臣. *Shiguo chunqiu* 十國春秋. Beijing: Zhonghua Shuju, 1983.

Wu Xueling 吳雪伶. "Nanshiren: Nüxing huayu de shenhuazhe: Tangdai gongyuan shi chuangzuo zhuti kaocha zhi er" 男詩人: 女性話語的深化者: 唐代宮怨詩創作主體考察之二. *Luoyang shifan xueyuan xuebao* 洛陽師範學院學報, 2009.12, 102–6.

———. "Nüshiren: Nüxing huayu de zifazhe: Tangdai gongyuan shi chuangzuo zhuti kaocha zhi yi" 女詩人: 女性話語的自發者: 唐代宮怨詩創作主體考察之一. *Luoyang shifan xueyuan xuebao*, 2008.6, 37–40.

Wu Zhaoyi 吳兆宜 et al. *Yutai xinyong jianzhu* 玉臺新詠箋注. Beijing: Zhonghua Shuju, 1990.

Wu Zhida 吳志達. *Zhongguo wenyan xiaoshuo shi* 中國文言小說史. Jinan: Qi-Lu Shushe, 1994.

Xia Zuen 夏祖恩. "Qingdai yeshi de shixue diwei chutan" 清代野史的史學地位初探. *Fujian shifan daxue xuebao* (Zhexue shehui kexueban) 福建師範大學學報 (哲學社會科學版), 1995.1, 101–6.

Xie Siwei 謝思煒. *Bai Juyi shi ji jiaozhu* 白居易詩集校注. Beijing: Zhonghua Shuju, 2006.

Xing Peishun 邢培順. "*Zhao Feiyan waizhuan* tanlun" 趙飛燕外傳探論. *Zhonghua nüzi xueyuan Shandong fenyuan xuebao* 中華女子學院山東分院學報, 2009.1, 58–63.

Xiong, Victor Cunrui. *Historical Dictionary of Medieval China*. Lanham, Md.: Rowman and Littlefield, 2017.

Xiong Ming 熊明. *Han-Wei Liuchao zazhuan yanjiu* 漢魏六朝雜傳研究. Shenyang: Liaohai Chubanshe, 2004.

———. "*Zhao Feiyan waizhuan* kaolun: Jian lun Han Wei Liuchao zazhuan dui Tangren chuanqi de yunyu yu qidao" 趙飛燕外傳考論: 兼論漢魏六朝雜傳對唐人傳奇的孕育與啓道. *Guji yanjiu* 古籍研究, 2005.2, 58–65.

Xiu Xinyu 修新宇. "Lun Liaodai dihou: Xiao Guanyin shige de yishu tedian" 論遼代帝后: 蕭觀音詩歌的藝術特點. *Chifeng xueyuan xuebao* (Hanwen zhexue shehui kexueban) 赤峰學院學報 (漢文哲學社會科學版), 2009.6, 1–3.

Xu, Jay, ed. *Tomb Treasures: New Discoveries from China's Han Dynasty.* San Francisco: Asian Art Museum, 2017.

Xu Jian 徐堅. *Chuxue ji* 初學記. Beijing: Zhonghua Shuju, 2005.

Xu Liming 須黎明. "Shuangfeng bing zhi chuan er mei: *Zhao Feiyan biezhuan* shangxi" 雙峰并峙傳二美: 趙飛燕別傳賞析. *Gudian wenxue zhishi* 古典文學知識, 1998.3, 29–31.

Xu Tong 徐熥. *Jinfeng waizhuan* 金鳳外傳. In *Xuelin manlu* 學林漫錄, vol. 15. Beijing: Zhonghua Shuju, 2000.

Xue Hongji 薛洪勣. *Chuanqi xiaoshuo shi* 傳奇小說史. Hangzhou: Zhejiang Guji Chubanshe, 1998.

———. "Wan Qing 'huanghou xilie xiaoshuo' shulüe" 晚清 '皇后系列小說' 述略. *Ming-Qing xiaoshuo yanjiu* 明清小說研究, 2006.3, 75–80.

———. "*Zhao Feiyan biezhuan*" 趙飛燕別傳. In *Zhongguo gudai xiaoshuo baike quanshu* 中國古代小說百科全書, ed. Liu Shide 劉世德 et al., 744–45 Beijing: Zhongguo Dabaike Quanshu Chubanshe, 1993.

Xue Ruisheng 薛瑞生. *Yuezhang ji jiaozhu* 樂章集校註. Beijing: Zhonghua Shuju, 1997.

Yan Kejun 嚴可均. *Quan Hanwen* 全漢文. In *Quan shanggu Sandai Qin Han Liuchao wen* 全上古三代秦漢六朝文. Beijing: Shangwu Yinshugan, 1999.

Yan Wanzhang 閻萬章. "Liao Daozong Xuanyi huanghou fu wei Xiao Xiaohui kao" 遼道宗宣懿皇后父爲蕭孝惠. *Shehui kexue ji* 社會科學輯, 1979.2, 114–19.

Yang, Shao-yun. "The Politics of Omenology in Chengdi's Reign." In *Chang'an 26 BCE: An Augustan Age in China*, ed. Michael Nylan and Griet Vankeerberghen, 323–46. Seattle: University of Washington Press, 2015.

Yang, Zhiyi. *Dialectics of Spontaneity: The Aesthetics and Ethics of Su Shi (1037–1101) in Poetry*. Leiden: Brill, 2015.

Yang Gang 楊崗. "Xian-Qin zhi Qin-Han de xunxiang xisu wenhua" 先秦至秦漢的熏香習俗文化. *Xibei nonglin keji daxue xuebao* (Shehui kexue ban) 西北農林科技大學學報 (社會科學版) 11.4 (2011): 174–79.

Yang Hongnian 楊鴻年. "Huben Yulin" 虎賁羽林. In *Han-Wei zhidu congkao* 漢魏制度叢考. Wuchang: Wuhan Daxue Chubanshe, 1985.

Yang Hongxiu 楊鴻修. *Gongdian kaogu tonglun* 宮殿考古通論. Beijing: Zijincheng Chubanshe, 2001.

Yang Jialuo 楊家駱. *Su Dongpo quanji* 蘇東坡全集. Taipei: Shijie Shuju, 1989.

Yang Qing 陽清. "Zhao Feiyan gushi ji qi xiaoshuo bianzou" 趙飛燕故事及其小說變奏. *Minsu yanjiu* 民俗研究, 2013.5, 111–17.

Yang Quan 楊權. *Xin wude lilun yu Liang-Han zhengzhi: 'Yaohou huode' shuo kaolun* 新五德理論與兩漢政治: '堯後火德' 說考論. Beijing: Zhonghua Shuju, 2006.

Yang Zhishui 楊之水. "Lantang yu xiangshui" 蘭湯與香水. *Zijincheng* 紫禁城, 2011.4, 92–98.

Yanyansheng 艷艷生. *Zhaoyang yanshi* 昭陽艷史. In *Zhongguo jinhui xiaoshuo baibu* 中國禁毀小說百部. Beijing: Zhongguo Xiju Chubanshe, 2000.

Yao Mian 姚勉. *Xuepo ji* 雪坡集. Siku quanshu ed.

Yong Rong 永瑢 et al. *Siku quanshu zongmu* 四庫全書總目. Beijing: Zhonghua Shuju, 1987.

Yoo Hee Jun 유희준 and Min Dong Kuan 민동관. "Munhak munhwa: *Maebijŏn* ŭi kungnaeyuipkwa pŏnyŏgyangsang" 문학 문화: 매비전 (梅妃傳) 의 국내유입과 번역양상. *Pigyomunhakyŏn'gu* 비교문학연구 27 (2012): 255–89.

You Li 尤李. "*Fenjiao lu* ji qi shiliao jiazhi kaoshi" 焚椒錄及其史料價值考釋. *Guji zhengli yanjiu xuekan* 古籍整理研究學刊, 2011.6, 103–7.

Yu Xiaohong 俞曉紅. "*Da-Song Xuanhe yishi* zhong de *Shuihu* renwu gushi" 大宋宣和遺事中的水滸人物故事. *Xiandai yuwen* 現代語文 22 (2010): 14–16.

Yuan Lükun 袁閭琨 and Xue Hongji 薛洪勣, eds. *Tang-Song chuanqi zongji* 唐宋傳奇總集. Zhengzhou: Henan Renmin Chubanshe, 2001.

Yue Shi 樂史. *Lüzhu zhuan* 綠珠傳. In *Biji xiaoshuo daguan: Wubian* 筆記小說大觀: 五編, comp. Lidai xueren 歷代學人. Taipei: Xinxing Chubanshe, 1983.

———. *Yang Taizhen waizhuan* 楊太真外傳. Shanghai: Shanghai Guji Chubanshe 2002.

Yun Zhu 惲珠. *Hongxiangguan shicao* 紅香館詩草. Qing woodblock print, no date.

Zeng Gong 曾巩. *Zeng Gong ji* 曾巩集. Beijing: Zhonghua Shuju, 1984.

Zeng Ya 曾亞. "Lun Ming-Qing xiaoshuo zhong de Sui Yangdi" 論明清小說中的隋煬帝. *Ming-Qing xiaoshou yanjiu* 明清小說研究, 1994.2, 161–66.

Zeng Zao 曾慥. *Leishuo* 類說. Siku quanshu ed.

Zhang, Aidong, and Wayne Schlepp. "Xiao Guanyin: Her Tragic Life and Melancholy Poems." *Journal of Song-Yuan Studies* 28 (1998): 213–21.

Zhang, Zhengjun. "Anonymous, 'The Tale of the Plum-Blossom Consort' 梅妃傳." In *Song Dynasty Tales: A Guided Reader*, ed. Zhenjun Zhang and Jing Wang, 55–78. Hackensack, N.J.: World Scientific, 2017.

———. "Qin Chun 秦醇, 'Supplementary Biography of Empress Zhao: The Flying Swallow' 趙飛燕別傳." In *Song Dynasty Tales: A Guided Reader*, ed. Zhenjun Zhang and Jing Wang, 1–15. Hackensack, N.J.: World Scientific, 2017.

Zhang Ao 張鷟. *Chaoye qianzai* 朝野僉載. Siku quanshu ed.

Zhang Chengjian 張乘健. "'Changhen ge' yu *Mei Fei zhuan*: Lishi yu yishu de weimiao chongtu" 長恨歌與梅妃傳: 歷史與藝術的微妙衝突. *Wenxue yichan* 文學遺產, 1992.1, 51–58.

Zhang Chunhong 張春紅. "*Shiyi ji* chuangzuo de shenqihua zhuiqiu" 拾遺記創作的神奇化追求. *Xizang minzu xueyuan xuebao* (Zhexue shehui kexue ban) 西藏民族學院學報 (哲學社會科學版) 31.2 (2010): 73–77.

Zhang Kan 張侃. "Shitan Xiao Qi dui *Shiyi ji* de zhengli he piping: Cong xiaoshuo pipingshi de jiaodu jiayi kaocha" 試探蕭綺對拾異記的整理和批評: 從小說批評

史的角度加以考察. *Fudan daxue xuebao* (Shehui kexueban) 復旦大學學報 (社會科學版), 1995.2, 82–87.

Zhang Nie 張嵲. *Ziwei ji* 紫微集. Siku quanshu ed.

Zhang Peiheng 章培恒. "*Daye shiyi ji, Mei Fei zhuan* deng wupian chuanqi de xiezuo shidai" 大業拾遺記, 梅妃傳等五篇傳奇的寫作時代. *Shenzhen daxue xuebao* (Renwen shehui kexueban) 深圳大學學報 (人文社會科學版) 25.1 (2008): 106–10.

Zhang Xiang 張翔. "Shuangmian guanzhao: Boshanlu: Chutu shiwu yu yongwushi de huzheng" 雙面觀照: 博山爐: 出土實物與詠物詩的互證. *Liaoning shifan daxue xuebao* (Shehui kexueban) 遼寧師範大學學報 (社會科學版) 36.3 (2013): 395–401.

Zhang Xiaofeng 張小鋒. "Zhengshuo Zhao Feiyan" 正說趙飛燕. *Wenshi zhishi* 文史知識, 2006.8, 73–79.

Zhang Xiaoming 張曉明. "Lun Handai huangzu de wenxue chengjiu" 論漢代皇族的文學成就. *Qingdao daxue shifan xueyuan xuebao* 青島大學師範學院學報 23.1 (2006): 70–75.

Zhang Xiuhua 張秀華. "Cong jinwen cailiao kan yin chai liao sanshong jili" 從金文材料看禋柴燎三種祭禮. *Mudanjiang daxue xuebao* 牡丹江大學學報, 2009.2, 3–4.

Zhang Xiuying 張秀英 and Huang Haiyan 黃海艷. "*Da-Song Xuanhe yishi* he *Shuihu zhuan* zhong de Yang Zhi luocao zhi bijiao" 大宋宣和遺事和水滸傳中楊志落草之比較. *Qiqihaer shifan gaodeng zhuanke xueyuan xuebao* 齊齊哈爾師範高等專科學院學報, 2006.3, 50–51.

Zhang Ying 張英, Wang Shizhen 王士禎, Wang Tan 王惔, et al., comps. *Yuding yuanjian leihan* 御定淵鑑類函. Siku quanshu ed.

Zhang Yu'an 張玉安. "Han Wei Nanbeichao buyao yanjiu" 漢魏南北朝步搖研究. *Yishu tansuo* 藝術探索 26.2 (2012): 6–14.

Zhang Yunhua 張雲華. "Lun Beichao funü de duhan fengqi" 論北朝婦女的妒悍風氣. *Shixue jikan* 史學集刊, 2008.6, 99–104.

Zhang Yuniang 張玉娘. *Lanxue ji* 蘭雪集. In *Yuan shi xuan: San ji* 元詩選: 三集, comp. Gu Sili 顧嗣立. Taipei: Taiwan Shangwu Yinshugan, 1983.

Zhangjiashan Ersiqihao Hanmu Zhujian Zhengli Xiaozu 張家山二四七號漢墓竹簡整理小組. *Zhangjiashan Hanmu zhujian (Ersiqihao mu): Shiwen xiudingben* 張家山漢墓竹簡 (二四七號墓): 釋文修訂本. Beijing: Wenwu Chubanshe, 2006.

Zhao Xiupei 趙修霈. "Song chuanqi 'diangu lihe' de chuanqi shoufa—yi liupian Song chuanqi wei li" 宋傳奇 '典故離合' 的傳奇手法—以六篇宋傳奇爲例. *Wen yu zhe* 文與哲, 2009.12, 165–94.

Zhao Youwen 趙幼文. *Cao Zhi ji jiaozhu* 曹植集校注. Beijing: Renmin Wenxue Chubanshe, 1984.

Zheng Chenggong 鄭成功 and Zheng Jing 鄭經. *Yanping erwang yiji* 延平二王遺集. Taipei: Shijie Shuju, 1957.

Zheng Fu 錚甫. "Han Chengdi zhi si yu 'yinghou shouxin': Cong *Zizhi tongjian* guanyu tianren ganying de yize jizai tan qi" 漢成帝之死與 '熒惑守心': 從資治通鑒關於天人感應的一則記載談起. *Zhonghua wenhua luntan* 中華文化論壇, 1999.1, 124–28.

Zhongguo Guji Shanben Shumu Bianji Weiyuanhui 中國古籍善本書目編輯委員會, ed. *Zhongguo guji shanben shumu: Shibu* 中國古籍善本書目: 史部. Shanghai: Shanghai Guji Chubanshe, 1998.

Zhongguo yeshi jicheng Bianji Weiyuanhui 中國野史集成編輯委員會 and Sichuan Daxue Tushuguan 四川大學圖書館, comps. *Zhongguo yeshi jicheng* 中國野史集成. Chengdu: Ba-Shu Chubanshe, 1993.

Zhongguo yeshi jicheng xubian Bianweihui 中國野史集成續編編委會 and Sichuan Daxue Tushuguan, comps. *Zhongguo yeshi jicheng xubian* 中國野史集成續編. Chengdu: Ba-Shu Chubanshe, 2000.

Zhou Chunjian 周春健. "Zhounan 'Zhongsi' shi jiaoyi fawei" 周南螽斯詩教義發微. *Zhongshan daxue xuebao* (Shehui kexueban) 中山大學學報 (社會科學版) 51.2 (2011): 144–52.

Zhou Zhongfu 周中孚. *Zhengtang dushu ji* 鄭堂讀書記. Shanghai: Shangwu Yinshugan, 1959.

Zhu Mu 祝穆. *Gujin shiwen leiju* 古今事文類聚. Shanghai: Shanghai Guji Chubanshe, 1983.

Zhu Rundong 朱潤東. *Badai zhuanxu wenxue shulun* 八代傳叙文學述論. Shanghai: Fudan Daxue Chubanshe, 2006.

Zhu Shengfei 朱勝非. *Ganzhu ji* 紺珠集. Siku quanshu ed.

Zhu Ziyan 朱子彥. "Qin-Han hougong zhidu shulun" 秦漢後宮制度述論. *Xueshu yuekan* 學術月刊, 2000.6, 81–87.

INDEX

CPSIA information can be obtained
at www.ICGtesting.com
Printed in the USA
BVHW070745160521
607088BV00004B/6

9 780295 748757